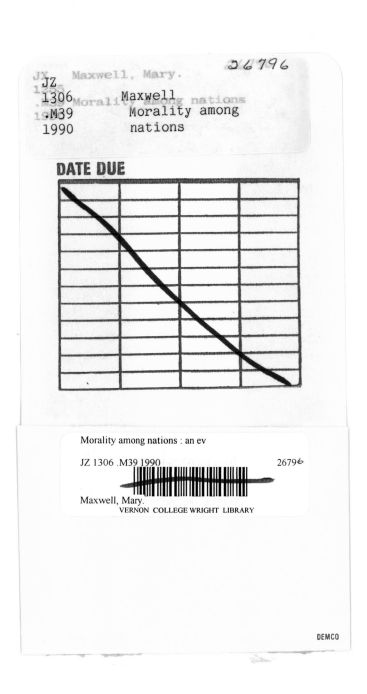

Morality among Nations

SUNY Series in Biopolitics

Brian A. Gladue, EDITOR

Morality among Nations

an Evolutionary View

MARY MAXWELL

●●●●●●●●●●●●●●●●●●●●●●●●

State University of New York Press

Published by
State University of New York Press, Albany

©1990   State University of New York

For information, address the State University of New York Press,
State University Plaza, Albany, NY 12246

Library of Congress Cataloging-in-Publication Data
Maxwell, Mary.
　Morality among nations : an evolutionary view / Mary Maxwell.
　　p.　cm. — (SUNY series in biopolitics)
　Includes bibliographical references.
　ISBN 0-7914-0349-1. — ISBN 0-7914-0350-5 (pbk.)
　1. International relations—Moral and ethical aspects.
2. Sociobiology.　I. Title.　II. Series.
JX1255.M39　1990
172'.4—dc20
　　　　　　　　　　　　　　　　　　　　　　　　　　89-27881
　　　　　　　　　　　　　　　　　　　　　　　　　　CIP

10　9　8　7　6　5　4　3　2　1

To E.O. WILSON
humanist, conservationist, friend

Contents

Preface

Several Christmas Eves ago I attended Midnight Mass at a small church in London. The advertised sermon was "World Peace." Judging by the young age of the preacher and the fact that antinuclear protests were strong in Europe at the time, I assumed that he might exhort the congregation to take some sort of action towards disarmament. Instead, he told us that if we each had love and peace in our hearts, "like Christ, the Prince of Peace," then the world would be right. I left the service feeling rather annoyed at that well-intentioned person, but had only a vague sense of why he was wrong to draw such a direct line between the wishes of individuals and the behavior of nations. Later, I had the opportunity to delve into that matter with some academic gusto. One result is this book, which attempts to provide a more satisfactory picture of the relationship between human morality or goodwill and the outcome, or possible outcome, of world affairs.

It is my hope that this book will be useful to those who are already familiar with the debate about international morality, especially as I have provided a new critique of that debate from the perspective of evolutionary biology. As well, I hope that this volume can serve as an introduction to those who have no previous exposure to the subject. I have endeavored to make both the philosophical section and the biological section self-contained, and to furnish a useful bibliography at the end.

Acknowledgments

I must thank many people and several institutions for assisting me. The following persons commented on one or more chapters of this book: J.J.C. Smart, George Maxwell, Sissela Bok, and F.H. Hinsley. A completely different earlier version was read by Paul Corcoran, Jack Donnelly, Paul Keal, and Jonathan Schonsheck. These scholars all helped me significantly; I feel grateful to them in inverse proportion to the gentleness of their criticism. I also wish to thank the anonymous reader who suggested that I add an "afterword" to put my work in context.

I received valuable bibliographical leads from Tim Hardwick, Jim Blight, Graham Nerlich, and Peter Lawler. Anne Whicker held my hand while typing the manuscript—no mean feat. Bob Catley tried to keep me on the realist straight and narrow. Mark Oliphant plied me with articles from the *Bulletin of the Atomic Scientists,* and shared his wisdom. Ron Garson, Latin grammarian, cured me of some of my favorite expressions. Antonio Santos and Ruth Ellickson burned the midnight oil, word-processing. My husband George waited it out even to the edge of doom. I am very grateful to these many teachers and friends for their time. I should say that mention of their names is not meant to imply endorsement: some agree with my ideas, some disagree, and one, at least, disagrees vehemently.

I had the use of four excellent libraries for research: The Barr Smith Library of the University of Adelaide, Australia; the British Library at the London School of Economics and Political Science; the Hugh Owens Library of University College, Aberystwyth, Wales; and the Andover Library at Harvard Divinity School. The University of the United Arab Emirates provided a tranquil setting in which to compose the final draft. For all of this, I am extremely aware of my good fortune. I was additionally helped, in terms of exposure to new publications, through my membership in the Association for Politics and the Life Sciences, the European Sociobiological Society, and the Authors Guild.

I should also like to acknowledge some of the broad influences on my work. First, there is the magnificent book, *The Perfectibility of Man,* by the Australian philosopher John Passmore, which does not even get a mention in my text, but which is the most thumbed-through volume in my collection. Second, there is a series—not officially a series, but a progression of anthologies in international relations theory—from Herbert Butterfield and Martin Wight's *Diplomatic Investigations,* to Ralph Pettman's *Moral Claims in World Affairs,* to Michael Donelan's *The Reason of States,* to James Mayall's *The Community of States.* These gave me delight and sustenance. I later was attracted to the international law writings of Richard Falk and Adda Bozeman—simultaneously—and these helped shape the present work (thus proving how catholic one's taste can be!). Pierre van den Berghe influenced my thinking in ways other than indicated in the one major reference I make to his book, *The Ethnic Phenomenon,* particularly by his relentless depiction of the brutal side of international behavior. I thank all these writers for their inspiration.

The greatest intellectual debt I owe in this book is to the late Hedley Bull, who encouraged me in a nascent version of this project shortly before his death in 1985. His lecture, "International Anarchy in the 1980s," delivered at the University of Adelaide in 1983, directly led me to undertake the study of international relations and to pursue a degree in that field. I share with Bull's other colleagues their sadness at the loss of such a great mind. Here I take the liberty of quoting from the introduction to his book *The Anarchical Society* (with permission of Macmillan Press, London):

Of course, I do not wish to imply anything so absurd as that this study is "value free." A study of this kind that did not derive from moral and political premises of some kind would be impossible, and, if it were possible it would be sterile. What is important in an academic inquiry into politics is not to exclude value-laden premises but to subject these premises to investigation and criticism, to treat the raising of moral and political issues as part of the inquiry. I am no more capable than anyone else of being detached about a subject such as this. But I believe in the value of attempting to be detached or disinterested, and it is clear to me that some approaches to the study of world politics are more detached or disinterested than others. I also believe that inquiry has its own morality and is necessarily subversive of political institutions and movements of all kinds, good as well as bad.

I respectfully appropriate those sentiments and concerns for the study at hand.

Introduction

If death defines the human condition, injustice defines
the social one. There is a duty, national and international,
to reduce it as much as possible. But there is no
definitive victory.
                                        — *Stanley Hoffman*

International morality is a subject of growing interest among both scholars and the public. It is something that one is forced to think about, as the
occasions for international moral — or immoral — exchanges multiply in a
world of interdependent nations. Certain social transactions, perhaps *most*
social transactions, seem to most people to have a rightness or wrongness
about them. Among those that involve international factors are: the issue
of resources (do people in one country have any claim over the natural
resources of another?); the issue of migration (is there a moral obligation
for nations to accept refugees, or to protect migrant workers?); the issue
of covert operations (under what circumstances is it right for one nation
to destabilize the government or economy of another?); and the issue of
armaments (is it wrong to stockpile nuclear weapons or chemical weapons,
or to sell conventional arms to both sides engaged in war?).

Yet there is little consensus on these or similar issues, and there is a
dearth of fundamental ethical argument available to give guidance. The
philosophy of international ethics is at a primitive stage. There is also, I
observe, a considerable amount of confusion generated by the existence
of actual international helpfulness and non-helpfulness. Under the category of helpfulness we see, for instance, that when one country is visited
by a natural disaster such as an earthquake, the governments of other
nations, without any discussion, send generous relief in the way of money,
manpower, and technical aid. By contrast, massive malnutrition is a
problem that does not usually elicit international response, even when it
is well-publicized and continues for decades. Here, non-helpfulness is the
accepted reaction; this perhaps spreads the impression that international
morality, or at least international conscience, is a quite arbitrary thing.

Another instance of helpfulness consists of the concern shown by
outsiders for the political repression of their fellow human beings in
particular countries. Thus, the blacks victimized by apartheid in South
Africa, and certain political dissidents in the Soviet Union receive, almost
without question, the sympathy of the outside world, and the perpetrators
of these repressions are widely denounced. Yet this is oddly selective:

events in other countries seem equally worthy of attention, but they are more or less ignored. Even genocide often appears to be "acceptable." Jack Donnelly has recently observed:

> In the last twenty-five years we can point to barbarous atrocities in Burundi and Rwanda, the decimation of Kampuchea under Pol Pot and his successors, the death of between a fifth and a third of the population of East Timor during its forcible incorporation into Indonesia, and the systematic massacre of Indians in Paraguay and Guatemala among other countries. Humanitarian intervention was not even attempted—by all indications, not even seriously considered—in all of these cases.[1]

In short, I believe that the very coexistence of routine helpfulness and routine non-helpfulness is a large factor contributing to public confusion about international morality.

Certainly in the contemporary world of interdependent nations, the meager theoretical development of the concept of international morality presents a major intellectual challenge. The challenge is to find out what international morality really is. Is there any "map" to the right and wrong of international behavior? Is there any fundamental basis for judging certain international acts to be moral or immoral? Is there any ultimate source of obligation among nations? Or is the very idea of morality completely out of place in international affairs, and perhaps even—as some have said—a harmful notion?

Research Sources

I shall tackle those questions as directly as I can in this book. It is my intention to examine the entity, "international morality," under various lights, as thoroughly as possible. I initially selected three academic fields from which to draw research for this subject, namely, international relations theory, ethical philosophy, and sociobiology. For reasons which I shall mention below, ethical philosophy did not yield much insight in my study, but sociobiology, surprisingly, did. The subtitle of this book—"An Evolutionary View"—refers to the fact that *humans evolved*, a long time ago, in ways that continue to affect international relations today.

The format of this book is as follows. Part One "Traditional Arguments concerning International Morality" draws its material from the traditional literature of international relations theory. Part Two "Sociobiological Hypotheses Pertinent to International Morality" draws most of its material from sociobiology and anthropology, and some from social psychology. Part Three "Critique and Conclusions" points to an interesting—I would say startling—relationship between the ideas from those first two parts. Let me now introduce the three areas of research related to international morality.

International Relations Theory

International relations as a specialized academic discipline has existed only since 1919. In its first couple of decades it had as its main subject matter international law and international organization. This reflected public concern with ways of preventing war, following the Great War. Later, beginning in the 1940s and 1950s, it switched its focus to *power* and *interest* in the international arena, rather than legality or morality. The power-politics approach continues to dominate the field of international relations, and many academics explicitly distance themselves from "normative" concerns. Nevertheless, both in Britain and the United States there has remained at least some scholarly engagement in the intellectual problem of international morality, and by the 1980s some universities were offering courses entitled "International Ethics," taught by international relations experts.*

The traditional literature concerning international morality that is used by international relations theorists includes the writings of political scientists, philosophers, social theorists, international lawyers, and even theologians. Hence the names of Saint Augustine, Machiavelli, Hobbes, Grotius, and Kant appear in Part One of this book, as well as more recent writers such as Niebuhr, Morgenthau, Bull, Falk, and Bozeman. Most of these writers, particularly the early ones, did not set out explicitly to investigate the fundamental nature of international morality. Rather, they wrote about some issue of their day, such as war, sovereignty, the rights of the individual, the nature of community, or the role of reason. Yet their *indirect* comments on the moral relationship among nations have been raised to the status of major pronouncements—"dogma" to some—on the subject of international morality.

In Part One, I present twelve major views on international morality. In order to demonstrate vividly that the theorists are divided, I have chosen six "for" and six "against." Their arguments constitute what could be called the positive and negative positions on international morality. The negative position takes the general stand that "there is not and cannot be a moral relationship among states." The positive position holds that "rules of morality apply to all human transactions, whether the actors be individuals or states." The six arguments to be listed under the negative position are those of: national interest, international anarchy, nationalism, national sovereignty, group immorality, and cultural

---

*These courses may make use of anthologies such as *International Ethics: A Philosophy and Public Affairs Reader*, edited by Charles Beitz, Marshall Cohen, Thomas Scanlon and A. John Simmons; *Ethics and International Relations*, edited by Anthony Ellis; and *Boundaries: National Autonomy and Its Limits*, edited by Peter G. Brown and Henry Shue.

pluralism. The six arguments to be listed under the positive position are those of: cosmopolitan morality, natural law, the society of states, the just war, human rights, and world order.

While my list of twelve is certainly not exhaustive, I believe I have captured the major facets of the "for" and "against" arguments. For each of the twelve I try to put as persuasively as possible the unique justification given by its author in defense or refutation of the idea that there is a moral relationship among states. As the reader will see, these justifications are as contradictory as they are compelling—thus a thorough exposure to them seems to bring us no nearer an answer to the question "Is there a moral relationship among states?" Students of international relations theory who look no further than their own discipline cannot resolve this problem; it is at an impasse.

Ethical Philosophy

It had been my plan, therefore, to go outside of international relations and its related discipline, political science, to ethical philosophy proper. Here the research was unexpectedly thin, although I hasten to say that there is currently a renaissance in ethical discussion of international issues, such as the revival of Christian just-war theory with special reference to nuclear war, and the extension of the idea of domestic justice to the international sphere.

My reasons for finding ethical philosophy unilluminating as to the core concept of international morality are twofold. First, the history of Western ethical philosophy, from Socrates up to the late nineteenth century, is a collection of separate ideas rather than a cumulative body of knowledge such as that of science. Many ethical philosophers started from different "first premises" and faced different historical circumstances. For instance, Plato was interested in finding the just society, while the Stoics and Epicureans were trying to prescribe the good life for the individual. Where Hume was keen to discover the innate moral sense that makes people judge things as good or bad, the Utilitarians wanted to judge governments and laws by their ability to assure the greatest happiness for the greatest number. Kant, Marx, Mill, Nietzsche, Sartre—all philosophers have had very different starting points and contemporary concerns. These philosophers not only do not help us to discover what *international* morality is, they do not lead to any particular conclusion as to what *morality* is.

Second, since the early twentieth century, the major inquiry of ethical philosophy, namely the question of "What is right?" or "What is good?" stopped being an important—nay, stopped being a respectable question in the Anglo-American academic world. The *Principia Ethica* of G.E. Moore, published in 1903, and A.J. Ayer's *Language, Truth, and Logic*, published in 1936, led, in different ways, to a rejection by ethical philosophers of their traditional role in commenting on "the good." All they could comment on was what it means to say that something is good. (Some said it meant merely to express one's emotions or to propagate one's interests.)

My own belief is that these philosophers were on the right track in declaring as futile the search for an objective, external, discoverable moral truth. Typical of so much of the intellectual achievement of the twentieth century, their work consisted of uncovering deception and irrationality. However, their stance inevitably intimidated their fellows from taking a professional interest in the normative ethical issues of the day. (By "normative" I mean concerned with prescribing standards.) A glance through almost any philosophical journal—until fairly recently—reveals a discussion carried on in abstract terms and making little if any reference to vital social issues. Thus, ethical philosophy does not provide us with the material we need, to discuss or develop international morality. (As I have acknowledged, however, some of the writings categorized as international relations theory in Part One are in fact works by philosophers.)

Sociobiology

A third area to which I then turned was sociobiology. More precisely, it turned to *me*, in that certain ideas which I had learned from sociobiology kept haunting me while I tried to concentrate on international morality. As I shall argue in Part Two of this book, sociobiology—or, more generally, the study of the biological evolution of human nature—provides major clues to both morality and international relations.

Sociobiology's clue to *international relations* is fairly straightforward. It consists of the hypothesis that humans evolved in small groups and that intergroup hostility was a factor in the evolution of such behaviors as group loyalty and violence toward enemies. A behavioral characteristic of almost any group is to treat its members one way and nonmembers another way. The rightness of this is loudly proclaimed by the group in question and furnishes a "group morality." Correspondingly, it supports intergroup immorality or amorality, in a way that often contradicts the standard morality of its members—for example, it contradicts the "absolute" prohibition against killing.

Sociobiology's clue to *morality* is more complicated than its clue to international relations, and much more has been written about it.* The aspect of it that is relevant to our study is primarily the discovery that *the impulse to moralize*, or to be concerned with the rightness and wrongness

---

*Full-length works include Peter Singer, *The Expanding Circle*; Michael Ruse, *Taking Darwin Seriously*; Lionel Tiger, *The Manufacture of Evil*; and Richard Alexander, *The Biology of Moral Systems*.

of things, *is innate*. The genetics of altruism, as we shall see, furnishes the key to the evolution of moral emotions in humans. Thus, our moral sensibility is a "given," and because of it we construct moral opinions. Later in time, rule-making and the formulation of ethical principle become established as cultural institutions, but in the first instance they are based on human nature. Just as Hans Morgenthau and other political scientists have claimed that power is an instinct that must be reckoned with,[2] I like to say, using sociobiological theory, that a sense of morality is also instinctive and must be reckoned with.

As will be discussed in Part Three of this book, some ideas from these sociobiological researches shed new light on the traditional arguments concerning international morality. In fact, the evolutionary approach results in an important explanation of the dichotomy between the aforementioned negative and positive positions. Namely, I shall claim that the theorists who say "there is not and cannot be a moral relationship among states" are essentially defending *group morality* over the "standard" kind of morality. They assert, in essence, that the group and its welfare have priority over all other considerations. On the other hand, those theorists who say "rules of morality apply to all human transactions whether the actors be individuals or states" are affirming that the tendency of morality, once developed, is to take all human relations into its compass—including the relations between groups. They believe that "standard morality"—and the cultural and intellectual development of ethical principles—become ascendant over crude group morality in the long run.

This book then is both an expository presentation of the history of thought on the subject of international morality, and a critique of that thought using primarily the new insights of sociobiology. I am not unaware that sociobiology is controversial, and criticisms of it will be incorporated at appropriate places in the text. Nevertheless, I do not think that application of it to international relations theory is reckless at this stage. On the contrary, I think that what sociobiology has to say about the nature of morality and the nature of international relations are two of the "missing pieces" in all previous discussion on the subject of international morality.

The reader should be forewarned that this book does not jump into actual contemporary issues in international morality. It starts out with a careful philosophical review of the problem, in which the reader will be expected to bear with some rather intricate detail—then he will be asked to follow a fairly close argument about human evolution. The payoff, however, is that a grounding in these two areas prepares him to think about international morality in a constructive and novel way later. Knowledge of the material contained in Parts One and Two is prerequisite, in my estimation, for 'doing anything' about contemporary problems of international morality.

Part I

Traditional Arguments concerning International Morality

2

The Negative Position

> *The Rights of Man were transformed into universal*
> *conquest without, it seems, any theorizing more sophis-*
> *ticated . . . than the statement by Genet which Fox quoted*
> *in the House of Commons: "I would throw Vattel and*
> *Grotius into the sea whenever their principles interfere*
> *with my notions of the rights of nations."*
>
> — *Martin Wight*

Introduction to Part One

Part One, "Traditional Arguments concerning International Morality," encompasses Chapters 2, 3, and 4. Chapter 2 presents six arguments that constitute what I call the *negative* position on international morality. I choose to discuss the negative position before discussing the positive position since the negative position currently dominates the academic field of international relations and is also widely accepted by practitioners of politics and diplomacy. The six arguments that constitute the *positive* position will then be presented in Chapter 3.

In each of the twelve sections, I shall encapsulate the argument as succinctly as possible; this will necessarily entail some sacrifice of the variation within each idea. Its origin, its major contributors, and the main thrust of the argument will be noted. So as not to give the reader a "rosier" view of each argument than is warranted, I shall follow each with a list of the major criticisms to which it has been subjected. Furthermore, the chapters on the negative and positive positions will be followed by a chapter that compares the merits of those positions. (Chapter 4).

Definitions

I must mention here that my phrase "arguments concerning international morality" has a very restricted meaning. By the term "international morality" in Part One, I mean to focus on the problematical *existence* of a moral relationship among nations. That is, I am interested only in philosophical statements about whether such a relationship does or does not exist. I am not, for now, interested in judging the actual moral behavior of nations, or even identifying the international issues that have moral significance. (After all, if it could be proven that nations do not have a moral relationship among themselves—as do individuals—it would be pointless to list international moral issues and impossible to judge a nation's "moral behavior".)

My choice of the twelve arguments below was the result of an inventory in which I tried to find all available worthwhile philosophical statements about the existence, or nonexistence, of a moral relationship among nations. In some cases, such as that of Hobbes, I extracted the author's "argument concerning international morality" from his larger theories about other things. In other cases, such as that of Bozeman, the argument was expanded by me from rather isolated comments by the author. The decision to give the uniform label "argument" to these twelve somewhat uneven offerings stems from my desire to show that each *argues* for the existence, or nonexistence, of a moral relationship among states. Thus, each of the six arguments supporting the negative position says "There is no moral relationship among states *because of such-and-such a reason*". In Niebuhr's argument, for example, the reason is the social-psychological one that "humans acting in groups are not as conscience-bound as humans acting individually".

There is one other term that must be defined here at the outset, namely, the word "theory." As just stated, I shall uniformly label the twelve ideas "arguments" when I am specifically presenting their case for or against international morality. But frequently I shall refer to their more general function, which is as explanatory theories of some aspect of international relations. My use of the word "theory" in those instances is not meant to credit them with being rigorous scientific theories. Of the twelve arguments below, the two which are most often called "theories" in the literature, namely the theory of the just war and world-order theory, are perhaps the least deserving of that name. (They are more like policy recommendations.) The fact is that the word "theory" has many definitions, and it is difficult to avoid these more relaxed usages. *The American Heritage Dictionary* gives three definitions of the word *theory*: "1. Systematically organized knowledge applicable in a relatively wide variety of circumstances . . . 2. Abstract reasoning; speculation 3. Broadly, hypothesis or supposition." My references to "theory" throughout this book will fit mainly under the second and third definitions.*

---

*The professional use of the term "theory" in political science is, in any case, not cut-and-dried. As John Garnett observes in his book, *Commonsense and the Theory of International Politics* (p.4), "In the literature of international politics, the meaning of the term theory is not yet sufficiently settled to justify any kind of unilaterally stipulated restrictive definition . . . Here, more often than not, terms like 'model,' 'approach' and 'concept' are used interchangeably with 'theory,' and at this stage of the subject's development it seems sensible to regard them, not as alternatives to theory, but as varieties of it . . ." Multiple usages of the word "theory," are also identified by James Dougherty and Robert Pfaltzgraff in their book, *Contending Theories of International Relations* (pp. 11-12).

The Negative Position

Let us now look at the most persuasive arguments that deny the existence of, or in some cases the desirability of, international morality. On the whole, they hold that "there is not, and cannot be, a moral relationship among states." Some of the writers who defend this position claim to do so from a neutral standpoint, that is, they are just reporting the facts of life without commentary. In others, we find a barely disguised rationalization for, or even a celebration of, national selfishness, while in others there is a tone of regret: the dynamics of international politics are said to be dictated by necessity and the results may be called "tragic."

Of the six arguments to be presented here, the first two, those of *national interest* and *international anarchy*, arose in the sixteenth and seventeenth centuries. These discuss the nature of power and competition, and imply that something in human nature prevents morality from working in world politics. The next two, the arguments of *national sovereignty* and *nationalism*, became prominent in the eighteenth and nineteenth centuries. They emphasize mainly the nature of the state and the rights of the state and thus glorify the state over the international community. The last two, the arguments of *the immorality of the group* and *cultural pluralism*, are creatures of the twentieth century. They use a sociological approach to argue that certain characteristics of groups and cultures prevent the formation of an international morality.

In summarizing their position, that "there is not, and cannot be, a moral relationship among states," I use the word "states" to mean "nation-states." In most instances the word "nations" would be equally appropriate; however, I wish to concentrate on nations as political entities, rather than as ethnic groups or cultures.

The National Interest

The first argument that supports the negative position concerning international morality is that of the *national interest*. It holds that *the essential, perennial relationship among states is one of competition and self-help, and hence moral considerations are irrelevant*. The advice which national interest writers offer to the statesman is that he should attend first to his nation's survival, and second to the furtherance of its interests. There is apparently a moral principle involved here—that of protecting the nation, or of guarding the *salus populi*. However, another feature of national interest theory is more straightforwardly amoral. It emphasizes "the facts of life." In the real world, it says, international relations are characterized by aggression, deceit, and the play of power politics. The national leader must, perforce, follow the rules of the game: he must meet his opponents on their own terms. To wish instead that the world were a more moral or idealistic place is to engage in naive fantasy. The national interest approach is associated with, and holds some tenets in common with, the theories of *raison d'etat, realpolitik,* and realism.

It could be said that a national interest position was adumbrated as early as the sixteenth century. Niccolo Machiavelli (1469-1527) is considered one of the earliest realists, and also a father of political science. He broke with the medieval tradition of describing how the world *should* work, and wrote instead his observations of actual human behavior. As Raymond Gettell notes, Machiavelli "separated politics and ethics even to the point of scandal and paradox."[1] It was Machiavelli's desire to develop a "scientific" view of statecraft, to teach the Prince how to go about dealing with the problems of power. He famously exhorted the Prince to be guided by expedience, not moral principle, choosing, for example, cruelty over justice, if that made his rule more efficient. "It is necessary for a Prince wishing to hold his own to know how to do wrong and to make use of it or not according to necessity."[2]

Machiavelli's emphasis could thus be said to be on "prince interest" rather than on national interest, except that he sometimes equated the two. While never having any illusions about the selfish personal motivations of princes, Machiavelli saw that strong leaders could save the state from ruin. Eager that the republic of Florence not be invaded by foreign armies, he argued that any action could be justified. The Prince "need not make himself uneasy at incurring a reproach for those vices without which the state can only be saved with difficulty."[3] The moral theme here is that a greater good justifies the abandonment of moral principle.

The rightness of pursuing the national interest is widely accepted today. Foreign policy is to be conducted in an amoral way. Covert operations, for example, are practical ways of dealing with enemies or rivals, to be judged only according to their success, not according to moral criteria. One rule of thumb here is: if the other side does it, we must do it. This public repudiation of moral standards may seem uncharacteristic of the West. The intellectual defense of the national interest is, I believe, related to a sudden reaction against *idealism* in international political theory that came about in the 1940s. This reaction was based both on the discovery of philosophical flaws in the idealist position, and on historical events. Such things as the League of Nations and the Kellogg-Briand pact were predicated on a faith in the "decency" of nations. When this faith was shattered in the 1930s there was room for new theorizing as to the realities of international politics, and a need to explain the behavior of nations according to such concepts as the national interest.

The new school of thought that came about is broadly labelled *realism.* In 1940, the British diplomat E.H. Carr published *The Twenty Years' Crisis, 1919-1939: An Introduction to the Study of International*

Relations. In that book, Carr achieved a remarkable *coup* over idealism by lumping all idealist theories into a category which he disparagingly labelled "utopian." Hans Morgenthau elaborated the realist position brilliantly and boldly in his 1948 book, *Politics among Nations*, which became the leading textbook of international relations in the United States for four decades. In most of his writings Morgenthau explicitly advocated the national interest; he recommended exclusive attention to power politics, and the banishing of moral consideration from foreign affairs.[4] In the following remark by Morgenthau we hear the echo of Machiavelli:

> *Why should we deny Jefferson's cunning, say, in the Puget Sound affair, the cruelty with which the Indians were treated, and the faithlessness with which the treaties with the Indians were cast aside? We know that this is the way all nations are when their interests are at stake—so cruel, so faithless, so cunning.*[5]*

Morgenthau had emigrated from Hitler's Germany to the United States and was obsessed with the need to show the American government how power politics works.[6] He exerted a major influence on the U.S. State Department, particularly by way of his disciples, such as George Kennan in the 1950s and Henry Kissinger in the 1970s. This was a most dramatic instance of academic theory persuading the practitioners. As John C. Garnett has put it, American policy-makers "swallowed Realism hook, line, and sinker."[7]

For our purposes in this study, it can be seen that the national interest argument supports the overall negative position that "there is not and cannot be a moral relationship among states." It gives two reasons for this (both of which appear to be "moral" reasons). The first, mentioned above, is that the protection of one's own state is a greater good than, say, concern for other states. The second is that incorporation of moral principles into foreign policy should be eschewed because it is both inappropriate and potentially harmful. Kennan particularly developed the theme that morality is not only irrelevant in international affairs, it is a positively dangerous commodity since it may lead to crusading fervor and lack of reasonable perspective. In his 1952 book, *American Diplomacy: 1900-1950*, Kennan deplored "the carrying over into affairs of states of

---

*It would be misleading if this brief presentation portrayed Morgenthau as someone personally unconcerned with the moral significance of international politics. In various writings, such as *Scientific Man versus Power Politics* and *The Purpose of American Politics*, he showed that a nation's foreign policy is constrained both by moral principle and by public opinion, and that ideals help to shape a nation's "purpose," including its international purpose. Likewise, E.H. Carr should not be caricatured as a one-sided thinker. He recognized that a shift from idealism to pure realism would deprive us of all imagination and motivation.

the concepts of right and wrong: the assumption that state behavior is a fit subject for moral judgment"—a position which he reiterated as recently as 1986.[8] Thus, various scholars have given an ethical dimension, as it were, to amorality in foreign policy.

Finally, let me say something further about realism. It is outside the scope of this book to present the general tenets of realism.* However, two large themes carry over from the realists' ideas to lend general support to the negative position on international morality. The first is their emphasis on *necessity*, rather than, say, reasoned preference. Realists believe that certain forces in the world, or perhaps ultimately in human nature, determine the outcome of international events. This belief naturally devalues any effort to make nations behave ethically. The second theme is realism's emphasis on the *autonomy of politics*—that is, its autonomy from other spheres of activity such as law, economy, or ethics. In my estimation it is the sophisticated appeal of these two themes that has most assisted the rise of realism to its important position in academia.

In 1985 Michael Banks found realism to be still the foremost "paradigm" in international relations.[9] Obviously the success of realism owes much to its great explanatory power: it provides a very credible description of the world political scene. At the same time I believe it is worth noting that additional factors, such as factors in the cultural background, help to make this theory particularly welcome. For example, *academically*, realism and power politics are appropriately scientific-sounding, and satisfy the requirements of professional specialization: political scientists are able to isolate politics from ethics in order to focus exclusively on the operation of power. *Popularly*, the Machiavellian ethics associated with realism seem acceptable to the layman; as Stanley Hoffman notes, these appeal to the "machismo of might and to the selfish instincts suppressed by Christian ethics."[10] *Politically*, realism's emphasis on the national interest would naturally appeal to powerful Western nations, who have nothing to lose by endorsing the realistic status quo as opposed to conjuring up idealistic reforms.

---

*The following sources would yield a reasonable collection of realism's tenets: Martin Wight, *Power Politics*; Hans Morgenthau, *Politics among Nations*; Raymond Aron, *Peace and War*; and Kenneth Thompson's biographical work, *Masters of International Thought*. A recent philosophical critique of realism can be found in Michael Joseph Smith, *Realism from Weber to Kissinger*. The structural variant of realism appears principally in Kenneth Waltz, *Theory of International Politics*, and is discussed in Richard Little, "Structuralism and Neo-Realism." "The Poverty of Neo-realism" by Richard Ashley, and replies to it, such as Richard Gilpin, "The Richness of the Tradition of Political Realism," can be found in *International Organization's* "Symposium on the New Realism." (Vol. 38, 1984)

The cultural setting of the twelve arguments concerning international morality will be further discussed in Chapter 4. For now we must turn to a discussion of the criticisms of national interest.

Criticisms of the National Interest Argument

Despite its strong intellectual hold, the idea of national interest is not without its challengers and critics. There are flaws in the argument. For example, as Marshall Cohen points out, it is false to assume that people in a modern democracy give their leaders *carte blanche* to do anything and everything on the nation's behalf. That would be like saying, Cohen argues, that stockholders will always insist that their drug company sell thalidomide so long as it increases profits.[11]

There is also the charge that the term "national interest" may be a misnomer, since it is often merely the interests of certain elites that are at stake. Analysts from Charles Beard[12] in 1934 to Noam Chomsky and Edward Herman[13] in 1982 have demonstrated that American foreign policy is often made for the benefit of narrow economic interests rather than for, and sometimes contrary to, the interests of the nation as a whole. Here, the phrase "national interest" is merely a device to rally loyalty. Similarly, the term "national security" may cover a multitude of sins: Hoffman warns us to be alert to "the tinsel Machiavellianism that prostitutes the notion of national security in order to justify shabby or deluded external interventions."[14]

Additionally, the national interest argument can be criticized for trying to make of itself a moral idea. It seems to me that realism and national interest theory ring more true when they do *not* pretend to endorse moral principle. The claim that a statesman is acting most morally by protecting his own nation is, at best, an irritating distraction when one is trying to discuss how nations should treat one another. Moreover, Morgenthau and Kissinger add a further twist by making *possibility* the touchstone of moral behavior in a statesman.[15] For example, Kissinger holds that to try to do the impossible, such as to try to enforce human rights abroad, is immoral. This kind of talk so perverts the usual meaning of the word "moral" as to make the national interest argument appear merely propagandist.

International Anarchy

The second argument that supports the negative position on international morality is that of *international anarchy*. The word "anarchy" means "without rule," and it is certainly very significant for international relations that world society has no government and no ruler. The international-anarchy argument holds that *while the members of domestic societies have formed a social contract with one another and so live in a civilized* manner, the nations of the world have never formed a contract and therefore continue to act savagely toward one another. According to this view there is no such thing as justice on the world scene, nor is there any overriding authority. There is also no room for trust. Any enthusiasm which a given state may feel about forming relationships with other states should be tempered by skepticism and suspicion towards its neighbor.

The architect of the theory of international anarchy* is Thomas Hobbes (1588-1679). Like Machiavelli, Hobbes was fascinated by Renaissance science and by the possibility of using a scientific approach to understand politics. A friend of Galileo and a contemporary of Newton, Hobbes was interested in the laws of motion. His portrayal of natural man in a perpetual state of violent conflict was probably derived both from the idea of physics and the reality of social chaos during the English civil war. His "billiard ball" imagery, of states bumping up against one another in an anarchic world, has remained central in international relations theory until recent times.

Hobbes' primary interest was in civil society, not in international anarchy. The latter idea was developed only briefly, in one chapter of his *Leviathan*.[16] Hobbes' main concern in *Leviathan* was to establish the obligation of the citizen to obey the sovereign, and for this he used the device of social contract. By contrast, he said, the world of states has not made a contract, its members do not have above them a common power to keep them in awe, and they do not constitute a society. This type of analogy led Hobbes to some surprising logic. He wrote:

> To this Warre of every man against every man, this . . . is consequent: that nothing can be Unjust. The notions of Right and Wrong, Justice and Injustice, have there no place. Where there is no common Power, there is no Law: where no Law, no injustice. Force and Fraud, are in Warre the two Cardinall vertues.[17]

In other words, law precedes morality rather than the other way around. Since there is no world law, moral obligations do not apply to states. Thus Hobbes would exempt even civilized nations from having to treat foreign states in an ethical—or even a "civilized"—manner.

A less controversial aspect of Hobbes' work is simply his emphasis on the need for self-defense. All nations are insecure, hence they must put "Spyes upon their neighbors" and have "Garrisons and Guns upon the Frontiers of their Kingdoms".[18] This view has recently been updated by Andrew Bard Schmookler in his book, *The Parable of the Tribes*. He

---

*This theory of international anarchy bears no relation to the philosophy of anarchism, which holds that all forms of government are oppressive and undesirable.

notes that if there were ten tribes on Earth and nine of them wanted peace, it would eventually come to pass that all ten would be warlike because of the need to guard against the ruthlessness of the one aggressor.[19] It hardly needs to be said that international anarchy theory, like national interest theory, enjoys widespread belief today.

Criticisms of the International Anarchy Argument

Numerous challenges to Hobbes' model of international society are current. Hedley Bull has argued, in *The Anarchical Society*, that states *do* form a society, even in the absence of a ruler, and that the limiting of aggression and the keeping of promises ("*pacta sunt servanda*") are two of that society's central concerns.[20] Ian Brownlie notes that the typical interaction of state with state is not savage in quality, but is in fact humdrum. Whether in matters of civil aviation, commerce, or immigration, states routinely follow international law; warlike interactions are the exception, not the rule.[21]

Other writers have criticized Hobbes' billiard-ball model of states. The *dependencia* theorists complain that the Hobbesian model inaccurately implies that states are equal in power whereas they are very unequal. This Marxist-inspired view holds that a better model would be that of an octopus, representing the advanced, rich nations, whose tentacles suck wealth from the Third World.[22] A third major criticism is that Hobbesian imagery improperly portrays states as the only actors in world affairs: Robert Keohane and Joseph S. Nye, Jr. show that there are many transnational interactions occuring today which do not involve states, and that economic institutions and non-governmental agencies can be important actors in dealings with states.[23]

Finally, as to Hobbes' idea of the ubiquity of security concerns, Sissela Bok notes that preoccupation with defense can be a self-fulfilling prophecy. Clausewitz and others in the past recommended the use of "worst-case scenarios" in prudent defense planning, but today modern technology has removed almost all limits to what an enemy could conceivably be conjuring up. Bok writes:

> The mutual distrust between nuclear powers has become self-perpetuating; it creates the very evidence which reinforces it. . . . Each nation imagines the enemy's most ingenious and devastating schemes and then [actually implements the means] of retaliating with enough severity to deter anyone from putting such schemes into action.[24]

Bok does not think that resignation to such a spiral of behavior is necessarily warranted—as long as the strategies of trust, mistrust, and deception become better understood. She notes, "Since distrust grows through reciprocal and repeated actions, it stands to reason that it can also be cut back thus."[25]

National Sovereignty

The third argument that supports the negative position on international morality—that "there is not and cannot be a moral relationship among states"—is that of *national sovereignty.* It holds that *states have a right to freedom and dignity.* (The sovereign right of nations can be seen as comparable to the liberal right of individual freedom). In a sense, this theory could be listed under the positive position on international morality because it holds that states *do* have a moral obligation toward one another—namely, the obligation to respect one another's independence. However it seems more appropriate to list national sovereignty under the negative position, since it excludes all obligations *except* the one of mutual respect. In its contemporaray usage, furthermore, national sovereignty is a doctrine that frequently proclaims the rights of states against the "rights of humanity." David Luban notes that the sovereignty idea can be "a major moral enemy of the human rights movement, inasmuch as attempts at sanctions or interventions against human rights offenders are inevitably denounced as violations of their sovereignty."[26]

As F.H. Hinsley has recorded, arrival at the very idea of sovereignty, in the domestic sense, was a great achievement in the late Christian era. It depended partly on the rediscovery, in the thirteenth century, of Greek writings concerning the notion of the *polis,* the body politic.[27] Its effect was to *limit* state authority by enlarging the role of popular consent. The idea of *multiple* sovereignties took even longer to develop. "Men had to overcome immense obstacles before they could conceive of the world they inhabited as being a world composed of separate political communities."[28] Most of all, Hinsley says, they had to rid themselves of the notion that Christendom was a single community and that natural law was the supreme authority.[29]

When they did accomplish this, the resulting doctrine of national sovereignty, in the seventeenth and eighteenth centuries, had the effect of *enhancing* the power of the state. It sanctioned the secular power of the state, and allowed *raison d'etat* to dictate foreign policy. Andrew Linklater contends that certain major writers on international law at that time, such as Vattel and Pufendorf, were philosophically sympathetic to natural law, but they compromised by defending the sovereign state as sacrosanct.[30] What they could have done, as Pufendorf himself earlier suggested, was to show that the sovereigns were "still subject to the natural law, and so were obligated, of course, to draw up only such rules of sovereignty . . . as were agreeable to that law."[31]* Instead they settled for a dichotomy of

---

*Linklater develops this idea more fully in his book, *Men and Citizens in The Theory of International Relations,* in which he argues for a more cosmopolitan ethics.

private and public ethics, resulting in a "morality of statecraft" whereby "the sovereign as trustee for the welfare of the community, must deny the validity of principles which are normally observed in the conduct of purely private relations."[32]

The incompatibility of natural law with the law of sovereign states will be discussed in the next chapter. Here we might dwell on the state's immunity from external moral criticism as a feature of the national sovereignty doctrine. Statesmen today make full use of this privilege of immunity. Article 2 of the United Nations Charter requires that no member engage in "the threat or use of force against the . . . political independence of any state." This article is frequently invoked against external criticism of a state's domestic policies. Leo Kuper observes that the United Nations has come to function rather like a gentleman's club in which members politely look the other way in regard to each other's wrongdoings. By thus supporting one another's sovereignty, they guarantee similar immunity to criticism for themselves.[33] An example of the importance which sovereigns attach to "national privacy" can be seen in the regulation stipulating that petitions submitted to the United Nations Commission on Human Rights by injured parties are to be handled by that body in secret. Maurice Cranston has described this a "a situation worthy of Lewis Carroll."[34]

Perhaps the most direct example of the concept of national sovereignty working against the practice of international morality, or at least humanitarianism, can be seen in the history of the Genocide Convention. In 1948, while memories of the Holocaust were still fresh, many nations signed the Genocide Convention which promised that nations would bypass the protection of national sovereignty in order to rescue persons from genocidal massacres. Yet in clear instances where information of genocides has reached the United Nations in time for action to be taken, such as regarding Cambodia in 1975 or Burundi in 1972, no action was taken.[35] In fact the only time that the word "genocide" has been used in an official condemnation of state behavior by the United Nations was against Israel in connection with the 1983 massacre by Christian Phalangists in the Palestinian Camps.[36] This was predictable, in that Israel has been treated as a "pariah" state in the United Nations, not a full-fledged member of the gentleman's club enjoying immunity to criticism.

Criticism of the National Sovereignty Argument

By focussing on the rights of the sovereign state, the doctrine of national sovereignty overlooks or denies the rights of smaller entities such as individuals, or larger entities such as humanity. That logical dilemma is certainly the major criticism that can be made of the national sovereignty argument. However, there are three other important criticisms to be noted. The first is simply its inaccuracy as a description of the real world.

Interventions abound, for instance, that of South Africa in Botswana in 1985, that of the Soviet Union in Afghanistan in 1979, or that of the United States in the Dominican Republic in 1964. So the imagery and rhetoric about the sovereign equality of states is simply misleading. As Hoffman notes, "What produces interventions . . . is the perennial dialectic of relations between the weak and the strong."[37]

The second criticism concerns the ontologically false analogy between states and persons. Marshall Cohen points out: "It is far from obvious that because individual men have a natural right of self-preservation, states do as well . . . The death of a state does not require the loss of single life. Indeed it may even save some."[38] Charles Beitz claims that conceiving of nations as largely self-sufficient, purposive units leads to the erroneous normative conclusion "that states, like persons, have some sort of right of autonomy that insulates them from external moral criticism and political interference."[39]

The third criticism is the same one that applies to laissez-faire economics. States are seen as analogous to individuals in the liberal manner, each being a free agent pursuing its own interest. But this, Beitz says, implies "an indifference to the distributive outcomes of their economic interaction."[40] Thus the concept of sovereignty, which promotes the equality of states, hides the facts of economic dependency and exploitation.

Nationalism

The fourth argument that supports the negative position on international morality is that of *nationalism*. It *proclaims the nation itself as the greatest value.* Of course, nationalism is usually not presented as a formal theory. Rather, it is often merely an expression of patriotism, or an appeal to ethnocentrism. However, there are several philosophical justifications of nationalism that give it a sort of intellectual respectability. Three of these, which will be discussed below, are: the idea of the general will or the collective good; the romantic claims in support of cultural diversity; and the argument that ethnic self-determination is a valid political goal.

Collectivist theories, concerned with the social good, portray the nation, or the community, as more fundamental and more important than the individual person. Before any philosophers thought up theories of the social good, collectivism no doubt prevailed naturally. For thousands of years of human prehistory and history, the group *was* more important than the individual — individualism itself being an artifact of modernity. The first consciously-created scheme for the social good recorded in Western philosophy is Plato's *Republic*. Here, justice is thought to be comprised of the willing participation of each person in his social and occupational role.[41]

For our purposes, however, the key writer on the social good is Jean-Jacques Rousseau (1712-1778) whose collectivist idea of the *general will* influenced Kant, Hegel, and Marx. Rousseau's collectivist conclusions can perhaps be traced to his belief that man is fundamentally social rather than egoistic. Whereas Hobbes had implied that egoistic persons joined society for the benefit of security, Rousseau postulated that only in society did persons fulfill their real human nature. In *Du Contrat Social* he wrote:

> The passing from the state of nature to the civil society . . . puts justice as a rule of conduct in the place of interest. . . . It is only then, when the voice of duty has taken the place of physical impulse, and right that of desire, that man, who has hitherto thought only of himself, finds himself compelled to act on other principles, and to consult his reason rather than study his inclinations.[42]

In Rousseau's work, the word "contract" does not imply a covenant by which people mandate certain powers to a thereby accountable ruler. Rather, in the social contract "each of us puts his person and all his power in common under the supreme direction of the general will."[43] As Cranston notes, this general will is not to be confused with the will of the majority; the general will is a normative concept whereas the will of all is merely an empirical concept.[44] Moreover, Rousseau says, "Whosoever refuses to obey the general will shall be compelled to do so by the whole body. This means nothing less than that he will be forced to be free."[45]

The significance of Rousseau's work for the argument of nationalism is that it leads to an exaltation of nation and state, based on a semi-mystical idea of union. He wrote, "In place of the individual personality of each contracting party, this act of association creates a moral and collective body [and thus receives] its unity, its common identity, its life and its will."[46] In the case of the new states of the twentieth century that had to mobilize politically-backward populations, a philosophy of the general will proved to be a useful apology for centralized authority. At the same time it assisted the rhetoric about the sacredness of the state and perhaps made more credible the claim of charismatic leaders to be the personification of the nation. The underlying tactic of nationalist thinking, it seems, consists of a conflation of different entities into one. As an example, the Soviet delegate to the United Nations was heard to say, upon abstaining from voting for the Universal Declaration of Human Rights in 1948, "In a society where there are no rival classes, there cannot be any contradiction between the government and the individual, since the government is in fact the collective individual."[47]

A second philosophical underpinning for modern nationalism is the romantic idea that humanity consists of the separate cultural achievements of particular peoples. Johann Gottfried von Herder (1744-1803) opposed the French Enlightenment idea of rational progress which implied that the eighteenth-century achievement in art and science was the standard of civilization. He proposed instead that nonrational aspects of cultures, including primitive ones, have been essential to the development of the human spirit.[48] Besides valuing diversity, romanticism also glorified emotion, spirituality, and imagination; it encouraged rebellious poetry and music. The resulting works, such as those of Wordsworth, Thoreau, Chopin, or Wagner, in turn fuelled nationalist sentiment, a feeling of pride in the greatness of one's nation. The romantic love of Nature assisted the theory that a "people" was a natural unit, related by blood and tied to the soil.

Romantic ideas contribute to a negative approach to international morality in at least two ways. First, their spirit is anti-cosmopolitan. As Linklater states, "The historicists took humanity to be not an essence shared by all men, but the totality of cultural configurations."[49] Hence, "horizontal moral ties between individual members of world society are deemed illusory; what is objectively necessary is the separation of men into political communities."[50] Second, the idea of each culture fulfilling its specialty can lead to the moral claim that each has a divine mission to succeed, even in competition with other nations. Friedrich von Treitschke claimed, "Every people has the right to believe that in itself certain forces of the divine reason find their highest expression."[51] He glorified war as "not barbarism but a holy ordeal which rightly determines the destiny of peoples."[52]

After the theories of collectivism and romanticism, the third idea underpinning nationalism is the defense of ethnic integrity. This kind of nationalism, associated for example with Mazzini's nineteenth-century drive to unite Italy, is based on the principle that the political and national unit should be congruent.[53] Ernest Gellner defines nationalism as "a theory of political legitimacy, which requires that ethnic boundaries should not cut across political ones."[54] In the mid-twentieth century, the call for ethnic unity, also known as self-determination or national liberation, was one of the moral ideas guiding decolonization. Paradoxically, at the same time, calls for "national unity" had to be made in new states whose borders had incorporated diverse ethnic groups in the days of colonial rule. Leaders in these states had to use such symbols as the flag, Independence Day, and historic heroes, in the task of "nation-building." Today, claims for secession and irredentism are less successful, with the most intractable cases being the ones where the contenders are approximately equal in historical claim or in political and military strength.

The position of nationalism as a "negative argument" concerning international morality obviously has to do with the fact that the protection of "one's own people" can mean utterly callous treatment of anyone else.

As Gellner points out, "a territorial political unit can only become ethnically homogeneous ... if it either kills, or expels, or assimilates all non-nationals."[55] In living memory, tens of millions of people have been killed or deported in actions undertaken to preserve the existence, or the honor, or the purity of nations. Thus, John Dunn calls nationalism "the starkest political shame of the twentieth century."[56]

Criticisms of the Nationalist Argument

Firstly, all of the theoretical aspects of nationalism can be subjected to criticism. When writers such as Rousseau and Hegel define freedom as conformity, they simply twist the word "freedom" beyond recognition. At best it could be said that a person who gives up the pursuit of his own interest in favor of the welfare of the group gains freedom from bad conscience, or freedom from the dangers of rebelling against authority. The proposal that something like a "general will" actually exists is unsupported metaphysics. The concept can be seen as a philosophical sleight of hand; it provided Rousseau with a way out of the conflict between self-interest and duty to society.

Secondly, the romantic claim that each culture perfects its special achievement in isolation is only partly true. There has been immense borrowing of material and ideational culture in all ages. In a similar vein, the claim that an ethnic group is related by blood is more or less nonsense. As Pierre van den Berghe points out, the white population of Australia, a collection of immigrants from European countries, cannot be said to be a group of kinsmen. Even people in a relatively homogeneous nation such as Japan have only a fictional relationship to one another.[57]

Thirdly, nationalist doctrine may be criticized on the grounds of its moral ambiguity. As Dunn notes, "Cultural nationalism at home, practised between consenting adults in national privacy or bravely if somewhat furtively devised within someone else's imperial domain" may be harmless or even edifying.[58] But, at the same time, he notes, we feel the "moral shabbiness" of nationalism readily enough just because it "does violate so directly the official conceptual categories of modern ethics, the universalist heritage of a natural law."[59]

The Immorality of Groups

The fifth argument that supports the negative position on international morality is that of the *immorality of groups*. It holds that *a group of persons does not act ethically, as a body, in a way that reflects the typical behavior of its individual members*. Rather, there are certain characteristics of group behavior which lead to a lower moral standard for the group. The author of this theory is the Protestant theologian Reinhold Niebuhr (1892-1971) who was a church pastor and teacher at Union Theological

Seminary in New York. During the 1920s he became disenchanted with idealism and tried to work out a moral and social theory that realistically took "sin" into account. He defined his "Christian realism" as: "the disposition to take all factors in a social and political situation, which offer resistance to established norms, into account, particularly the factors of self-interest and power."[60] Although directly influential as a public commentator on such subjects as democracy and Marxism, his impact on international relations theory came about largely because he influenced such diplomats and scholars as Morgenthau and Kennan. Morgenthau called Niebuhr the greatest political thinker of his generation; Kennan referred to him as "the father of us all."[61]

Niebuhr's major contribution to the negative position on international morality was made in his book, *Moral Man and Immoral Society*, (which, he later said, should have been called *The Not So Moral Man and His Less Moral Communities*).[62] His theory combines several observations. The first is that large groups, such as whole countries, do not have direct contact with each other, and the members cannot perceive each other's needs or sympathize as they would on a face-to-face basis.[63] A second factor making it difficult for groups to act with a conscience is that "the mind, which places a restraint upon impulses in individual life, exists only in a very inchoate form in the nation."[64] Thirdly, there can be no ethical action without self-criticism, but such criticism is "usually thwarted by the governing classes and by a certain instinct for unity in society itself."[65] That is, "Every society [regards] criticism as a proof of want of loyalty."[66]

Fourthly, Niebuhr finds that there is an ethical paradox in patriotism which has almost completely escaped notice, namely, that patriotism transmutes individual selflessness into national egoism. Loyalty to the nation is a high form of altruism, yet "the unqualified character of this devotion is the very basis of the nation's power and of the freedom to use the power without moral restraint."[67] Oddly, then, it is the unselfishness of individuals which makes for the selfishness of nations! Hence it is a vain hope to think that international problems can be solved merely by trying to increase the morality and sympathy of individuals.

Fifthly, "there is an alloy of projected self-interest in patriotic action. The man in the street, with his lust for power and prestige thwarted by his own limitations" indulges those lusts vicariously in his nation's successes.[68] Sixthly, there is a perennial weakness in the moral life of individuals, namely, hypocrisy, which "is simply raised to the nth degree in national life."[69] Nations seem able to get away with blatantly hypocritical explanations for their actions. Niebuhr cites, as an example of national hypocrisy, President McKinley's statement that before deciding to annex the Philippines "I went on my knees and prayed to Almighty God for light and guidance [and then I saw that we must] take all the Filipinos, and uplift and civilize and Christianize them . . . for whom Christ also died."[70] But the height of hypocrisy, Niebuhr says, is "the Preamble of the Treaty of the Holy Alliance in which the reactionary intentions of Russia, Prussia, and Austria . . . are introduced in words reeking with dishonest religious unction: 'Their majesties solemnly declare . . . to take as their sole rule the precepts of holy Religion, precepts of righteousness, Christian love, and peace.' "[71] In short, Niebuhr says "No nation has ever made a frank avowal of its real imperial motives."[72]

R.M. Hare, also, believes that there are certain characteristics of inter-national action which do not fit the routine of inter-individual morality. He defines moral thinking as "subjecting one's own interests, where they conflict with those of other people, to a principle which one can accept as governing anyone's conduct in like circumstances."[73] However, he notes, morality includes the pursuit of broad *ideals* as well as merely the reconciliation of *interests*, and nations in conflict with each other are as likely to be in conflict over ideals as over interests.

> Where an ideal is involved in the conflict . . . the situation is much more difficult; for ideals have a universalizability of their own and therefore resist [reconciliation, or bargaining]. This is most clearly evident in international politics . . . [and so] conflicts became much more intractable.[74]

Criticisms of the Immorality-of-Groups Argument

It is hard to find challenges to the theory of the immorality of the group, although Niebuhr offered one himself. Late in his career, according to James F. Childress, Niebuhr "worried that his realism had become 'excessively consistent' and had obscured the residual capacity for justice and devotion to 'the larger good,' even in collective life."[75] A similar criticism has been made of realism in general. Referring to Morgenthau's book, *Politics among Nations*, John C. Garnett comments, "Generations of students were so gripped by a brilliantly convincing view of the world that they were unable thereafter to see anything except crude 'power politics'."[76] According to Garnett, "the value of . . . concepts is that they help us to order data that would otherwise be unmanageable, and alert us to patterns and relationships which might otherwise elude us . . . however, some concepts can be so persuasive that they blinker the vision of those who hold them."[77]

Relatedly, Michael Banks reminds us that "the study of international relations must be regarded as part scholarly inquiry, part ideological discourse, shared among scholars, commentators and practitioners in all parts of the world."[78] "Each set of ideas," he says, "either strengthens or weakens existing reality, and thereby alters it."[79] So the very presence in society of ideas such as Niebuhr's may influence the moral behavior of nations. Of course these criticisms of realism, or indirectly of Christian realism, do not dispute the specific observations which Niebuhr offered concerning group behavior. I personally cannot locate any logical flaws in Niebuhr's theory of group immorality and am unaware of any scholars having attacked it directly.

Cultural Pluralism

The sixth and final argument to be listed here in support of the negative position on international morality is that of *cultural pluralism*. It holds that *international morality is impossible because there is no international cultural consensus about moral values.* Each nation, or each major region of the world, has a coherent system of values and attitudes, and a way of life based on age-old practices and religious beliefs. Some of these differ so profoundly from the Western way that there can be no meeting of the minds internationally. The main spokesperson for this argument is Adda Bozeman.*

Bozeman originally stressed the infeasibility of international law in her 1970 work, *The Future of Law in a Multicultural World.* The occasion for that book was the rapidity of political modernization of the globe and the appearance of new Third World states after World War II. Many of these states came into being by revolutions copied from the West; they had not, however, passed through the political and intellectual stages of the West. Bozeman stresses that the world view of the Christian West includes a certain orientation to time and certain expectations about the development of the individual personality, which underwrite our sense of law and contract, but which are not shared by other major cultures.

In regard to time, for example, she says of Asia and Africa, "Since the past is trusted as the abode of truth . . . it will perforce instruct or dominate the present."[80] That the Greeks were committed to the cultivation of rational yet daring thought she sees as the exceptional event, giving rise to the idea that "the uncertain future may be partially divested of its unpredictability by human effort."[81] In the words of Ortega y Gasset, "No human grouping can overcome the primary disposition toward time [that is, a conservative concern with order and constancy] unless it becomes somehow receptive to the individual and his innovating thought."[82]

---

*There is another argument concerning cultural pluralism that goes deeper than Bozeman's thesis. I refer to the case against the imposition of "common purposes" made by Terry Nardin in his book *Law, Morality, and the Relations of States.* Nardin relies on the conservative political philosophy of Michael Oakeshott which holds that small groups can associate voluntarily for common purposes, or ends, but not whole nations—and certainly not international society itself. Nardin emphasizes the propriety of developing legal *procedures* that are international, but not constructing a morality for the world.

To have the individual as the center of attention is also a Western phenomenon. "Asian and African traditions had been at one for millennia in stressing the primacy of the group, assigning essentially role-playing functions to the individual, and keeping thought subordinate to custom and authority."[83] For example, Bozeman says, the "original system of Buddhist ethics had been aimed at developing a non-political mentality, withdrawn from the concerns of acquisitive and self-defensive action."[84] In the West, on the other hand, "forms of social order have here been called into being for the express purpose of accomodating individualism.[85] All European legal systems converge upon "the person." "The person is capable of suffering and inflicting wrongs [and] the individual can commit himself voluntarily and rationally in association with others. . . . Law has been consistently trusted in the West as . . . the most effective agent of social control."[86] By contrast, no possibility existed in either the Orient or Africa "of disengaging 'law' as a separate system of norms, of fathoming 'contract' as a structuring principle for human relations, and of rendering rights and obligations in the language of legal abstractions."[87]

Of the Muslim world, Bozeman states that after the eleventh century "all the great problems of knowledge had been solved, once and for all, by the revealed word of God. . . . By rejecting rational modes of thought, the Arabs rendered themselves constitutionally distrustful of all abstract or *a priori* universal concepts, such as 'the law of nature', ideal justice, and the like."[88] In Africa, she notes, the clue may be the lack of literacy over the centuries. Hence even today, there is "no deeply rooted interest in theory and philosophy [because these] presuppose a well-developed relation to writing."[89]

In short, the Western way of looking at things is parochially Western, even if paradoxically it is universalist in its theme. We may be accused of missionary zeal and cultural imperialism in our attitude to other cultures. Bozeman concludes, "Obsessed with the task of creating an egalitarian, world-spanning conceptual order, reluctant to face up to natural diversity and disorder in human affairs, we have tended to force our preferred structures and typologies . . . upon institutions. . . ."[90]

Numerous other writers support various observations of Bozeman. For example, R.J. Vincent, writing about human rights in China states, "Individuals come last. . . . Indeed there is some doubt about whether they come anywhere at all."[91] Lucian Pye believes that Asians have never been able to demand popular consent for governments because the paternal structure of authority has been highly valued there.[92] Hedley Bull notes that "In China, Central Africa, Pakistan and Saudi Arabia, human rights in the Western sense are not regarded as morally valid."[93]

Max Stackhouse, in a cross-cultural survey of the creedal roots of human rights, finds that there are essential differences in the understanding of justice between, say, the United States and India. For the United States, the public law in the Liberal-Puritan view is an approximation of universal moral law.

> Each person is seen as equal before the law, whatever his estate or social condition. Justice is thus best served when all ties of blood, class, birth, group membership, previous behavior, and religious opinion are left out of consideration, for then the court has a greater chance of being fair, impartial, and unprejudiced. . . . In the Hindu view [on the other hand], it was precisely the social ties of persons—ties of family, caste, and religion—that were the clue to the identity, the being of persons, and hence to the *particular* cluster of rights and duties by which they were to be judged.[94]

James Piscatori finds that Jeffersonian ideas of men being born with inalienable rights could never be part of the Islamic outlook. The message given to Muhammad makes it clear that men must submit to Allah and "whosoever do not become the Lord's servants have no legitimate claims against him."[95] Moreover, the "individual's due" is also conditional on his obedience to government. "The intimate Islamic connection of religious and political functions, unlike the Christian West's dualism of Caesar's and God's due, obviate the need for a rival institution to check the validity and the power of the regime."[96] In general, Piscatori says, "Rights do not attach to men but to the Creator: it is more appropriate, [within Islam] to refer to the *privileges* of man."[97]*

Criticisms of the Cultural Pluralism Argument

Criticisms of cultural pluralist ideas are several. Firstly, on a practical point, international law is not necessarily infeasible because of diversity of cultures. International law is practiced not by cultures but by states. The political leaders of almost all states—exceptions may be made for contemporary theocracies—do "understand" Western concepts of law and contract, although they may choose not to submit to international law where it connotes Western hegemony. Secondly, time does not stand still: the historical trend has been for more and more states to join the European-based society of states, and to subscribe to its documents, and

---

*This kind of discussion often raises the objection that Islam has, and always has had, a highly developed system of human rights. Indeed it is true that the dignity of the person is a notable feature of Islamic society, and the Qur'an calls for compassion toward, and protection of, the weak and disadvantaged. What I am discussing here, however, is the idea of a "right" which is thought to inhere in the person, and the lack of this particular concept in any culture except that of the modern West. That lack purportedly makes for a non-unity of values and limits international legal development.

hence, ideas. The Preamble to the U.N. Declaration of Human Rights says that the declaration is a "common standard of achievement for all peoples."[98] As Hoffman remarks of those who have signed it merely for political effect, "If countries have been hypocritical enough to put [human rights] in their constitutions, they might as well be asked to do something about them."[99]

The third and more profound criticism of writings such as Bozeman's is that they are based on Western arrogance. Bozeman implies that Westerners have the last word on all subjects moral and that "our" ideas of justice, rights, and law are true, and our rational cast of mind objectively the best. But it can easily be objected that other societies' moral ideas are just as good, or better. The African writer Asmarom Legesse notes that "When forced to choose basic values, societies rank them differently,"[100] and that Africans rank the value of the community above that of the individual. In the Western tradition, he says, "the individual is held in a virtually sacralized position. There is a perpetual, and in our view obsessive, concern with the dignity of the individual."[101]

The individual is portrayed in Western literature as "fighting to preserve his domain against the oppressive forces of society" but, Legesse says, "no aspect of Western civilization makes an African more uncomfortable" than this.[102] The heart of African culture is egalitarian and antiheroic in character."[103] Moreover, most African cultures "have mechanisms of distributive justice that ensure that individuals do not deviate so far from the norm that they can overwhelm society."[104] For example, "The emperors and noblemen of Ethiopia were expected to die in poverty after lavishing their subjects with gifts." No one is allowed to break out at the top, but no one should fall out at the bottom, either. Thus, "Among the Nyakyusa of Tanzania local communities organize themselves into cooperative work crews that ensure that every farm is brought up to the community standard."[105] The cornerstone of the African Socialism of Julius Nyerere has been that "every man [has] an equal right to a decent life before any individual has a surplus above his needs."[106]

The foregoing African view is scarcely different from a statement which Stackhouse makes, based on Western thought:

> The decisive class for the future of humanity is the middle class. All should join it. When people are too poor or too rich; when they are powerless or so powerful that they can be corrected by no one; . . . when purpose is reduced to survival or has no end larger than self-realization— when this happens, something is fundamentally wrong with the world.[107]

In short, Westerners' judgments of "inferior cultures" may often be found to be made in ignorance.

Summary. To summarize this chapter, there is strong evidence to support the negative position on international morality, namely, that there is not and cannot be a moral relationship among states. Some of the arguments I listed relied on human nature, others on the imperatives of *raison d'etat*, and others merely on the fact of diversity, in order to demonstrate the difficulty of establishing an international morality. Some seemed to justify amorality, while others were more apologetic in tone. As may be expected, the three arguments which use the word "national"—national interest, national sovereignty, and nationalism—stressed a positive value. Indeed it can be argued that "the realist approach is saturated with normative presuppositions that accord moral primacy to the state and its security interests."[108]

On the whole, the negative view of international morality tends not to be gleeful about international *immorality*. Even Machiavelli appears to wish that morality could prevail. "A prince cannot observe all those things which are considered good in men . . . he must . . . not deviate from what is good, if possible, but be able to do evil if constrained."[109] The catch seems always to be the impossibility of it, owing to the peculiar fact that morality operates well within states or nations, but, for some reason, not among them. I shall subject this idea to further analysis later; for now we must take up the opposite side of the argument, the positive side.

3

The Positive Position

> The structure of human activity on a global scale necessarily has a normative element that is best studied in relation to the place of law. To deny law this role is to give way to the nihilism of the age.
>
> *Richard Falk*

If I have done my job effectively in the preceding chapter, the reader is now persuaded that there is not and cannot be a moral relationship among nations. Both the "evidence" and the "logic" against such a moral relationship are overwhelming. But now let the reader hear the arguments in support of the positive position! They, too, are, I believe, overwhelming. The positive position could be stated simply as "There *is* a moral relationship among nations." That manner of expressing it would show it to be the exact opposite of the negative position. However, for reasons that will become evident later, I prefer to phrase the positive position on international morality as "Rules of morality apply to all human transactions, whether the actors be individuals or states."

There are some significant differences in the approaches of the two positions. The negative arguments concentrate on the nature of the state, and the nature of the international arena, to explain why there can be no moral relationship. By contrast, the positive arguments concentrate on the nature of morality itself. Hence, some of the major concepts we will find discussed in this chapter are: law, justice, rights, duties, and values. A second point of contrast is that the negative arguments such as national interest, international anarchy, and national sovereignty, emphasize the practical, political aspects of international relations, while the positive arguments are more interested in the rational and reformist aspects.

This chapter summarizes six arguments that support the positive position on international morality. The first two, those of *natural law* and of *cosmopolitan morality*, are of ancient origin. They emphasize the enduring moral law and its universal applicability. The next two, the arguments of the *society of states* and *the just war*, have been important since the states system began, which is sometimes dated to the Treaty of Westphalia in 1648. Those two discuss particular opportunities for moral behavior among states. The last two, the arguments of *human rights* and

31

world order, are typical of twentieth-century thinking: they offer radical plans for organizing global affairs.

Natural Law

The first and most encompassing argument to be listed in support of the positive position on international morality is that of *natural law*. It holds that *even in the absence of world government, and despite the problem of cultural pluralism, there is still a universal standard of right and wrong.* Natural law proponents believe that there is a self-evident law, a law engraved in the human heart, which applies to all humans everywhere. Morality is not conventional, changing with time and place, but is fixed and is knowable. In the words of Cicero:

> True law is right reason in agreement with Nature; it is of universal application, unchanging and everlasting. Its commands urge us to duty and its prohibitions restrain us from wrong-doing . . . we need not look outside ourselves for an expounder or interpreter of it.[1]

There are two historical sources of the natural law idea. The first is Aristotle. He held the teleological view that all things must unfold according to their nature (*physis*) or purpose. The nature of humans is both biological and intellectual: people act to fulfill their instinctive desires and their urge to find a higher morality. At the beginning of his *Nicomachean Ethics* he wrote: "The Good has been rightly defined as 'that at which all things aim'."[2]

For Aristotle, the law which humans should follow is somehow contained within human nature itself. This idea passed into modern theory largely through the work of St. Thomas Aquinas who incorporated Aristotelian naturalism into Christian theology. Aquinas held that natural law guides individuals in three areas: self-preservation, procreation, and the pursuit of the knowledge of God.[3] If behavior does not serve those ends it is wrong. Thus, for example, the Catholic Church regards as sinful the practice of contraception and homosexuality because they are "unnatural," that is, they do not serve the ends of procreation.

The second source of natural law theory is Stoic thought. The philosophers of the Stoa, beginning with Zeno (295-261 BC), worked out an elaborate cosmology to explain the harmonious order of the universe. They postulated an animating force in the world, made of some pure, ether-like substance, called *pneuma* ("fiery breath").[4] This organizing principle was also known as the world-soul or Logos, or Reason. All nonhuman creatures act in conformity with the world soul. Humans, too, despite their personal freedom of action, can voluntarily choose to follow this natural law. An individual who chooses a disciplined, "stoic" life through the use of reason is acting in a partnership with God.[5] A major implication of Stoic thought is that the possession of reason makes all people equal citizens of a cosmopolis, a world community: this will be discussed later under "cosmopolitan morality."

The significance of natural law for our discussion of international morality stems from the fact that it is sometimes proposed either as a guide for international law or as a source of judgment of the behavior of individual states. The most dramatic use of natural law in an international context occurred this century at the Nuremberg Tribunals. There, the prosecutors identified the category of "crimes against humanity." These included the "extermination, enslavement, deportation and other inhumane acts committed against any civilian population ... *whether or not in violation of domestic law*"[6] (emphasis added). In other words, the immorality of these acts was self-evident; the fact that they had been declared legal in a certain sovereign state was considered irrelevant. But such an event as the Nuremberg judgments is very rare, and can be said to have occurred only because the world was scandalized by Nazi atrocities. Today, for example, there has been no international legal action to identify the crime against humanity which can reasonably be said to be implicit in the stockpiling of nuclear, chemical, or biological weapons.

The historical relationship between natural law and international law can be outlined as follows. The Romans first worked out a *jus gentium* (law of nations) in order to govern the many diverse tribes in the Empire. This *jus gentium* was said to contain those universal principles of law that were practised everywhere because of human nature rather than because of local convention. As such, the *jus gentium* was more or less interchangeable with the *jus naturale*. Later the Romans made use of the Stoic natural law idea in order to obtain a broader theoretical base for the *jus gentium*. Roger Scruton notes, "The *jus naturale* came to function as a standard against which all civil law could be judged, and was elevated by Cicero into the repository of reflective criticism and justification of positive law."[7]

Roman *jus gentium* was, however, not inter-national law, since all nations were part of the Empire. Indeed, even for over a thousand years after the fall of Rome there was no need in Europe for a true international law: the states of the Holy Roman Empire were unified in their deference to papal authority. Moreover it was a central metaphysical belief of the Christian religion that God was the author of a universal order. Saint Augustine (354-430) proposed that the very existence of separate states was artificial, a result of punishment for sin. By the seventeenth century, however, following the Reformation and Counter Reformation, it was no longer possible to maintain the fiction of a united Christendom: the states of Europe were constantly warring. Geoffrey Stern writes, "with the devastation of the German states in the Thirty Years War, the need to base their relations on a minimum of mutually acceptable standards of 'good' and 'just' behavior had become for the governments of western Europe an inescapable necessity."[8]

Hugo Grotius (1583-1645) is a transitional figure between natural law and international law. His *De Jure Belli Ac Pacis* of 1625 was a compendium of all kinds of law and how they relate to one another. Grotius importantly distinguished between divine law and volitional law, thus carving out a secular realm in which jurisprudence could subsequently operate. His understanding of how states would settle their disputes— "without using Mars as their arbiter"—included the expectation that reason and natural law would prevail. Richard Falk observes:

> What Grotius attempted . . . was to provide the foundation for a new normative order in international society that acknowledged the realities of an emergent state system and yet remained faithful to the shared heritage of spiritual, moral, and legal ideas that any Christian society could still be presumed to affirm as valid.[9]

Morever, he says, Grotius believed "that restraint and decency could be grounded in law despite the realities of the new age of statist diplomacy."[10]

Grotius was wrong. Natural law was not sufficiently compelling, in itself, to cause sovereign states to restrict their activities. The type of international law which came into being in the following centuries was, as Wight put it, a codification of *realpolitik*.[11] The only basis of international legal obligation that could be found was that of *consent*. Thus, providing that sovereigns agreed to certain rules by treaty, or more loosely, by custom, these laws could be binding on them. If this legal aspect was absent, the moral aspect would not be effective. Emmerich de Vattel made the transition from Grotian thinking to this next stage by declaring that natural law still applied, but that the first principle of natural law in the international context was the law of the sovereignty of the state!

Vattel's book, *The Law of Nations*, published in 1759, became a handbook for diplomats. In its Preface, he wrote, "The rules and decisions of the law of Nature cannot be purely and simply applied to sovereign states. . . . [They] must necessarily undergo some modifications in order to accommodate them in the nature of the new subjects to which they are applied."[12] The modifications, of course, were in favor of "state morality." Andrew Linklater points out that an earlier theorist, Samuel von Pufendorf, had also concluded that "the state rather than natural law should be central in determining human conduct" and that this is "tantamount to the assertion that the state and not the individual is the fundamental personality in world politics."[13]

In short, international law based on the *consent of sovereigns* is incompatible with the theory of a natural law that imposes itself by *moral force.* Yet natural law has not entirely disappeared from the international scene. Wight notes the following irony:

> International law seems to follow an inverse movement to that of international politics. When diplomacy is violent and unscrupulous, international law soars into the regions of natural law; when diplomacy acquires a certain habit of cooperation, international law crawls in the mud of legal positivism.[14]

Criticisms of the Natural Law Argument

There are two main criticisms of natural law. The first concerns its original metaphysical bases, either the Aristotelian teleological basis or the Stoic cosmological basis. Both have been disproven by science. There is no evidence for purpose in Nature, nor for harmony—quite the opposite in fact: evolution is random, and Nature, as Peter Medawar has shown, is "messy."[15] Much less is there evidence for a fiery breath that guides the Universe. These challenges to the metaphysical bases are not too damaging, though, since the argument about the compelling moral law did not seem to need such underpinning. As Ralph Pettman notes, natural law has often been dismissed as a "value judgment masquerading in absolute metaphysical terms."[16]

The second criticism is a pragmatic one, namely, that natural law cannot work in a system of sovereign states, and so to advocate it is futile. As mentioned, there is occasional use of natural law in official fora, such as at Nuremberg. Article 7 of the Nuremberg Charter states "The official position of defendants, whether as heads of state or responsible officials in government departments, shall not be considered as freeing them from responsibility or mitigating punishment." David Luban notes the following paradox: "By making even sovereigns legally liable for their deeds, Article 7 denies that the sovereign is the sole source of law in his state; it thus denies the doctrine of sovereignty itself."[17] The Nuremberg and Tokyo trials have been deemed "victor's justice" by some; it is noteworthy that no similar war-crime trials have followed. For example, Lt. William Calley, convicted of killing one hundred and nine non-enemy civilians at MyLai, was not brought before any international judge. Private groups of citizens have staged international trials, such as the Bertrand Russell Tribunals and the Lelio Basso Tribunals,[18] but the results of these have not, to say the least, become recognized as international law.

Cosmopolitan Morality

The second argument that supports the positive position on international morality is that of *cosmopolitan morality.* It holds that *moral obligations are pan-human.* Cosmopolitan moralists either ignore the existence of state boundaries, or view the state, and politics generally, as obstacles to justice and humanitarianism. There are two ideas within the theory of cosmopolitan morality: that of cosmopolitanism, and that of the universalness of morality.

Cosmopolitanism, the idea that all humans are brothers by virtue of their shared reason, was introduced by the Stoics. It was a departure from parochialism that had incalculable consequences for Western history. First, it influenced Saint Paul's decision to allow baptism to the Gentiles. Saint Paul, a Jew trained in Greek thought, wrote to the Galatians: "There is neither slave nor free, there is neither male nor female; for ye all are one in Christ Jesus." Second, cosmopolitanism influenced Roman law. Cicero, the interpreter of Greek Stoicism for the Romans, brought in the notion of equality in the first century. By 212 AD the Emperor Caracalla proclaimed: "All those who live within the borders of the Roman Empire are Roman citizens." Despite the reality of local and national loyalties, cosmopolitanism is an idea that is deeply embedded in Western thought.

The other idea, that of the universalness of morality, is likewise taken for granted. As R.J. Vincent notes, the term "universal morality" is a tautology.[19] One aspect of the universalness of morality has to do with the extending of sympathy or concern to all people including foreigners. Judith Lichtenberg observes, "The continual movement . . . of humanistic thought generally [is] to enlarge the moral community . . . from self to family to tribe to nation, and ultimately to the whole human race."[20] Michael Donelan states, "The inclination of our being to prevent ills and wrongs to others knows nothing of race, religion and the like."[21] T.H. Green, in the nineteenth century, remarked that we have "an ever-widening conception of the range of persons between whom the common good is common."[22]

Another aspect of the universalness of morality has to do with the fact that moral rules are derivable from universal principles; these do not vary according to circumstance. Immanuel Kant considered it to be an intrinsic feature of a moral rule that one could will it to be applicable to all agents.[23] As Linklater notes, the trend toward universalistic morality correlated with the historical development of freedom and self-determination. The "philosophical historians," notably Kant, Hegel, and Marx, suggested that history was made possible by the existence of free creatures—those who had "the capacity to initiate action."[24] Thus, if there be such a thing as moral progress, it must consist of the increasing willingness of humans "to live in a world governed by rational principles which [they have] freely imposed upon themselves."[25]

The significance of cosmopolitan morality in a discussion of international relations is that it gives a focus of opposition to statist morality. It particularly challenges the doctrine of national sovereignty in two areas: that of humanitarian intervention, and that of international economic justice. In regard to the former, Donelan notes that our moral sensibilities cannot stop "at the waters' edge":

> The principle of the common good means that the internal affairs of other states are our business. For we desire as men conditions of life that are for the good of all men; a state has independence only to implement this. If the system for the production of food in a state is such that some starve; if the political arrangements are a tyranny; ... outsiders are rightly concerned and the rulers of the state are in principle accountable to them.[26]

Similarly, Beitz comments about the principle of national sovereignty in regard to South Africa and Cambodia, in the following philosophical manner: "One might ask why a principle that defends a state's ability to pursue an immoral end is to count as a moral principle imposing a requirement of justice on other states."[27]

Beitz is also a leading theoretician in the second application of cosmopolitan morality, namely to international economic justice. He holds that the social contract approach to distributive justice, as now practised in domestic societies, should be extended globally, since the actual economic interchanges of the contemporary world are international. Beitz notes that "the intuitive idea is that it is wrong to limit the application of contractarian principles of social justice to the nation-state."[28] This, he says, is because of such things as "the increasing sensitivity of domestic societies to external economic, political, and cultural events" and "the increasing impact of international arrangements . . . on human well-being."[29]

Our moral relationship to all humans, however, may seem too vague to inspire any particular action. One way to make these relationships more specific is to establish a correlation between rights and duties. Henry Shue claims that the very existence of rights implies the existence of rather specific duties. Having a right means "that the relevant other people have a duty to create ... effective institutions for the enjoyment of what people have rights to enjoy."[30]

Shue particularly emphasizes the duty of all people to avoid depriving others of their rights. This duty "must be universal and therefore applies to every individual and institution, including corporations."[31] So, for example, if an agribusiness firm wishes to grow an export crop in a poor country, it must compensate the peasants who previously grew their own food on that land, such as by paying them a wage adequate for the purchase of a similar amount of food.[32] Richard Barnet concurs: "Millions of people," he says, "are uprooted from the land and are physically separated from their traditional food supply. [These farmers] would have to be paid on a scale commensurate with the cost of imported food . . . A corporation that is not willing to pay on such a scale is committing a clear violation of human rights."[33]

Criticisms of the Cosmopolitan Morality Argument

The criticisms of the idea of cosmopolitan morality are numerous. Firstly, there is something unrealistic about the claim that humans have the same sympathetic predisposition toward every member of the human race. As Karl Popper notes, the New Testament notwithstanding, you cannot love every person as yourself. To love is a privilege for family and friends, not to be confused with the more limited obligation to treat all persons impartially and with respect.[34] Secondly, in regard to economic justice, there is the charge that the cosmopolitan theorists are not reading the facts correctly: the world is *not* a unified economic system. Some businesses, such as mining and finance, do have concentrated control of a worldwide market, but there are also many local systems of agriculture, commerce, and manufacturing. The social contract approach therefore does not always apply on a global scale.

Thirdly, a more general criticism of cosmopolitanism is linked to the contemporary critique of liberalism, and of abstract theories of justice such as that of John Rawls. This critique faults the modern view of the human as being too atomistic. It argues instead that the individual arises out of a social community; he is not a self-sufficient entity, and he has particular moral responsibilities as well as general ones. As Michael Sandel puts it, the self is "encumbered."[35] Fourthly, there is a question as to whether the cosmopolitan moralists would really be as ready as they claim to be, to give up the rights of states, of groups, or of cultures. Hedley Bull calls their bluff by noting the following:

> If the idea of the world common good were to be taken seriously, it would lead to the consideration of such questions as how the immigration policies of states throughout the world should be shaped in the general interest, which countries . . . have the most need of capital and which the least . . . or what outcomes of a host of violent civil and international conflicts throughout the world best conformed to the general interests of mankind.[36]

The Society of States

The third argument that supports the positive position on international morality is that of the *society of states*. It consists of a modest claim about morality in which the society of states is pictured as *a group of sovereigns, who, rather than pursue solely their own national interests, act with some restraint for the good of the whole.* "The good of the whole" in this context means the good of all sovereign states rather than the good of humanity. The society of states is sometimes called "international society."

This theory is a rebuttal of Hobbes' description of international anarchy. It sees international society not as savage but as characterized by a modicum of good will and mutual aid. This description was originally limited to Christian Europe but now is often said to apply worldwide. At the very least, there are certain items which states agree on. Terry Nardin lists the following: the states' rights to independence, legal equality, and self-defense; duties to observe treaties, to respect the immunity of ambassadors, to refrain from aggression, to conduct hostilities within the laws of war, to respect human rights, and to cooperate in peaceful settlements of disputes.[37]

Some writers theorized about the society of states in ideal form. Christian Von Wolff (1679-1754) imagined a *civitas maxima*, a great community of states. He emphasized that this was to be only a legal fiction, not an actual world government. The various states, he assumed, would logically form a social contract with one another, just as individuals had done within particular states. Wolff came to this idea under the influence of Leibniz's philosophy of the pre-established harmony of the universe.[38]

The Abbé de Saint-Pierre, starting from a different viewpoint—reaction to the horrific bloodshed of the wars of the Spanish succession—also sought an ideal way in which states could act as a community. In 1713 he wrote his *Project for Perpetual Peace*, which gave rise to further developments and reactions by Rousseau, Kant, and Bentham.[39] Saint-Pierre envisioned a federal union of states in which war would be controlled. A state wanting to go to war would first have to put its case up to arbitration. Some of Saint-Pierre's ideas were written into the Hague Convention of 1899, and later became part of the League of Nations model.[40] For instance, in the League, a member state planning to declare war had to submit its plan and wait six months for the League to make a decision on it.

There will probably always be proposals for an idealized society of states, since the very idea seems logically compelling. Other writers, however, particularly those with actual experience in diplomacy have emphasized that in reality, international order, and to some degree, international amity, is maintained through more practical devices. Principal among these devices is the *balance of power*. This practice of forming alliances against a strong power in order to prevent its absolute dominance was first seen in Europe in the coalition against Philip II of Spain. It was also implicit in the Peace of Westphalia, which marked the end of the Hapsburg pretensions to universal monarchy, and was made a conscious objective of international society in the Treaty of Utrecht of 1713.[41]

Henry Kissinger, among recent diplomats, has been the outstanding exponent of balance-of-power theory. He notes of the 1970s:

There was a difference in the Chinese and American approaches to international relations. China's was in the great classical tradition of European statesmanship. The Chinese Communist leaders coldly and unemotionally assessed the requirements of the balance of power little influenced by ideology or sentiment. They were scientists of equilibrium. . . . Only one principle was inviolate: No nation could be permitted to be preeminent, however fleetingly, over the combination of forces that could be arrayed against it. . . .[42]

By contrast, he says, the Americans have no conceptual framework for so cold-blooded a policy. Theirs is "a tradition of equating international conflicts with legal disputes and invoking juridical mechanisms for their resolution, a view considered naive by the Chinese."[43] He adds, "We in the Nixon Administration felt that our challenge was to educate the American people in the requirements of the balance of power."[44]

Just as Kissinger regrets the public lack of understanding of this key principle, Bull regrets that "in scholarly analyses of the subject it has been slipping into the background."[45] He also shows that in this century there has been a tendency to demonstrate the idea of international society less through the evidence of actual cooperation of states and more on principles showing how they *should* behave, such as those of the Kellogg-Briand Pact or the Charter of the United Nations. This emphasis on a reformed society of states, he says, leads to the neglect of those institutions which play a central role in the maintenance of international order:

There has developed the Wilsonian rejection of the balance of power, the denigration of diplomacy and the tendency to seek to replace it by international administration, and a return to the tendency that prevailed in the Grotian era to confuse international law with international morality or international improvement.[46]

Bull also points out that the three goals of international society: the balance of power, the preservation of independence of individual states, and the keeping of peace, operate strictly in that order of priority. The formation of alliances and spheres of influence, involved in the balance of power, can obviously cause small states to lose their independence. In regard to the partition of Poland in 1772 by Austria, Russia, and Prussia, Burke and Gentz had argued that this was "a departure from the true principles of the balance of power, which enjoined respect for the independence of all states, large and small alike."[47] No, says Bull, the partition of Poland was not a departure from the principle of the balance of power but simply an application of it. Indeed, the principle is one which is always most important to the large powers, who are in fact the custodians of international order.[48]

Obviously, then, the society-of-states argument differs greatly from the other arguments that constitute the positive position, particularly that of cosmopolitan morality. It is opposed to the idea that international society is populated by citizens rather than by sovereigns; it is also against any schemes for international justice which place the responsibility for justice in an entity other than the state. W.H. Smith notes, "For the foreseeable future the most effective principles of justice will be those found within the nation-state. There is no simple way in which they can be extended to mankind at large."[49] Nevertheless, this theory defends the importance of order in the world as a prerequisite for justice. In short, it believes that the maintenance of the states system *is* the basic ingredient of international morality.

Criticisms of the Society-of-States Argument

Criticisms of the society-of-states argument are aimed both at the theoretical premises and at its empirical accuracy. The theory appears to stake its credibility on the record, so let us look at the record. There has been much international cooperation when no-one's national interest needed to be sacrificed, for example, in the unified effort to rid the world of smallpox. In many matters, however, the record of interstate solidarity has been unimpressive. Evan Luard notes of the League of Nations, that, "It was based on collective security, 'the principle of each for all and all for each', the rule that, whenever an act of aggression occurred the whole community would combine to defend the victim"[50] but this quickly fell apart. No state intervened when Italy invaded Ethiopia, Japan invaded Manchuria, or Germany invaded Czechoslovakia. The United Nations, as well, has been unable to obtain collective action. For example, its call for a boycott of Rhodesia in the 1970s met with little success, since each state assumed that other states would "cheat," in accordance with their economic interest.

In regard to the willingness of nations to submit to international law when their interests are at stake, it need only be pointed out that very few of the 170 nations have signed the Optional Protocol giving jurisdiction to the International Court of Justice, and only 14 have adhered to the interstate complaints procedure set up by Article 41 of the Covenant on Civil and Political Rights.[51] The United States, out of economic motives, failed to sign the Law of the Seas Treaty, one of the most comprehensive efforts to share the "world heritage" equitably.

Criticisms are also levelled at the theoretical (or perhaps ideological) premises involved in the society-of-states idea. These criticisms come predictably from both realists and idealists, since the society-of-states idea occupies a middle position between the two. According to a model made famous by Martin Wight, there are historically three types of international relations theories: *Realist*, such as that of Hobbes and

Machiavelli who defend national interest; *Rationalist*, such as that of Grotius and later society-of-states theorists; and *Revolutionist*, such as that of Kant who looks for a community of mankind.[52] Some idealist critics think that the idea of international society is too conservative— and may even find in Rationalism a disguised Realism.[53] Richard Falk criticizes statist logic in general for its failure to realize that "the *whole* is necessarily prior to the *parts* in matters of ecological stability and military security."[54] Kantian cosmopolitanists such as Beitz find that it is senseless not to have a principle to guide the distribution of the benefits and burdens of social activity on an international scale.[55]

Realists, in turn, criticize Rationalism for being idealistic in its emphasis on law and cooperation. According to Raymond Aron, "If law cannot and must not ever precede by too great a gap the values already felt by the common conscience, the moment has not yet come legally to force states to judge for themselves without appeal to a superior authority."[56] Similarly, Bull notes, "Although the solidarity exhibited by international society may increase in the future, just as it may decrease, it can still be argued that in the twentieth century the Grotian conception has proven premature."[57]

The Just War

The fourth argument in support of the positive position on international morality—that rules of morality apply to all human transactions, whether the actors be individuals or states—is that of the just war. It holds that *the making of war can be subject to moral judgment.* Just-war theory began as a theological doctrine in the fifth century, with Saint Augustine, and became a secular matter of international law in the early modern period, such as in the writings of Vattel. Just-war theory has two parts: *jus ad bellum*, which defines the circumstances in which it is just to go to war, and *jus in bello*, which prescribes certain restraints during the course of war. Both ideas attempt to put some moral structure into the practice of violence.

Saint Augustine was first led to theorize about *jus ad bellum* during the barbarian invasions of the Roman Empire. James Turner Johnson observes:

> Given Augustine's deep positive feelings for . . . Rome, and Roman culture as he knew them in the late classical era, it is remarkable that, when these were attacked and in desperate danger of being overwhelmed by invaders from the north, he found it necessary to *justify* Christian participation in their defense.[58]

Yet he *did* find it necessary because, morally, war was such a breach of the Christian principle of nonviolence. Saint Augustine's justification for these wars against the barbarians was mainly that of self-defense. However, he set out more specific criteria for just wars, criteria which are still referred to today, for example: the leader declaring war must have the proper authority; he must have the right intention; the means used must be proportional to the ends; war must be used only as a last resort; and it must have peace as its goal.[59]

For many centuries, the wars undertaken by Christians had the theme of saving the Christian religion, such as against the Moors in Spain, and the Crusades to liberate the Holy Land. A new problem arose, however, when the Spanish conquered South America. The *conquistadores* tried to justify their treatment of the Indians on grounds of the right to force Christianity on these heathens. The Spanish jurist and theologian, Franciscus de Victoria, argued against this in his book *De Indes et De Jure Belli Relectiones* in 1557. The Indians, he said, were a separate community, not under the authority of the Pope, so a law of nations must be appealed to here; religion could not be forced upon them. On the other hand, Victoria declared that under natural law the Indians had no right to prevent the free passage of traders and missionaries; if they did so, the Spanish could fight in self-defense.[60] A similar point was argued later by Grotius in his *Mare Liberum*:

> If . . . it was right to take up arms because innocent passage was refused across foreign territory, how much more justly will arms be taken against those from whom the demand is made of the common and innocent use of the sea, which by the law of nature is common to all?[61]

Vattel, in 1749, continued to rely on natural law, in the sense of self-evident right and wrong, in his adjudication of just war. Any party who is unjustly attacked has every right to take up arms, but

> whoever . . . takes up arms without a lawful cause can absolutely have no right whatever. . . . He is guilty of a crime against the enemy . . . he is guilty of a crime against his people whom he exposes to danger. He is guilty of a crime against mankind in general whose peace he disturbs, and to whom he sets a pernicious example. Shocking category of miseries and crimes! Dreadful account to be given to the King of kings![62]

Nevertheless, despite Vattel's implied shock at the behavior of sovereigns, the "age of sovereigns" was by then a hundred years under way and would continue for at least another two hundred years. During this period, Hoffman notes, "war was treated essentially as a morally neutral fact and therefore could be indulged in by states whenever they had a reason for it."[63] Just-war theory either ceased to be discussed or was used as a rationalization for statist activities.

At the end of the first World War, there was, again, impetus for thinking about the rightness and wrongness of war, and attempts were made to define and outlaw "aggression." By the mid-twentieth century a new category was being debated as a just cause of war, self-determination, as was an older category, humanitarian intervention.[64] In recent years considerable attention has been given to the theory of *jus ad bellum* in connection with nuclear war.[65] For example, some ask: how can the prescription of "proportionality" be observed when the effects of radiation could destroy all life? Christian theologians have argued that even the manufacture of nuclear weapons may itself be immoral.[66]

The second aspect of just war theory, *jus in bello*, concerns "moral rules" to be imposed on belligerents to mitigate the overall amount of suffering and damage in war. Today these laws are codified in the Geneva Conventions, and include categories of protected persons and categories of forbidden weapons. Among the protected persons are: civilians, medical personnel in the battlefield, soldiers attempting to surrender, and prisoners of war. Among the prohibited weapons (in the 1980 Convention) are: bombs with nondetectable fragments that embed in persons' bodies; incendiary weapons dropped from the air, such as napalm, in populated areas; and mines and boobytraps placed indiscriminately, unless they are the kind that self-destruct after the combat period. Geoffrey Best notes that these three types of weapons are "small beer" compared to the long list that has been proposed by various groups.[67] It reflects the fact, he says, that "the law of war can never be more than a compromise between what men's humane desires make them wish to do, and what the release of their combative proclivities in war drives them to do."[68]

It must be said that in general the Geneva Conventions are taken remarkably seriously. Most armies today train their soldiers in these rules, and respect for the Red Cross flag in the battlefield is almost unquestioned. Nevertheless, *jus in bello* is subject to cultural standards. Richard I. Miller observes in his 1975 book, *The Law of War*, that "prisoners of war taken in East Europe will be treated according to the attitude of the local population, while in Latin America the social status of a rebel is critical in determining his treatment."[69] He writes:

> Moreover, the humanitarian prohibitions against torture, humiliation and degradation of prisoners are completely at odds with the cultural tradition of Malaysia and, particularly, Indonesia. Southeast Asians have developed humiliation and degradation of the person to a fine art.[70]

Criticisms of the Just-War Argument

Three criticisms of the just-war argument may be noted. First, the theory is unfair to nations which are dissatisfied with their present share of power, wealth, or territory. John Burton comments, "It is not an accident that the doctrine of just war is advanced by academics and representatives from a powerful nation. [It argues] that any attack on the status quo is unjust and illegal."[71] Second, it would appear that the doctrine has become a political and rhetorical tool. Hoffman remarks, "Notions such as self-defense or community causes . . . risk producing the maximum hypocrisy." In a world of self-help, he says, "all states ought to be under suspicion" in regard to their interpretation of the just war.[72]

Third, in the twentieth century, technological advances in warfare have made most of the *jus in bello* provisions impractical. "Obliteration bombing" began in World War II, and the atomic bomb was used against Japan as a logical military step despite the fact that it could in no way discriminate among combatants and noncombatants. Since the 1950s a new phenomenon—nuclear deterrence—has arisen, for which just war theory can offer little moral guidance. As Field Marshal Lord Carver notes, the concept of deterrence abounds in illogicalities and paradoxes. He writes:

> If one wishes to deter war by the fear that nuclear weapons will be used, one has to appear to be prepared to use them. . . . But if one does so and the enemy answers back . . . one is very much worse off. . . . To attempt to reduce the risk in order to make the threat more credible—through some form of limited nuclear war . . . begins to make that risk more acceptable and therefore less of a deterrent. . . . To call the results defence or security is to make a mockery of the terms.[73]

Human Rights

The fifth argument that supports the positive position on international morality is that of *human rights*. It holds that *the rights of human beings have priority over the rights of states.* Unlike the theories of natural law and cosmopolitan morality, which do not offer specific political prescriptions, human rights may seem, at first glance, to offer a solution to international moral problems. Human rights is as much a program as a theory: it promises to "make the world right" for the human being. It focuses on the dignity and worth of the person, and implies that other matters, such as the behavior of governments, are subordinate. After all, that is the essence of Western political philosophy.

The internationalization of human rights began in the last century. The outlawing of the slave trade, for example, was proposed as a legal goal by the Congress of Vienna in 1815;[74] minority rights and labor rights were granted by treaties under the League of Nations. However, the United Nations Universal Declaration of Human Rights of 1948 is considered to be the first major statement that all people everywhere possess certain rights. The declaration was passed by the General Assembly without dissenting vote. Two United Nations documents which clarified these human rights became available for signature in 1976, namely the Covenant on Civil and Political Rights, and the Covenant on Economic, Social, and Cultural Rights.[75]

It is possible to look at human rights activities of the last few decades as either a great success or an almost complete failure. The successes have been mainly in articulating the specific rights, in educating people about them, in monitoring and protesting specific violations, in setting up some machinery for enforcement, and in putting sufficient pressure on Western governments to make them take some international action.[76] The failures have been mainly in two areas: the incompatibility of international human rights with the states system, and the ideological impasse in the West's and East's respective interpretation of human rights.

In regard to the first failure, the states system gives high priority to the value of state sovereignty: this makes human-rights law unenforceable across state borders. The extent to which the covenants are "law" in the first place is questionable. They are multilateral treaties, but there is no world law, as such, much less a world enforcer of law. Theoretically a human rights case could come before the International Court of Justice, but so far none has done so. It is, however, the usual practice for international law to become part of the national law of the countries that sign the treaties. Thus it is possible for international cases to come before domestic courts: this has happened on several occasions.[77]

In general, the mere existence of "legal" human rights does not do much to alter the human condition. The populism of the human rights movement distracts from the basic fact that the treaties were made by sovereign states. Bull comments, "Claims that [the covenants] express not the consent of states, but 'the general will of the world community' are an aspiration rather than a description of actual trends."[78]

The second failure of the human rights movement has to do with the uncompromising attitude of East and West about their philosophies of rights. There are three kinds of rights: civil or political, social or economic, and group rights. Civil rights (sometimes called "negative rights") have to do with freedom from coercion or interference by government—such as the right to free speech, assembly, and a fair trial. While the West sees these rights as fundamental, the Soviet Union has seen them as unnecessary or wrong. Bull notes,

> To preserve the gains of the revolution, the Communist Party must keep a firm grip on the helm of the ship of state, and to concede individual rights that would be used by the enemies of the working class to loosen this grip would be a betrayal of the revolution.[79]

While Westerners associate the liberal theory of natural rights with the value of equality, socialists see it as a class-based idea. They believe, Kuper observes, that liberalism is

> an ideology of the rising bourgeousie. Man is viewed . . . as an egoistic individual pursuing his selfish interests with a minimum of interference. [This] legitimizes inequality. What is the significance of the right to property for those without any possible means of acquiring property?[80]

The second group of rights, social or economic, also known as "positive" rights, includes the freedom to do one's duty, and also includes the right to receive certain benefits from society, such as food or education. Although this area is the specialty of the Communist countries, the West does not strongly disagree about it, since the welfare state is now a familiar part of life in liberal societies too. In short, civil rights are the most contentious one on the international scene.

The third category of rights, group rights—the specialty of the Third World—is contentious also. Group rights include the political rights of racial minorities and/or the economic rights of poor nations. The documents reflecting such rights are the United Nations Declaration on the Granting of Independence to Colonial Countries and Peoples of 1960, and the unofficial Universal Declaration of the Rights of Peoples proclaimed by a conference in Algiers in 1976.[81] The point of contention here, for the West, is that these rights often imply a sort of collectivism in which the individual can be repressed by the ruler in the name of nationalism or racial pride. Eugene Kamenka suggests that group rights be given validity only when they extend, rather than destroy, civil rights.[82] He writes:

> Peoples, in other words, are above all, people, members of the human race. As such they are entitled to dignity, respect and the recognition that they are fully members of the human race. They are not entitled to immunity from outside or internal criticism of their dominant customs, practices and traditions in so far as these are themselves destructive of respect for persons, of moral compassion and of the recognition of the moral equality of all people.[83]

Criticisms of the Human Rights Argument

Two interesting criticisms have been raised about human rights—one pertaining to its program, and one to the philosophical theory that underwrites it. The first is that it is meaningless or even cruel to "entitle" someone to a privilege that he can never obtain. Many of the rights listed in the United Nations documents are pie-in-the-sky, considering the lack of political and economic development of some nations. For example, Article 24 of the 1948 Declaration states, "Everyone has the right to rest and leisure, including . . . periodic holidays with pay."

Accordingly, A.J.M. Milne has made the useful suggestion that rather than enlarging the number of rights we should drastically cut them. He points out that *law* can work only if the agreed-upon *morality* is there, and it is only there for a minimum number of rights. Milne identifies the following as those human rights for which all cultures have the ethical infrastructure: 1. the right to life, 2. the right to respect for one's dignity as a person, 3. the right to be dealt with honestly, for instance to have promises kept, 4. the right to justice, that is, to have one's interests fairly considered, 5. the right to freedom from unprovoked violence and arbitrary coercion, and 6. the right to aid, so far as is possible, for relief of one's distress.[84] These rights, he says, are simply part of social relations as such; no particular ideology or philosophy is needed to justify them. It may be noted that these rather simple rights have rather obvious correlative duties, the identification of which, as Henry Shue says, is an important step toward the enforcement of human rights.[85]

The second criticism of human rights theory refutes the philosophical notion that rights are somehow intrinsic to the human person, rather than being the products of specific political and historical developments. Talk about natural rights was once referred to by Bentham as "a perpetual vein of nonsense"[86] while for the contemporary philosopher, Alasdair MacIntyre, belief in rights is on a par with belief in witches or unicorns.[87] It is now becoming realized that there is simply no foundation for the Jeffersonian statement that men are *born* with rights, or that rights are self-evident. They can only arise in the context of a particular culture and concrete circumstances.

Acceptance of this fact may go some way towards breaking the ideological impasse over rights—at least on the Western side. For instance, it is beginning to be admitted that political rights preceded economic rights in the historical English and American case, but that this chronological sequence is not a sacred formula. The chronology that "rights begin at breakfast" may make more sense today in countries where the populace is too malnourished to fight for its civil rights. R.J. Vincent has recently recommended that advanced Western societies, particularly the United States, give up their futile concentration on civil rights abroad, and start by contributing more to economic rights. He agrees with Shue that the right to subsistence is basic, that is, it is essential to the enjoyment of all other rights.[88]

World Order

The sixth and final argument to be listed in support of the positive position on international morality is that of *world order*. It holds that *values, not willy-nilly factors of power, should guide international relations.* The world-order approach does not base itself on any particular tradition in political science or philosophy. In fact, its methodology could be compared more to that of economics, in its cost/benefit analyses, or to sociology in its study of general trends in society. However, its subject matter has directly to do with international morality. The exponents of world-order studies take as their main object of study the values and goals of society. They tend to think of the world as a unit, and more or less ignore state boundaries. This is not because they fail to appreciate the power of the state, and the states system, but because they prefer to highlight other important forces in the world, such as rapid technological change, or the deterioration of the natural environment.

Preceding the academic world-order studies of the 1960s and '70s, there were attempts by American activists to establish world order through some sort of world government. In 1948 and 1949 the United States House Committee on Foreign Relations heard testimony in which proposals were made to strengthen the United Nations by giving it more authority over sovereign nations.[89] There was also a United World Federalists group: it believed that decisions made only in the unilateral interest of particular nations would again lead to world war, this time nuclear war. The World Peace Through World Law movement, led by Grenville Clark,[90] advocated U.N. supervision of world disarmament, and the consequent establishment of a transnational police force to assist states in maintaining their territorial integrity. These plans did not succeed and are not considered viable today.

Since 1968 there has been a more scholarly World Order Models Project (known as WOMP) under the direction of Saul Mendlovitz. WOMP invited members of both Western and non-Western cultures to create "relevant utopias" for future world order. Although their mandate was broad, the members first agreed on a set of four major values to guide their planning. These were: the minimization of violence, the maximization of economic well-being, the maximization of social and political justice, and the protection of ecological quality.[91] Major books to come out of this effort included *A World Federation of Cultures: an African Perspective* by Ali Mazrui,[92] and *The True Worlds: a Transnational Perspective* by Johan Galtung.[93] Since 1978 there has been a new phase in WOMP's effort: it is less preoccupied with formal organizations and more concerned with popular movements and grassroots initiatives. Indeed Richard Falk says, "it is probably a greater mistake these days to associate world-order studies with world federalism than with libertarian anarchism."[94]

World-order theorists obviously do not consider normative research to be out of bounds in political science. They follow both what is going on in the world—say, economically or demographically—and the normative effects of these things. They try to evaluate whether these trends are what people really want or intend. Robert Johansen believes that keeping one's attention focussed on values in the world can be more illuminating than merely studying the workings of power. "The value impacts of specific foreign policies . . . provide intellectual handles by which one may grasp [the direction of social change]."[95] Statesmen, he notes, often disguise their policies in order to obscure the real beneficiaries.[96]

World-order students claim that their own ideological position is not fixed *a priori*. Rather, according to Falk, they

> seek to evolve a globalist ideology that draws on *liberalism* to check the abuse of state power in the relations between governments and people, on *socialism* to depict a humane set of economic relations based on societal well-being, [and] on *ecological humanism* to reorient the relations between human activity and Nature.[97] (emphasis added).

Falk also claims that world order writers "keep an open mind" about the role of the state. However, he, along with Samuel Kim and Saul Mendlovitz, believes that "statecraft oriented around short-term concerns is incapable of preventing nuclear war, conserving resources, regulating population growth, achieving human rights, protecting the environment, or securing a healthy world economy."[98]

In regard to the future of the states system, world-order theorists distinguish between their own approach, which is one of *systems-transformation*, and the more conservative approach, which they call *systems-maintenance*. According to Falk, the notable systems-maintainers are Aron, Bull, and Hoffman. A feature of their approach is "its hostility toward 'normative' conceptions of world order that stress the pursuit of valued goals as the object of inquiry."[99] Those writers want, instead, to envision a world order which allows the present states system to flourish. Thus, Falk includes David Rockefeller and the Trilateral Commission in that same group. "Those who control the dominant institutions of government and business seek above all else to discover the means to sustain the system.'[100] Bull's "muddling-through-with-the-states system view," he says, has as its normative contribution a "neo-Machiavellian type of advice to the prince, in effect, a counsel of prudence given in a spirit of urgency in an era of global politics beset by the pervasive menace of nuclear warfare."[101]

By contrast, the systems-transforming approach propounds the need to transform international relations by diminishing the role of sovereign states in certain respects.[102] Thus, as mentioned, the new phase of the World Order Models Project is populist. It seeks to find ways "to mobilize a variety of groups working in widely disparate arenas for peace and justice, often in opposition to official state policy."[103] This approach does not have much faith in political elites or even in such institutions as the United Nations. Johansen recommends "a world assembly [that] would set general policy respectful of global humanist values. It would be organized to represent peoples, nongovernmental organizations, states and regional groups."[104]*

Criticisms of the World-Order Argument

Criticisms of world-order studies range from the superficial to the more important. One does not have to search far to locate these criticisms, since world-order theorists continually incorporate them into their own publications. Thus they readily admit that their work can be accused of "moral arrogance,"[105] of being full of platitudes,[106] and of "substituting advocacy for analysis,"[107] and they acknowledge that they may have "cried wolf" about ecological deterioration.[108]

The two most important criticisms are those of *ethnocentrism* and *infeasibility*. WOMP has sought, and obtained, the participation of Third World members, yet the project still maintains a Western, rationalist tone, and some find it to be an example of cultural imperialism. One of its participants, Rajni Kothari, proclaims

> The end of the era of Western dominance must also mean an end of the dominant Western world-view based on the theory of progress and the ethic of individualism. It also means the abandonment of the related assumptions of the relationship between knowledge and power on the ends of economic activity. . . .[109]

Fouad Ajami notes the hypocrisy of Western leaders who talk about world order in terms of intervening in places where dissidents are suppressed, but plead the principle of 'nonintervention' when the subject of Third World poverty comes up. "This approach postulates the existence of specific responsibilities to the world community on the one hand, but then proceeds to dilute the case for global norms when it comes to the rights of poor states."[110] He calls this a "cheap" kind of world order logic,[111] (this criticism does not generally pertain to world-order scholars, most of whom favor economic assistance to poor nations). It should also be noted that *leaders* in the Third World react with suspicion to any schemes, even academic ones, for global politics, which they see as a rerun of Western dominance. As Cornelia Navari points out, just as in

---

*I have emphasized the approach of Richard Falk and his colleagues in this section because they crystallize the issue of the priority of values. Other writers with a global outlook could also be called "world orderists." For example, Lester Brown, in his book, *World without Borders*, considers the worldwide phenomena of urbanization and unemployment. The term "world order" need not, of course, carry reformist connotations. Balance-of-power theorists are interested in world order, the world's bankers are concerned with the order of international finance, and so forth.

seventeenth century Europe, the leaders of new nations are obsessed with "the state" itself, and have no desire that states be federated.[112]

As to the charge of infeasibility—the claim that the state cannot be overcome anyway—world-order theorists have two answers. The first is "It doesn't matter." In other words, the point of the intellectual exercise is to understand the world better, not to succeed at revolution. The second answer is "Watch and see." World-order theorists claim to be in no particular hurry and believe they do see signs of shift against the traditional structure of the states system. Falk notes that even Lenin had no expectation that the Russian Revolution could succeed as early as 1917, and that in regard to Iran, everyone denied as late 1976 that there could be a revolution, yet by 1978 it was seen to be inevitable.[113] Moreover, who could ever have guessed the world transformation that would result from the preachings of Jesus of Nazareth?

Other Theories

In choosing six arguments to constitute the positive position on international morality, I selected from a wider group of candidates. Two criteria I used for selection were the currency of the argument today, and its credibility. Thus I omitted truly utopian prescriptions for a world state, whether these featured legal arrangements, military disarmament, or dramatic economic sharing. I favored instead the minimalist position on international society offered by the society-of-states theorists. It would not have been amiss, however, for me to have given an airing of Kant's utopian essay, *Perpetual Peace* which, though written in the eighteenth century, is farseeing on many issues.*

I could, as well, have discussed Integration Theory, especially since it is widely taught in university courses on international relations. This area of research, which began with Ernst Haas' study of the European Community,[114] and was developed by Karl Deutsch, seeks to discover how small political units join larger ones. Since integration theory is concerned with how wider loyalties are formed, it is certainly relevant to a study of the prospects for the development of a global mentality. However, its approach is mainly a practical one, not an 'ethical' one. Integration theorists are not, as such, interested in arguing that "rules of morality apply to all human transactions. . . ." Thus, none of them is, strictly speaking, a candidate for inclusion in this chapter.

---

*Sissela Bok has mined Kant's essay for ideas essential to a mitigation of hostile interstate relations in the late twentieth century, in her book *A Strategy for Peace*. She especially draws on Kant's insight that secrecy in government is inevitably harmful to the functioning of society.

Marxist-Leninist theory, also, is notably missing, again because of my restricted terms. Marx's own work on international relations is thin, and his expectation that persons would form class solidarity overriding national loyalties notoriously failed to materialize in 1914. Nevertheless, Lenin's theory of imperialism, borrowed from the English economist Hobson, has been developed substantially. For example, Immanuel Wallerstein hypothesizes that under the Dutch empire an international division of labor began as early as the sixteenth century and that the Industrial Revolution set up a framework of relations between the "core" and the "periphery" which still curtails the economic freedom of the peripheral states. The *dependencia* theorists, beginning in the 1950s, showed how neocolonialism operates in Latin America to maintain exploitation long after the formal colonial structure has ceased.[115]

The reason I declined to make explicit use of Marxist-Leninist theory is that it did not seem to qualify as a negative argument for international morality. It does not say "There is not and cannot be a moral relationship among states". It says—between its lines—something more like "There should be a moral relationship among states but this is honored mainly in the breach". As in most of Marx's work, the ethical desiderata is hidden beneath a purportedly scientific discussion about the laws of history.[116] I would agree, however, that the moral thrust of Marxist ideology—and its worldwide success in raising issues of economic injustice—must have a large, if indirect, influence on the positive argument for international morality.

Summary. To sum up this chapter, there is a long tradition that supports the notion of international morality—that is, the existence of a moral relationship among states. Only two of the arguments here specifically discussed the moral arrangements among nations, namely, the just-war theory and the idea of the society-of-states. The other four concentrated either on the individual or on humanity, contending that moral relationships actually take place at those levels. Thus the theory of cosmopolitan morality challenges the idea inherent in the doctrine of national sovereignty that rulers are exempt from universal moral laws. The human rights approach and natural law theory both suggest that a state's behavior can be judged by external standards, and that the state's right to sovereignty may in fact depend on its moral performance. World-order theory does not choose to comment on the relations among states. It focusses instead on the human interest—it shows incidentally, however, that states often act against this wider morality.

It is my hope that the reader now feels converted to the positive position, on the merits of these six arguments—at least for the nonce.

4

Assessment of the Negative and Positive Positions

> *That a civilization which has broken through immense barriers in almost every other direction should still hold views and pursue programs in international politics that it held and pursued when it was young—that is the outstanding failure of recent times.*
>
> F.H. Hinsley

Which side wins? Is it true that there is not and cannot be a moral relationship among states? Or is it true that rules of morality apply to all human transactions, whether the actors be individuals or states? In this final chapter of Part One, I shall evaluate the traditional arguments concerning international morality on their own merits. That is, before subjecting them to external analysis with the aid of sociobiology in Parts Two and Three, I shall examine them for internal soundness. Each of the twelve arguments was described and criticized individually in the preceding chapters; here they will be assessed in comparison with one another.

University courses sometimes serve these twelve—along with a few others—in smorgasbord style. The student is expected to pick and choose any or all according, apparently, to taste. But it is no doubt possible to find some means of judging the relative validity of the arguments. In the following sections I shall ask four leading questions: 1. Do the arguments incorporate, and depend upon, *unargued assumptions*? 2. Are the arguments universally applicable, or are they restricted to a particular *historical context*? 3. Do the arguments clearly acknowledge their *ethical premises*? 4. How successful are the arguments in distinguishing between *fact* and *value*?

Before asking these questions, however, it will be useful to review the negative and positive positions. I shall do this firstly by encapsulating the twelve arguments, and secondly by paraphrasing the overall negative and positive positions.

Encapsulation of the Twelve Arguments

The main points of the six arguments that constitute the negative position on international morality are as follows:

1. *National interest.* The relationship among states is that of competition and self-help. A statesman must discharge his duty by putting the survival of his own nation first. To bring moral concerns into international politics can be dangerous as well as futile.

2. *International anarchy.* There is no rule over world society and there is no social contract among nations. Nations are in a "state of nature" toward each other, hence no morality or justice is required. Skepticism or suspicion regarding the motives of other states is the prudent approach.

3. *National sovereignty.* There is one moral obligation among nations: to respect one another's independence. States are legally equal, and they are immune from external criticism. The rights of states are superior to the rights of humanity.

4. *Nationalism.* The community or collectivity is more real than the individual; the latter has a duty to the former. Each culture is an experiment in the good life, thus it is fitting for nations to try to outrank one other. Ethnic groups should seek national self-determination.

5. *Immorality of groups.* A group has a different kind of morality than an individual, owing to such things as lack of face-to-face contact, the suppression of self-criticism of the group, and the group's practice of hypocrisy. Patriotism paradoxically transmutes individual selflessness into national egoism.

6. *Cultural pluralism.* "International morality" is a hopeless concept: each group has a morality peculiar to its history and world view. The West's abstract, rational concepts of law and contract are based on certain orientations to time, to authority, and to the individual; these are not shared by others.

The main points of the six arguments that constitute the positive position on international morality are as follows:

1. *Natural law.* There is a right and wrong of human behavior that can be adduced by all reasonable human beings. This sense of right and wrong should guide the formation of international law. Sovereign rulers as well as citizens should be constrained by natural law.

2. *Cosmopolitan morality*. All humans are brothers and are citizens of a world state; sympathy can be extended to foreigners. The principles of morality are universalizable. If the state is an obstacle to morality, humanitarian intervention may be allowed. Economic justice should be international. Duties should be correlated with rights, even across borders.

3. *Society of states*. Sovereigns practice restraint, keep treaties, and act in the interest of maintaining the system. International society has been idealized about, as a war-preventing and law-abiding body; however, the strategies of diplomats, such as the balance of power, are what provide real order, and order is a prerequisite for justice.

4. *The just war*. To go to war justly, a sovereign must have authority and good intentions, and should observe proportionality. Wars of self-defense are typically just. Within the conduct of war, certain inhumane practices are forbidden, and noncombatants are to be protected.

5. *Human rights*. Rational human beings are worthy of the respect of their fellow man. Modern people have rights, such as the civil right of freedom from government coercion, and the social right of medical care. These rights should be enforced internationally by all available means.

6. *World order*. Individual states are incapable of handling the new agenda which includes worldwide problems of ecology, economy, and social justice. A value-centered approach is helpful here. The World Order Models Project seeks ideas from various ideologies and is interested in systems-transformation, perhaps by mobilizing people at the grassroots level.

Paraphrasing of the Negative and Positive Positions

The foregoing reflects a dissection of each individual argument. However I believe that students often think of the negative and positive positions as coherent wholes. In this section I shall use the same material as above, but forsake philosophical nuance in favor of being more polemical. I shall present a paraphrase of the negative position, adopting the tone of a student informing a fellow student who has not been exposed to the literature in question. This should better convey the force that the negative position, on the whole, possesses. Then I shall do the same for the positive position.

A Student's Defense of the Negative Position

"Look here [says our student], the question of whether states can behave morally toward one another is not one that has been neglected, nor is it an open question. Many great thinkers have worked on it and have concluded that for various compelling reasons, the concept of morality or ethics simply does not enter into interstate behavior. If every nation were willing to be Mr. Nice Guy, and if all nations had comparable values and a similar stage of advancement, then there might be a way for them to get together and work out laws, to which all would agree to be bound. But that clearly is not possible now. Note that it was tried, even in our century, with the League of Nations, but that proved a hopeless failure—a real joke.

"You have to realize that nations are selfish entities. Sometimes their actions seem justifiable: they may need to get at the resources of other nations as a matter of survival. Or, they may just be expansionist for expansion's sake. This seems to be a human trait, perhaps based on the search for glory. In order to guard against the inevitable rise of Napoleonic types, nations have traditionally formed balances of power, in which one powerful nation may gather several smaller nations around itself in an alliance against the dominant rival.

"It also has to be admitted that a strong nation can more or less do what it wants, vis à vis a weak nation. Many times in history strong nations have exploited or even obliterated weak nations. This is a fact of life, having to do both with human selfishness and with the structure of the world. Because of it, by the way, it is not morally commendable for a leader to take a pacifist stance. If he doesn't keep his nation prepared militarily he is actively tempting aggressors to attack, as Neville Chamberlain notoriously did at Munich in 1938.

"Besides the points I've made so far [continues our student], which are more or less morally neutral, there are also reasons why it is positively a good thing that nations do not have a moral relationship with one another. The first reason is the importance of national or cultural independence. Only when all the sovereign nations agree that the Prime Rule is for each to mind its own business, can each one set about performing its functions as it wishes. If you allowed anyone who thinks he knows best to interfere in the affairs of other countries there would be chaos. You'd also hear plenty of goodwill rhetoric being used to cover up the selfish motivations of the intervening power. We've seen this many times, for instance when India "helped out" in Bangladesh in 1971.

"So, it's reasonable policy for all statesmen to form an overriding agreement that they won't criticize each other's domestic affairs. At times this may mean that a people suffering from brutality or even genocide will not be saved by the outside world. But apparently people don't want to save their fellow men if it is inconvenient. If you think they do, please explain to me why "good nations" didn't try to help in Cambodia in the 1970s or Guatemala in the 1980s. Apparently, an individual who sees an individual suffering feels compelled to help, but not so a nation. Groups are simply less moral than individuals, even if they are composed of individuals. An enigma perhaps, but there you are.

"A second good reason for keeping "morals" out of international affairs is that some nations would get so morally worked up about eradicating evil that they would "fight to the last Afghan." Or they may insist righteously on the unconditional surrender of an enemy, as America unwisely did with Japan in 1945. Nations are also notorious for thinking that their culture is better than any other. It's obvious that each of the two superpowers thinks its ideology is pure and right, and the other's is sinful. If the superpowers had gone to war over this, the whole human race might have been wiped out. Note that in fact leaders in both the U.S. and U.S.S.R. behave pragmatically, not ideologically, on the world stage. For instance, America's sale of arms to Communist China makes no sense ideologically, but it's wise geopolitically. Leaders know how the game must be played and ideals are not part of this game. If you were in office, you'd learn it quickly, too, and you'd stop thinking about the morality of international relations.

"In short, people's natural instinct may tell them that something wrong or unfair is going on, internationally, but there's really not much that can be done about it. Whereas when a member of domestic society behaves in a reprehensible way his neighbors can call the police, in the international arena there is no authority to resort to—each nation just fends for itself. Nations and their relative strengths are the final determinant of who gets away with what. I assure you, this is *reality*."

A Student's Defense of the Positive Position

"Rubbish! [replies our other student]. You say it's not appropriate to apply the concept of morality to international activities, but I ask you how it is possible that any such activity—which may affect the welfare of millions of people in one fell swoop—could be exempt from moral concern. If you and I were two cave men standing here talking I could see how it might be possible for us to treat morality as some curiosity that could be dispensed with. But we are both products of Western civilization with its massive Judaeo-Christian influence, so we tend to think of all human affairs as subject to moral judgment. Moreover, we are products of the modern world wherein the behavior of a government is thought to be subject to the wishes and approval of the people. Indeed we look upon the enunciation of the rights of the individual—human rights—as our own major cultural achievement.

"At least partly, our belief in human rights comes from a belief in human equality. All members of the human race have some things in common. True, there is much cultural variation in behavior, but basically people like and dislike the same things. For instance, people like to bring up their children in good health, and they don't like to have their property stolen. All of this similarity gives rise to fairly universal laws. For this reason it seems to me that a general law prevails, and that nations are subject to it as well as individuals. An example would be that it is wrong for one nation to steal from another, just as it is wrong for one individual to steal from another.

"Of course I recognize that people act not only as individuals, but as members of groups, [continues our positive-position student]. Probably the only activity that individuals around the world engage in as fellow-earthlings is gazing at the moon. Group life is an important reality and I'll allow that groups have some rights, such as to try to survive and to practice their culture. But since there are many groups, and their interests may conflict, they should make efforts to compromise. The Golden Rule seems to be the conclusion that reason leads to. Groups can recognize other groups as having similar human wants and needs, and even "rights"—as themselves. This is not such a far-fetched proposal. Consider the Geneva Conventions. Here each nation has recognized, for example, that all wounded soldiers are in the same boat. So, mechanisms have been established to protect medical stations on the battlefield—something that a cynic may have said could never happen.

"I think we need to admit that there is a *direction to history*. The why's and wherefore's of international morality are not a function of a static structure of the world, nor of a fixed human nature. We should look at what is actually happening. On the one hand, *interests* are able to become more organized over time, as we see in the concentration of wealth and technological know-how. At the same time, *values* are able to become more organized and more "rationalized." Note how ecologists have made the public aware, in the last generation, of the priority of clean air and water—something that could have "gone by the board" if *interests* were the only factor that commanded power. I think that much of the argument that goes on, purporting to deal with the nation versus the individual, or the nation versus humanity, has instead to do with interest versus value.

"In short, [concludes our student] I do not buy your story that international morality is a nonsubject. It simply does not ring true to me. There cannot be a category of human affairs which defies moral consideration."

The negative and positive positions, when paraphrased in everyday language as above, may seem to sound equally correct and full of common sense. They *both* win: that is the dilemma to which this book is addressed. I shall now undertake the four questions listed at the beginning of this chapter, in an effort to see if we might find some damaging errors or lack of rigor in any of the particular theories which underwrite these positions— hoping that this might prove one position more valid than the other.

Unargued Assumptions

The first question to be asked here is: Do the twelve arguments incorporate—and depend upon—unargued assumptions? It has already been noted, in the criticisms of each one, that in many instances they *are* based on unargued assumptions, concerning either empirical data or metaphysical ideas. For instance, we saw that there are some unargued assumptions about *empirical data* among the negative writers. Thus, Hobbes was simply wrong about international anarchy: there is much international order. Some of the nationalists' empirical claims, too, are ill-formed, such as those concerning the alleged independence of cultural achievements, and the supposed blood relationship of compatriots. Likewise it was shown that the national interest view is misleading in its implication that statesmen always care for the interests of the whole nation, rather than that of only themselves or a narrow economic elite.

Among the positive writers, similar errors were noted in regard to empirical claims. Rights theorists are inaccurate in their claim that all men are born equal: nothing, empirically, could be further from the truth. Similarly far-fetched is the cosmopolitan assumption that people have natural sympathy for all their fellows: clearly there is a marked preference for kin and countrymen over strangers. World-order writers are wrong in their general imagery of the state as an obstacle to justice: states, with their laws and political organization, are the main providers of justice.

In regard to *metaphysical* ideas which would not generally be accepted today, I have already mentioned both the teleology and cosmology that underlie natural-law theory, and Rousseau's unsupported mysticism concerning the existence of the general will, and I endorsed Bentham's charge that "natural rights" are nonsense. Yet the supporters of natural law, nationalism, and human rights, respectively, seem undeterred by the fact that their work is based on questionable premises. My interest here is not so much in proving that these metaphysical ideas are wrong, but in pointing out that they are accepted uncritically by some international relations writers.

One particular unargued assumption pervades the negative position, and to my mind gives it an erroneous basis. I refer to the semi-metaphysical assumption that the state is itself a moral being, or that its actions must have some intrinsic moral quality; this thinking particularly affects the argument concerning national sovereignty and nationalism. I think it would be more logical if the negative position, (that there is and cannot be a moral relationship among states), would rely largely on admitting that states are inherently selfish and thus are unwilling to practice moral restraint internationally. Yet Niebuhr's theory is the only one of the six that is candid in this regard. It states that a group, by its very nature, has difficulty being moral since it is not like a moral person who has a conscience. Two other negative theorists downplay this point: Machiavelli tries to soften the explanation for the immorality of states by emphasizing the moral necessity of rescuing the nation from ruin; Hobbes takes the trouble to excuse the international behavior of states by reasoning that the laws of morality do not apply where there is no social contract.

Of course, it is natural for theorists to try to couch their ideas in some terms of "right." Michael Donelan observes, "For people know that right is the norm and not an aberration; no one ever appeals to wrong to justify his actions."[1] Naturally, too, we can expect state leaders to use moral rhetoric to conceal their real motives. The question is, to what extent do students accept this rhetoric and rationalization of national selfishness without noticing what is going on?

There are other related problems in the negative position. In the case of the national sovereignty argument, it is held that a state is entitled to freedom and noninterference because it is like a person. We may assume that this analogy depends on the idea that the sovereign speaks for the citizenry. Since the eighteenth century, the term "national sovereignty" has implied a contract between government and people; national sovereignty and popular sovereignty are strongly associated with each other. Today, however, only about 26 of the world's 170 states are in fact democracies, the rest being primarily one-party states or military dictatorships.[2] Despite this fact, the sacredness of the state which, for Westerners, comes of its compact with the people, is routinely extended to the 144 states that do not have a compact. The principal unargued assumption here is that *all* states, by nature of being called states, are deserving of certain rights and protection from external criticism.

There is also an assumption that states deserve national privacy so they can each conduct their culture's "historical experiment" without interference. This would seem reasonable grounds on which "the world" may morally agree to practice noninterference. It is, however, not what states have in mind. As Kuper shows, states make gestures of reverence toward national *privacy*, but their motivation is *self-protection*: they are willing to conform to club rules as the price of maintaining their own sovereignty. I do not intend the foregoing as an argument against state sovereignty: there are many reasons, not listed here, why state sovereignty is valuable and necessary. The point, in this chapter, is that when we choose between the relative merits of the negative and positive positions on international morality, we should not accept, as part of the negative argument, certain morally appealing ideas that are irrelevant to the issue.

Historical Context

The second question to which we must subject the arguments for and against international morality is: do they have enduring validity and universal applicability, or are they limited to the historical context in which they were first developed?

Some of the arguments make claims about human nature which might be expected to span time and place. Machiavelli's work is no doubt the best example. He cites enduring traits of human character—ruthlessness, deceit, lust for power—and also identifies the structural dynamics of politics. For instance, he shows that a prince must carry out some of the necessities of rule if he is not to be quickly replaced in office by a rival. It would be hard to fault Machiavelli on these observations, or on his deduction that a national leader is constrained against deviating too much from protection of his nation's interest in international politics. Nevertheless, when the setting changes from the fifteenth to the twentieth century, the relevance of Machiavelli's advice may be limited. For example, "national interest" may be hard to identify in an age when the world economy could collapse due to international debt, or when the normal exercise of a nation's military power could mean incineration of the globe.

In any case, most of the theories under discussion are not quite so broadly applicable as Machiavelli's. I believe it is worthwhile to take cognizance of the political and intellectual context in which each arose. For one thing, it may be noted that some of the ideas were developed in eras when there was greater or lesser concern with politics in general. Aristotle's ideas about man's social nature came about as a reflection of the well-developed political life of the Greek city-states; citizenship for free men in Athens was a full-time occupation. The Stoics, by contrast, were much less interested in political life, and turned their ethical inquiry to personal matters. J.V. Gough says of the Stoics, "In the bad days of the Roman Empire, at any rate, the main function of their philosophy lay in its consolation to the individual just man."[3] By the time of Augustine, political life was denigrated completely in favor of concentration on an other-wordly city of God, while at the dawn of the early modern period there was suddenly great concern again with affairs of state, both domestic and international. Such shifts in background would naturally call forth differing notions about the ethical position of politics.

For another thing, it may be significant to note the occupational position of the writers themselves. At least three of our major theorists had direct involvement in providing ideas to the governments or political factions, or both, of the day. They had to take a stand on crucial issues, and eventually paid a price: Machiavelli was tortured,[4] Grotius was sentenced to life imprisonment,[5] Hobbes went into exile.[6] It could be argued that because they were close to specific issues, their views are limited. On the other hand, quite the opposite could be true: that their vision was expanded by the need to support an urgent argument. In either case, specific historical events prompted their ideas to unfold.

Of course, it is not only events, but other *ideas*, that prompt ideas. Each of the twelve arguments has an intellectual context. The Stoics were reacting to the Sophists, Grotius was influenced by Bodin and Gentili, Vattel started his *Law of Nations* as a translation of Christian von Wolff's work (from which he quickly departed), Kant's *Perpetual Peace* reflects a Leibnitzian teleology that was imparted to him, also, by Wolff. Machiavelli and Hobbes, as we saw, were inspired by Renaissance science. Hans Morgenthau acknowledged that he was influenced as a student by the political theory of Max Weber.[7] Hedley Bull named Martin Wight as a mentor;[8] Richard Falk reports that the debate over the Vietnam War led him to crystallize his position on international law.[9]

In some cases, it is interesting to speculate on how a particular intellectual or practical problem which the theorist worked on early in life, would have formed the mold for his full-blown theory. Hobbes started out by translating Thucydides', *History of the Peloponnesian War*—certainly an auspicious departure point for the development of international anarchy theory. Regarding Herder's theory of the individuality of each *Volk*, Frank E. Manuel argues that it could possibly have been "merely a nativist reaction against contemporary frenchifiers of the German spirit."[10] He says:

> The superficial style of living in the German principalities where Herder spent his years was an imitation of the French court and in a sense his whole creative intellectual vision may be looked upon as a rejection of this artificially imposed way of life with its emphasis upon the progress of arts, science; and civility, defined in French terms.[11]

As for Grotius, his *Mare Liberum*, "Freedom of the Seas," published in 1609, may have given rise to his more general ideas about the laws governing international intercourse. This work is the record of a court case which he successfully argued, at the age of 21, in defense of the Dutch East Indies Company. That company had seized a Portugese vessel in compensation for its loss of trade in the East; Grotius argued that all nations were entitled to access to the high seas.[12] Could it be that if Grotius had been employed by the other, more powerful side, that he would not have concluded that natural law is the source of authority for international judgment?

In short, none of the twelve arguments are pure, "disembodied," or even particularly objective contributions to the debate about international morality. This is not to say that to be useful a political theory *should* be disembodied. On the contrary, every theory of this kind must have some real reference point. New positions on the subject, composed today, must refer to contemporary realities. Nevertheless, when older ideas are called into current service, they ought, I believe, to be critically evaluated as to their continuing accuracy, and with an eye to the historical and intellectual context that elicited them.

Ethical Premises

The third question that must be asked of the twelve arguments concerning international morality is: do they clearly acknowledge their ethical premises? Before pursuing that question let us note that all of the arguments, negative as well as positive, make normative prescriptions. From a number of these prescriptions that were already mentioned in preceding chapters the following is a sample: prisoners of war should not be killed; small countries should be sacrificed to preserve the balance of power; colonial rule should be overthrown; workers should be given holidays with pay; dictators should not be held accountable to outsiders; dictators *should* be held accountable to outsiders; cultural traditions should be protected; treaties should be kept; princes may break treaties out of expedience. In each case, the writer appears to take for granted that his audience would naturally agree with him: seldom is any explicit ethical argumentation provided. This is reasonable, since each of them is drawing on well-known and widely accepted ethical philosophies that exist in the cultural background.

Yet, we must ask, which *particular* ethical philosophies are being relied upon by each theorist? From the entire range of ethical ideas—about human nature, about moral motivation, about the proper social life—which come into play? Surprisingly, only two seem to have been used by all of our international relations theorists, namely, the philosophies of *natural law* and *social contract*.

Natural law takes as its major premise the universal phenomenon of conscience: rational human beings *know* the right thing to do. As we saw, the idea was developed in different ways by Zeno, Aristotle, Cicero, Aquinas, Grotius, Vattel, and the judges at Nuremberg. Natural law philosophy, I believe, informs all six arguments within the positive position. It directly accounts for natural law, cosmopolitan morality, the just war, and part of the society-of-states argument. It is also ancestral to the idea of natural rights, and the consequent belief that a government's *raison d'etre* is to fulfill such rights; thus the philosophy of natural law could be said to affect the arguments of human rights and world order as well. Indeed, the positive position "Rules of morality apply to all human transactions . . ." is a restatement of natural law.

By contrast, the ethical philosophy of social contract does not take conscience and duty as a starting point. Rather it is more skeptical about the human ability to be good. As its major problem for solution, it asks how selfish individuals can conform to requirements of social order. Hobbes resolved the dilemma uniquely by sorting out selfishness and cooperation into a temporal sequence. In the original state of nature, men were violent; life was "nasty, brutish, and short."[13] This caused men to be fearful of one another, and so for security they were willing to submit to a common power. Morality, for Hobbes, is not instinctive as it is in natural law theory, but is a matter of submitting to authority in exchange for benefits. Here, the principal motivation to be good is enlightened self-interest.

Rousseau faced the same basic questions as Hobbes about social relations, law, and government. He, too, sorted out a temporal sequence but a quite different one. Rousseau's legend of prehistory had three stages. In the first stage, man lived alone and was much like a beast with simple requirements and pleasures. He had no reason to be violent with other men; on the contrary, the feeling he had toward others was that of instinctive compassion—"the pure emotion of nature, prior to all kinds of reflection."[14] In the second stage, social life began—because resources became scarce. "Vast forests were transformed into pleasant fields which had to be watered with the sweat of men, and in which slavery and misery were soon seen to germinate . . ."[15] For Hobbes, social life was the solution, but for Rousseau it was the problem: it led to pride, jealousy, cruelty, and so forth. The rather extreme solution he proposed was that of alienation of oneself to the general will.[16] This general will often appears to be a metaphor for duty to society. (Hence Rousseau's work may be said to reflect natural law philosophy, despite the title of his book, *The Social Contract*.)

Hobbesian social-contract philosophy informs most of the arguments within the negative position on international morality, namely: national interest, international anarchy, and national sovereignty. Its pessimistic picture of man's moral nature is also shared by Niebuhr in his theory of the immorality of the group—although Niebuhr calls this by its theological name, original sin. Rousseau's ethical philosophy, of course, informs nationalism. As for the one remaining argument, Bozeman's cultural pluralism, there is no need to invoke any ethical premise: international morality is a non-problem in her scheme. Even domestic morality for Bozeman does not appear to require an explanation of human nature as either good or bad: people appear to practice morality according to cultural convention. Although Bozeman does not explicitly say so, it is this conventionality of morality—this freedom of morals from a controlling "human nature"—that makes cultural pluralism possible, and international morality impossible.

It should be mentioned here that two of the twelve arguments, namely, world order and human rights, attempt to construct an ethical system *de novo*, within which to define international morality. World-order theory asserts that certain *values* are the starting point from which the "shoulds" of policy follow. The four major values—the minimization of violence, the maximization of well-being and social justice, and the protection of ecological quality—were arrived at by negotiation among scholars, but it was assumed by them that these are commonplace values that obtain across all cultures. The policies required by these values involve major institutional reform, reform which would of course deprive the rich and powerful of some of their privileges; world order theory thus admits to being a utopian exercise in evaluation and planning.

Human rights theorists are less explicit about the social relationships between rich and poor. They, too, start with the "rightness" of such things as the freedom, dignity, and well-being of all individuals. They then proceed to argue that political and economic structures should be of such a form that these rights would be protected or provided. If this were pushed far enough, however, it would be seen that what Western human rights advocates have in mind is that everyone in the world live in a wealthy, advanced, democratic country. That is probably not possible: many of the benefits enjoyed by Westerners were a matter of historical luck, depending on small populations, abundance of land, and the opportunity to be "first" in technological development. Thus, human rights does not provide a sufficient moral theory. As noted, Henry Shue is trying to correct this by insisting that duties be correlated with rights, while A.J.M. Milne suggests that the total list of proclaimed moral rights be reduced to those whose moral basis—namely, participation in community life—is apparent.

From the point of view of ethical philosophy, the theories of world order and human rights fail to explain any mechanism of morality, such as the motivation to help others. They simply imply that all persons want to enjoy a good life and that social engineers can figure out how to arrange these benefits. Stanley Hoffman complains that world-order writers expect problems to "melt in the sunshine of [their] good example."[17] The most significant lacuna in these theories is undoubtedly their avoidance of discussion of competition and conflict. They fail to acknowledge any significant human drive towards cruelty and exploitation, although writers on world order and human rights do discuss the actual *results* of these traits. A third positive argument, that of cosmopolitan morality, makes no mention of unpleasant behavior, either actual or potential. The writings of both the Greek and Roman Stoics read like a report on the life of angels; some even imply that a reasonable person *cannot* do wrong.

In sum, one of the factors which has hindered direct comparison of the twelve arguments concerning international morality is their lack of explicit statement about their ethical premises. As a result, students are perhaps drawn to whichever position, negative or positive, is closer to their own ideological outlook, but these students may then be unable to defend their choice philosophically.

The Fact/Value Distinction

The fourth question to be asked is: how successful are the arguments in distinguishing between fact and value? That is, do they follow the academic rules of scientific objectivity? My research concludes that international relations theory, in general, fares poorly here. In this academic area, the doctrine of scientific objectivity is misunderstood and/or misused and has the overall effect of inhibiting a thorough analysis of the value propositions inherent in most of the twelve arguments concerning international morality.

There are two main problems here. The first is that students receive the impression that the negative and positive positions, as I have roughly divided them, correspond to the division between fact and value. Thus, for example, Morgenthau's work is "fact" because it talks about power politics; Falk's work is "value" because it delves into matters of social injustice. But that is not true, of course. *Both* of them talk about facts, for instance the facts of military preparedness in Morgenthau's case, or the facts of starvation in Falk's case. *Both* of them incorporate values in their approach to the problem, and in the solutions they offer. As a rule, it would probably be sensible to assume that there is very little in the way of disinterested study of such a vital field. K. Holsti claims "While some may argue that we have organized a field called international relations and politics because the phenomena are "there" the truth is that we study them because of a deeply held normative concern about the problem of war."[18]

The second problem is more complicated. It has to do with the fact that the study of international relations theory is a study of *theory*, which is not the same as the study of the world. When the student of this subject wants to reach a final judgment about international morality, ("*Is there a moral relationship among states?*") he must rely on the material contained in the various theories. He thus has to measure the worth of each theory; this can only be done by checking its performance against some external standards. In the case of checking the empirical claims of the theory, he can go to current sources of data. In the case of checking the *moral* claims he can analyze the moral reasoning of each. That is, without intruding his own moral preferences, he can apply standards of logic, consistency, or thoroughness. Owing to the intimidating presence of the fact/value tenet, academics may shrink from the prospect of judging moral claims—but if that is the subject matter of some of the theories at hand, how else can these theories be judged?

One of the few uses of this style of evaluation to be found in the international relations literature is provided by R.J. Vincent. He criticizes that use of the morality-of-states concept which implies that there are *only* states in the world. We must reject this claim, he says, on the basis of its philosophical error.

> Otherwise the morality of states would be a doctrine rationalizing blindness to central moral issues concerned with the treatment of individuals (for example, slavery), or of groups (for example, the principle of national self-determination), or . . . of the world as a whole (for example, the obligations attending travel on 'spaceship Earth'). A morality giving no sight of such central issues would be a third-rate morality whatever the argument of prudence that supported it.[19]

In other words, Vincent tries to hold the philosophy of the morality of states to some standard of reasonableness. I do not believe that Vincent need be accused of simply stating his own moral preferences or of violating the fact/value distinction. Rather, he is analyzing a certain moral theory on its face. This is clearly distinct from moralizing.

John C. Garnett has written:

> When [academics] have, to the best of their ability, accurately described the world as it is, they have completed their task; they can go no further. If they are tempted—and many are—to go on and moralize about the world they have described . . . then they overstep their academic mandate. At that point they hang up their gowns and don cassocks.[20]

I agree with Garnett that it is improper for professors to impose their ideological views about the world on their students. Yet there is such a thing as making an attempt to analyze moral statements with some objectivity. Thus I do not agree with David Easton who says: "The factual aspect of a proposition refers to a part of reality; hence, it can be tested by reference to the facts. . . . The moral aspect of a proposition, however, expresses only the emotional response of an individual to a state of real or presumed facts."[21] Easton's description of morals as being somehow indistinguishable from emotions is the type of fact/value distinction that inadvertently helps to *keep* the moral aspects of theories at an emotional, unanalyzed level.

Summary. To summarize this chapter, an attempt has been made to assess what I call the arguments concerning international morality, using internal criteria. Some of them were seen to be unreliable because they depend on unargued assumptions. Some lose their validity when taken out of their historical context. Most of them are deficient in acknowledging their ethical bases, and only two develop a moral theory explicitly, although they all make moral statements. Finally, the academic concern with the fact/value distinction tends to inhibit proper analysis of the normative content of these arguments. Because of all these circumstances, a student might find it difficult to research the central question "Is there a moral relationship among states?" The arguments are, *in toto*, a rich source of ideas about international morality, yet individually they remain unsatisfying.

I thus propose that we put aside these traditional writings for the moment and move to another area, that of evolutionary biology, to get some new light on our central topic. Part Two will present two major sociobiological hypotheses relevant to the subject of international morality, namely hypotheses about morality itself, and about the behavior of groups. Following that, Part Three will extend the critique of the negative and positive positions on international morality by applying this external knowledge.

Part II

Sociobiological Hypotheses Pertinent to
International Morality

5

The Biology of Morality

> *In brief, man is also a moral being. It is this side of man which the age of science has obscured and distorted, if not obliterated, by trying to reduce moral problems to scientific propositions.*
>
> —Hans Morgenthau

Introduction to Part Two

We now switch our focus from international relations theory to sociobiology, in the effort to find out more about international morality. In every age, philosophical ideas and social theories are partly dependent upon the prevailing scientific knowledge—Aristotle's biology, Hobbes' physics, and Locke's psychology being salient examples. In fact, many of the theories underwriting the positive and negative arguments in Part One contained some scientific premise about the world or about human nature, although these were not often made explicit.

The new discipline of sociobiology arose out of evolutionary biology in general; it also owes much to population genetics, ecology, and ethology in particular. E.O. Wilson defines sociobiology as "the systematic study of the biological basis of all social behavior."[1] Most practitioners of sociobiology are concerned with animal species other than humans; however, there is now a reasonably well-developed literature on human sociobiology.[2] In Part Two I shall concentrate on the two areas of human sociobiology that are of direct interest to a study of international morality. The first, in Chapter 5, concerns the biology of morality. The second, in Chapter 6, concerns the evolution of intergroup behavior. Following that, in Chapter 7, I shall discuss some of the criticisms and controversies of sociobiology.

The Biology of Morality

If it were discovered that human morality had some biological, genetic basis, this would presumably be of great interest to ethical philosophers and social theorists. The prevailing belief, after all, has been that moral behavior is *learned* and is culturally relative. Until now, the most convincing explanation as to how or why morality came about has probably been that of social contract. That theory holds that people will arrive at a rational decision to restrain their normal selfish or violent impulses in order to enjoy the benefits of social life. Any alternative to a moral law-abiding situation is perilous and therefore it is logical that people will opt to establish a moral system. Once it is established, the new members of society, that is, the children, pick up morality as habit or custom.

At least that is the best secular explanation. Most cultures have also persuaded their members that there are supernatural connotations to morality. Goodness is a spiritual quality: perfection exists in some abstract realm to which humans can aspire. Many of the great religions use a personified God as the example of pure moral behavior, and proclaim that sinful behavior goes against God's wishes. Even in the non-theistic philosophy of Immanuel Kant, good behavior is *intrinsically* right without respect to its beneficial social consequences.

The view that I shall present here pays no attention to either the social contract origin of morality or the alleged divine origin. It starts with a discussion of social behavior in the animal kingdom and shows how it is possible that a moral sense could have developed, under the pressure of natural selection, in hominid species ancestral to man. I shall argue that there is thus some human-nature grounding to morality, particularly thanks to the evolution of the moral emotions, and that these give rise to the cultural institution of morality.

It should be noted that the word "morality" is used in common parlance to mean many different things. It conjures up at least three realms of behavior: *order*, or social restraint, as indicated by laws and regulations; *welfare-provision*, including acts of mercy or generosity toward others; and *judgment*, as seen in the reasoning of judges, the justice-theories of philosophers, and the everyday moralizing of laypeople. In my discussion of the biology of morality I shall try to account, in sociobiological terms, for all of these behaviors. That is, I do not intend to narrow the ordinary definition of morality.

The outline of this chapter is as follows. A section on evolutionary theory will be presented first, and will be followed by a discussion of the main theory of sociobiology, namely, the genetics of altruism. I shall then outline two theories of the evolution of moral behavior in humans, namely Robert Trivers' theory of the moral emotions, and Richard Alexander's theory of interests. Then I shall discuss "other genetic predispositions for morality" and shall comment on the relative influence of genes and culture in the development of morality. Finally I shall inquire into the practical functions of human morality. The point of this exercise, of course, is to come up with an understanding of what morality is, so that we may later determine what international morality is.

Evolutionary Theory

The status of evolutionary theory within science today is that of virtually complete acceptance. In the mid-nineteenth century, Albert Russell Wallace and Charles Darwin independently discovered the key to diversity and change among the millions of species of plant and animal life. Their theory was that of *natural selection*, which requires three factors: 1. there is variation among individuals within species; 2. many more young are born than can survive to maturity; and 3. those that have characteristics best suited to their environment are the ones which survive and reproduce, passing on these "adaptive" traits to offspring.[3] Darwin published *On the Origin of Species* in 1859, still not knowing of what the hereditary mechanism consisted. Seven years later, the monk Gregor Mendel discovered, through his experiments with garden peas, the way in which the traits from both parents are combined in their offspring, and the law of dominant and recessive characteristics. His work went unnoticed until 1900 when the science of genetics began.[4]

Mendel, of course, did not know about genes, as such. The gene is a string of nucleotides shaped like a double helix or spiral staircase. It is known chemically as DNA and is located on the chromosomes. DNA appears in every living cell, suggesting that all life descended from one original cell. Genes carry the instructions of heredity and control the expression of traits by synthesizing the required enzymes; they are subject to occasional mutation by chemical accident or radiation. The genes for very specific anatomical and even behavioral traits have now been located on chromosomes in various lower animals. In man, over 600 of them have been located so far (out of about 100,000), such as the gene for Down's syndrome, which resides on Chromosome 21.[5]

It was not until 1953 that James Watson and Francis Crick "broke the genetic code."[6] By that time, however, the Darwinian theory of evolution had already been greatly augmented from many sources. Since the 1930s, scientists such as J.B.S. Haldane, R.A. Fisher, and Sewall Wright had been working out the mathematics of population genetics;[7] and biologists such as Theodosius Dobzhansky had observed natural selection in the laboratory by experimenting with fast-breeding species such as fruitfly.[8] Paleontologists had uncovered a wide range of fossils, dating the evolution of vertebrate life to 400 million years ago, and recorded the subsequent evolution of vertebrates from fish to reptiles, to amphibia, to birds and mammals. The field of ethology showed how "instinctive" behaviors evolved by natural selection: Konrad Lorenz, Niko Tinbergen, and Karl von Frisch received the Nobel Prize for this in 1973. In short, many biological sciences have corroborated Darwin's theory. It is the central, orthodox explanation of the living world.

The status of *human* evolution within biology is also strong. Biochemical evidence shows us to be very closely related to other primates.[9] Paleontology has provided reliable, if sparse, evidence of ancestral hominids who were transitional between apes and men. (These date to 3 million years ago and will be discussed below). Field studies of primates, such as Jane Goodall's long-term observations of chimpanzees,[10] have found that many behaviors or traits once thought to be uniquely human are present in animals: this suggests that they may be "genetic" rather than cultural.

The most startling new discovery of biology which relates to human evolution, however, did not come from work with primates, but rather from work with insects. I refer to the principal discovery of sociobiology by the entomologist William D. Hamilton in 1964, namely, the discovery of the mechanism of social life.[11] The social insects such as ants and bees have the most complex systems of social communication and cooperation of any nonhuman species, so it seems fitting that the biological basis of social life should have been found in them. In due course, Hamilton's theory, which is variously known as the theory of genetic altruism, kin selection, and inclusive fitness—or just "nepotism"—has been applied successfully to many mammalian species including primates.[12] Sociobiology, a new discipline of evolutionary biology, arose in response to this theory, to study the biological basis of society and social organization.

The Genetics of Altruism

"Altruism" is defined by *The American Heritage Dictionary* as "concern for the welfare of others as opposed to egoism; selflessness." As we shall see, biologists have found that acts of altruism may be acts of disguised selfishness, insofar as some benefit eventually accrues to the donor of an altruistic act. However, I believe it is useful to continue to use the word "altruistic" as in common parlance to indicate acts which are helpful to others and which at least *appear* to be unselfish.

Many animals perform altruistic acts. At first glance this seems peculiar. Why should an animal think of others? Unselfishness does not fit into the standard Darwinian theory of evolution. The rule of life is that only those traits come into being, or flourish, which can be passed on genetically between generations. Any trait which raises the "Darwinian fitness" of an individual animal, such as a trait which helps it to obtain food or find a nesting site, is likely to flourish. But a trait which *lowers* the Darwinian fitness (also known as reproductive fitness) of an individual, such as a trait for disease or incompetence, should die out: the individual will not live to reproduce the trait. All traits that incline an individual to be more helpful to his neighbors than to himself would seem to fit into this latter category of non-adaptive traits: the *neighbor* will live longer, or reproduce more, by virtue of the help he gets, while the "foolhardy" altruistic individual will die out, and his genetic trait for altruism will die with him.

Thus, animal altruism is, at first sight, a mystery. It puzzled Darwin who was aware of the extreme altruism of worker bees and ants. The altruism of bees even includes sterility: they sacrifice the chance to reproduce at all in favor of devoting their energy to helping other bees. But how could *sterility* possibly be an inherited trait? Morever, a certain species of termite has "soldiers" which explode their abdomen to secrete a chemical spray at the enemy, thus killing themselves as well.[13] But how could a trait for such suicidal behavior be genetic?

During the twentieth century, the problem of altruism, and more generally, the mystery of social cooperation, continued to be contemplated by biologists. Among these were R.A. Fisher, W.C. Alee, David Lack, J.B.S. Haldane, John Maynard Smith, and Vincent Wynne-Edwards. Haldane came close to working out the formula for genetic altruism.[14] The solutions that have now been found involve kin altruism and reciprocal altruism.

Kin Altrusim

The essential breakthrough came in entomology. W.D. Hamilton noted that Hymenoptera (ants, bees, wasps) have a peculiar mode of reproduction which causes sisters to be more closely related to each other than to their own daughters. Namely, they have 75% of their genes in common with siblings, and only 50% in common with offspring. Assuming, for the moment, that the "incentive" for reproduction is to push one's genes into future generations, it is better for these individuals to assist their sisters in reproduction, than to reproduce themselves. The net effect will be that by remaining "celibate" and behaving altruistically—in regard to energy spent helping siblings survive and reproduce—they may lower their Darwinian fitness but raise their inclusive fitness. "Inclusive fitness" is calculated by the number of one's genes that are *included* in future generations.[15]

This simple formula of kin altruism is the explanation for most altruism in animals. Of course, most species do not have the 75% genetic identity that makes the social insects so altruistic and socially cooperative. Mammals share only 50% of their genes with close relatives (except identical twins who share 100%). Mammalian social life is thus much looser than insect social life, with individual mammals remaining predominantly selfish.[16] The most prevalent instance of altruism in mammals is maternal; obviously, a mother raises her reproductive fitness by feeding and defending her young. In some mammal species these two things—food-sharing and defense—extend to other kin. In lion society, for instance, the mothers may suckle the cubs of their sisters, thus helping collateral descendants which have only 25% of their genes.[17]

Social defense may consist of as simple a behavior as giving an alarm call when a predator approaches. The individual that gives the call makes itself thereby more conspicuous to the predator; hence, such altruistic behavior seems nonadaptive. The animals in the immediate area, however, that are saved by hearing the call, are likely to be the relatives of the altruistic individual, rather than non-kin. Apparently, the instinct to give an alarm call is able to evolve because it helps a sufficient number of relatives. Crudely calculated, if the call saves more than two of the individual's relatives, which each have 25% of his genes (for example, 'nephews'), that is equivalent to saving one of his direct offspring. Helping ten relatives with 12½% common genes each (for example, cousins) is of greater genetic value (125%) than saving his own life. The mechanism of evolution involved here has been named "kin selection" by John Maynard Smith.[18] It differs from traditional natural selection in that the unit of selection is not the individual but the family.

The Selfish Gene

At the same time, Richard Dawkins points out that the unit of real importance seems to be the gene itself.[19] The "selfish" gene can be imagined as having a drive of its own: it is out to propagate *itself*, using whatever device it can, such as the individual or the family, to help its cause. This new way of interpreting evolution amounts to a Copernican revolution in biology, in which the individual, like the Earth, is no longer the center of the universe.

Richard Alexander, too, believes that individual survival is not what life is all about. He calls on the argument of G.C. Williams that the phenomenon of *senescence* demonstrates this. If individual survival *were* the thrust of life, we would no doubt live longer. The reason we break down after eighty years or so is not due to the cells' inability to carry on—after all, giant redwood trees can live for two thousand years. Rather, it must have to do with the reassortment of genes. The very fact that we frequently do things contrary to our survival interests, such as perform altruistic acts for relatives, or sacrifice our life in war, is a demonstration of the fact that it is the genes' survival more than the individual's survival that is controlling.[20]

In any case, the discovery of kin altruism and the concept of the selfish gene gave the needed clue to the biological basis of society. But now let us ask, what is society?

The Evolution of Society

As mentioned earlier, the social contract explanation for the origin of human society involves a moment in time when selfish individuals realized that they would be better off living in a cooperative society. That is not an impossible scenario for thinking, speaking human beings, but it could hardly explain the formation of societies in the animal kingdom. The majority of animal species, of course, do not have social life. Individual gnats and jellyfish, for instance, live only for their own survival. But in a fair number of bird and mammal species there is some social life, and in a few mammal species as well as in the social insects, there is a complex society in which the members have regularly patterned relationships and communication with one another. They act as a cooperative unit.

How can this be explained biologically? As discussed above, kin selection is the *mechanism* for the evolution of particular social behaviors. But the explanation as to *why* society came about is that *society is adaptive*. It leads to greater survival possibilities for its members (and their genes). Society itself can be thought of as an adaptation to the environment. Certain environments happen to present special opportunities or niches for creatures that can evolve a cooperative mode of living.

Very often, food supply is the environmental factor that "causes" the social adaptation to come about. Here, the evolution of society can be thought of as comparable to the evolution of an *anatomical* adaptation: the long legs of certain waterbirds, for example, came about to enable them to wade into the lake for fish. In a parallel way, food supply can cause a species to develop cooperative traits—elementary social life—as an adaptation to the environment. African wild dogs provide a clear instance of this. At one time there must have been an empty niche for a hunter of large game. That is, there were animals available on the plains but they were too big to be caught by an individual dog. A *pack* of dogs, however, could jointly fell the game.[21] So eventually the trait for cooperative hunting emerged in this species. Undoubtedly, the first group of wild dogs to evolve pack-hunting, in which individuals restrain their selfish impulses, consisted of related individuals: kin altruism was the mechanism. However in some species, as will be discussed below, it seems that reciprocal altruism can also evolve as a genetic trait. Here, unrelated individuals can enter into cooperative activities.

Cooperation in food-getting was mentioned as an explanation for the evolution of certain animal societies. Group defense is probably the other major explanation. In the case of ants, the ecological feature which prompted social evolution may have been either food supply or the need for group defense. In the case of primates, whose social evolution is of great interest in regard to the human species, it is most likely that the need for group defense was the key factor.[22] (Most primate species do not obtain food as a joint effort.)

Reciprocal Altruism

Besides kin altruism, there is another type of altruism that can evolve genetically, namely, reciprocal altruism. George C. Williams first proposed this in 1966, and Robert Trivers published the key article in 1971.[23]

Reciprocal altruism is based on an exchange of favors: "You scratch my back, I'll scratch yours." An individual can enhance his survival chances by doing favors for others if it is likely that the favors will be returned. Trivers states that certain criteria must be met: the individuals performing the altruistic acts must be intelligent enough to recognize one another and to remember favors; they should also live in a group which stays together for a time sufficient to allow enforcement of the pay-back rule. Reciprocal altruism may in fact have first evolved among relatives; however, the important point is that it can evolve among unrelated individuals.

Reciprocal altruism has been reported in mammals of high intelligence, such as baboons, chimpanzees, dolphins, and whales. In the case of chimpanzees, de Waal observes that Individual A assists Individual B in fighting off a rival; later B calls upon A to give similar assistance.[24] In the case of whales, Richard Connor and Kenneth Norris note that one or more individuals swim along under a sick companion, pushing it up to the surface for air.[25] Presumably those altruists can elicit similar help from the recipient later. Central to the hypothesis of reciprocal altruism is that the evolved behavior is instinctive: it is not dependent on conscious calculation of costs and benefits by the altruistic individual.

In species such as chimpanzee and whale, it is difficult to prove that the trait disposing individuals to perform altruism is genetic. Conceivably, each individual could invent the behavior anew by *recognizing* that a favor performed will merit a favor owed. In a less advanced animal, however, it is easier to see reciprocal altruism as instinctive. In 1984, Gerald Wilkinson reported in the journal *Nature* a case of reciprocal food-sharing in the vampire bat.[26] The vampire bat lives a particularly precarious life in that it must obtain food, namely, blood sucked from cattle, at least every three days or it will starve to death. Female bats, which associate in groups of about ten, have a system of sharing, in which a well-fed bat regurgitates blood to one which was unable to find a victim the preceding night. By experimentally capturing the bats on certain nights to deprive them of a feed, Wilkinson was able to record the exact direction of the altruism. The bats were found to be more likely to help those who had recently helped them, hence tit-for-tat reciprocity was involved.

The Impossibility of Gratuitous Altruism in Animals

It is not clear how the behavior of reciprocal altruism got started, but biologists agree that the trait for performing this reciprocal altruism could have flourished only if it helped the individual *performing* the altruism, not the recipient. Furthermore, as Trivers emphasizes, evolution by natural selection cannot work for the *good of the group*. There is no way that a trait can come into a species simply because it benefits the species: it always has to benefit the individual which possesses the trait.[27]

(An exception may be made for the case of group selection: that is a controversial matter that will be discussed in Chapter 6.)

In short, there is no gratuitous altruism in Nature. The cost/benefit analysis must always show the *donor* of altruism to be the winner. This may happen, as described above, where the returned favors are fairly similar. It may also occur by a formula in which the individual gives aid to a stranger in dire need, if the giving of the aid hurts the donor only a little but helps the recipient a lot. The example of saving a drowning stranger is often used here. Assuming that a person could save a drowning stranger merely by throwing out a rope, or otherwise not taking a great risk, it is worth it for him to do so in terms of the much greater return he may get some day—from any stranger—if *he* is drowning. So, Rule One of evolved reciprocal altruism is: help those who will help you at least equally on a tit-for-tat basis; Rule Two is: help those in great distress if the cost to you is small. Wilkinson found both rules to operate in the vampire bat species. As well as tit-for-tat reciprocity, he found that bats "in their final hours," closest to starvation, were preferentially fed.[28] This apparent welfare system must have come about because the starving bat receives a benefit that greatly outweighs its cost to the donor.

The Evolution of Human Morality

The foregoing discussion of genetic altruism does not provide us with an understanding of human morality. For one thing, altruism is not morality. Altruism is helpfulness, while morality—although it may include elements of helpfulness—has more to do with notions of right and wrong. Let me state emphatically that 1. I do not see morality in the animal kingdom—it is something peculiar to the human species (and possibly its hominid ancestors); and 2. I do not postulate a direct connection between genetic altruism and the fully developed human moral system. Rather, I propose that reciprocal altruism led to the development of "moral emotions" (Trivers' idea) and that the existence of *these* could cause notions of right and wrong to develop. These notions of right and wrong, in turn, resulted in the institutionalization of morality in human society.

The Hominid Species

The evolution of human morality must have taken place sometime before our species, modern *Homo sapiens*, was completely formed, which is thought to be about 40,000 or 50,000 years B.P. (Before Present). Indeed, all innate physical and mental traits of humans must have evolved before that date because shortly after that, the great migrations began. These migrations sent humans to all the continents; when their descendants were rediscovered by modern explorers they were recognized as being brothers to European man.

That logic furnishes us with the latest possible date of human evolution—namely, 40,000 years ago—but the earliest possible date is harder to discern. Mammals evolved as early as 225 million years ago; early primates evolved 65 million years ago; and apes diverged from monkeys about 30 million years ago. Within the ape line it appears from fossil evidence that orangutans branched off first, about 16 million years ago.[29] The fossil record of primates, from 16 million years B.P. to 3 million years B.P. is poor. However, there is a biochemical, rather than paleontological, method of dating evolution, which compares the similarity of chromosomes of various mammals. It indicates that the gorilla line broke off about 10 million years ago. It also indicates that a certain creature, living about 6 million years ago, was the ancestor to both the modern chimpanzee, and to the hominid line which culminated in the human species.[30]

Starting about 3 million years ago there is again good fossil evidence, such as that of the hominid specimen known as "Lucy."[31] There is also a set of very human-like hominid footprints, reliably dated to that period.[32] Hominids are divided into two genera: *Australopithecus* and *Homo*. *Australopithecus* (which includes "Lucy") may have lasted from sometime prior to 3 million years ago, up until 2 million years ago. This creature walked upright, was about 4 foot tall, and had a human-like skeleton. However, its brain size was only 450 cubic centimeters, similar to that of a modern chimpanzee.

Australopithecus was "replaced" by *Homo*, which is probably its direct descendant.[33] (This is disputed.*) The genus *Homo* is divided into two species: *Homo erectus* and *Homo sapiens*. *Homo erectus* is well known from the fossil record.[34] At least its *physical* characteristics are known, but its way of life can only be estimated from patchy evidence. For example, Glynn Isaac has described a *Homo erectus* site at Olduvai Gorge dated at 1.9 million years which has indications of communal eating habits.[35] The *Homo erectus* cave site at Choukoutien, China, dated at around 350,000 BC, shows evidence of the use of fire for cooking.[36] Tool use began early in *Homo erectus* and includes hand-axes which were most likely used for butchering animals. Tool use does not necessarily imply language use: it is not known whether *Homo* had language or not.

Homo sapiens has a much more complete social record. This species may have evolved as early as 250,000 years ago, judging from the large cranial capacity of the fossil skulls known as Steinheim man and Swanscombe woman—or even earlier. It is the Neanderthal type of *Homo*

---

*The "line of descent" is disputed in many ways. For a helpful roundup of the literature, see Graham Richards, *Human Evolution*. For informative photographs of hominid fossils, see John Reader, *Missing Links*.

sapiens, which lived from about 100,000 years to 60,000 years ago, that has plenty of evidence of housing, clothing, and large, cooperative group activities associated with its skeletal remains.[37] There is even a burial site dated at 60,000 years in Iraq whose decorations suggest religious belief.[38] Modern *Homo sapiens* begins with Cro-Magnon man, around 50,000 to 40,000 years ago, and has such incontrovertible evidence of hunting as the cave paintings of bison with arrows in their sides.

As stated above, the human genome was to a large extent completed by 40,000 years ago. That is, natural selection took place up until that time; most changes since then have been cultural. The main reason why evolution by natural selection has been curtailed is, of course, that modern cultural arrangements support individuals who, in harsher settings, would not live to reproduce. In sum, when we speak of the evolution of morality, or proto-morality in hominids, we are referring to some time between 3 million years ago and 40,000 years ago.

Trivers' Theory of the Moral Emotions

Robert Trivers believes that reciprocal altruism evolved in some species of animals, unaccompanied by any moral sense. However, he postulates that in the hominid line, certain emotions, which we can call the moral emotions, came about in relation to the behavior of reciprocal altruism[39] (particularly in relation to monitoring the give and take of the altruistic partners). These emotions include the feelings of guilt, gratitude, and moral indignation. I believe that these furnish the physiological basis of the phenomenon known as *conscience*.

Emotions, in general, are certainly biologically evolved. They consist essentially of discharges of sensation from the limbic system of the brain. In early mammals there are at least two primary emotions, pleasure and pain, whose rather obvious adaptive function is to guide the animal to do things essential to its survival. The pleasure of eating leads him to take nourishment, the pain of being bitten urges him to stay away from predators or competitors. In higher mammals there are more variations; for example, pain is differentiated into anger provoked by frustration, or anxiety in anticipation of pain. Carroll Izard has shown that in human babies, before the age of two years, a range of emotions emerges in a fixed sequence, including such pleasure emotions as joy and interest, and such pain emotions as shame or disgust. The fixed sequence suggests that these emotions are prepackaged, not completely dependent on the infant's learning or experience.[40]

Trivers suggests that the reason the moral emotions had to come about was to keep the adaptive behavior of altruism working in the face of the equally adaptive behavior of *cheating*. Once the behavior of altruism had entered our ancestral species' gene pool, he says, it was inevitable that the behavior of cheating would also come about: "You scratch my back, then I run away." An individual who can take advantage of the altruism of others, a so-called free-rider, will obviously gain in Darwinian fitness: he receives benefits at little cost. Gross cheaters, of course, would defeat their own purpose, since altruists would stop helping them; but subtle cheating is highly adaptive. Trivers states: "Natural selection will rapidly favor a complex psychological system in which individuals regulate both their own altruistic and cheating tendencies and their responses to these tendencies in others."[41]

Righteous indignation is perhaps the most important emotion involved in the practice of morality. Having this emotion gives a person leverage over others. He can make others fall in line not by threat of force but by mere contempt and "moralistic aggression." I am aware of only one report of possible "righteous wrath" in animals. De Waal described a case in which a female chimpanzee, name Puist, had supported a male, Luit, in chasing another male, Nikkie.

> When Nikkie later displayed at Puist, she turned to Luit and held out her hand to him in search of support. Luit, however, did nothing to protect her against Nikkie's attack. Immediately Puist turned on Luit, barking furiously, chased him across the enclosure and even hit him.[42]

De Waal speculates that this "retribution" indicates Puist's perception of unfair treatment. Since there is no extant species transitional between apes and modern man, we have no way of tracing the evolution of the moral emotions. Indeed, their evolution is only a hypothesis, but in the absence of any competing explanation for present-day moral feelings, it seems to me persuasive.

The way in which I believe human morality came about is as follows. The moral emotions, as Trivers says, evolved to monitor altruistic exchanges. Hominids began to experience such feelings as remorse, magnanimity, and righteous indignation. With this physiological equipment, individuals became *moralizers*: they started to sense a rightness and wrongness of the behavior of themselves and their fellows. Thus, moralizing arrived on the scene before morality itself! Note that nothing in the natural world has a moral quality to it as such. Even the altruistic deeds of animals are not moral: a bird giving an alarm call is not thought by other birds to act nobly.

At the beginning of this chapter I noted that the word "morality" applies to a large range of human activities, involving order, welfare-provision, and moral judgment. It is the last one—judgment—that we are discussing here, and I contend that it is the most central one. In *The American Heritage Dictionary*, the first definition listed for the word "moral" is "of or concerned with the judgment of the goodness or badness of human action and character; pertaining to the discernment of good and evil." It is this *concern* about goodness or badness that gives rise later to the belief that things are objectively right or wrong. Thanks to the moral emotions we start to *reify* good and bad things. We say sharing is a good thing, cheating is a bad thing. These evaluations are originally from Ego's point of view. Sharing is what he wants the other person to do for him; cheating is what he wants the other person to abjure. After a while, people set up "objective" rules about the rightness and wrongness of these acts, and are willing to follow the rules as the price to be paid for demanding compliance by others. Eventually the act in question appears to be intrinsically bad or wrong: "Cheating is a terrible thing!"

Later, then, we are equipped not only with the physiological apparatus basic to morality (which I take to be the moral emotions, rather than any particular instinct for altruism) but also with the perceived and reified *environment* of good and bad things. From thence it seems inevitable that cultures will institutionalize morality—whether in law, religion, or some more reflective modes of ethical reasoning.

Alexander's Theory of Interests

Richard Alexander has examined the evolution of moral behavior in a different way from Trivers and myself. His scheme does not basically conflict with that of Trivers. In fact he states "It is a common error to suppose that something additional to nepotism [kin altruism] and reciprocity is required to account for the structure of society."[43] Nevertheless, Alexander's plan is to account more directly for the adaptiveness of human moral behavior. He holds that the motivation for all action is egoistic *interest*, with the important proviso that Ego's interest includes reproductive, genetic interests—that is, inclusive fitness.

With this inclusion, Alexander claims to be able to resolve certain paradoxes in moral philosophy, notably that of the incompatibility of egoism and utilitarianism, and that of the moral dualism of human nature. "Essentially all authors consider pleasure or happiness as reward (benefit) and pain and suffering as punishment (cost), but none can explain in egoistic terms either the voluntary acceptance of pain or the pleasure of helping others."[44] The difficulty, Alexander says, is that these philosophers do not evaluate interests in the right currency, namely the currency of genes. If they did, they would see that pain can bring benefit!

Similarly, he notes, philosophers misinterpret a major point of moral behavior. They "regard morality in the behavior of an individual as consisting of a kind of altruism that yields the altruist less than he gives."[45] The reverse is true, Alexander insists: the altruist generally gets more than he gives. For one thing, he gets *reputation*. This is not an unsubstantial benefit: it means that others see the altruist as a reliable partner and so are likely to do more altruistic favors for him. In getting reputation, he also helps his family. Alexander believes that even a soldier who falls on a grenade, altruistically saving his platoon, may be winning points for his family, since he will later be seen as a hero and his relatives will be trusted, by association. Concerning the promises of religion, he remarks:

> If nepotism is our evolved function, then God (in the sense of *vox populi, vox Dei*) really can guarantee a reward "in Heaven," or after our individual deaths—or a kind of "everlasting life" (for our genetic materials) —as a reward for moral behavior during life.[46]

In his book, *The Biology of Moral Systems*, Alexander proposes that the rapid increase in brain size and intelligence during hominid evolution was related to social life rather than to, say, technology. He claims that advances in intelligence were largely advances in social skills, consisting of outmaneuvering one's fellows in the game of reciprocity. Even *self-awareness*, he believes, came about as "a way of seeing ourselves as others see us so that we can cause them to see us as we would like them to."[47] As part of this scheme, Alexander defines conscience as "the still small voice that tells us how far we can go in serving our own interests without incurring intolerable risks."[48]

In short, for Alexander, morality has nothing to do with genuine goodness, but with the serving of one's own interests. Of course, in post-evolutionary times there are larger systems of morality which go far beyond the inter-individual games he mentions. Of these, he notes: "Formal law, partly because it is written down, [may require] the 'creep' toward social systems that approach the idealized models of indiscriminate beneficence."[49] Even idealized moral systems, though, can still benefit the individual because they allow him to moralize about others. "Pressure is likely to be applied by each individual so as to cause his neighbor, if possible, to be a little more moral than himself."[50]

I personally favor Trivers' theory over that of Alexander's in that it better accounts for the drive which many people seem to have toward morality for its own sake. Alexander, along with others, is keen to show that altruism is not really altruism and that morality is not really morality. Rather, altruism is selfishness and morality is a game of interests. I admit that there is probably much merit to this—the behavior of moralizing seems often to encompass a lot of self-deception.

A conclusion about ethics which Alexander reaches is that if interests, and conflicts of interest, are the main stuff of human relations, then ethics should be concerned with compromises and contracts, rather than some futile search for pure moral truth. It seems to me that there is plenty of scope for such a hard-nosed approach in contemporary ethics. In fact, this view may be of particular value in the traditionally hard-nosed area of international relations.

Other Genetic Predispositions toward Morality

To complete the picture of the "biology of morality" we should note that besides the behavior of *judgment*, the other two behaviors subsumed under morality—*order* and *welfare-provision*—may also have evolutionary explanations. I propose that the order aspect of morality was aided in its development by the innate human predispositions for *obedience* and *conformity*, while the welfare-provision aspect was aided by the trait of *sympathy*.

Order. As Jane Goodall has documented, there is plenty of order in chimpanzee social life, much of it deriving from the ubiquitous presence of a dominance hierarchy.[51] While it is true that there is frequent fighting among mammals to establish or maintain their place in the hierarchy, there is also much resigned submission and "obedience." Animals frequently stay in line to avoid being battered by their superiors. Some human laws, as Marxists are quick to note, may have arisen merely as reinforcements of the already-existing power structure. It does appear that humans are willing to obey laws, as a matter of course. This penchant for a chain of command could be due in some measure to the primate background of the human species.

Besides obedience to superiors, there is also the more general habit of comformity. Humans seem to like regularity and discipline, and not tolerate much deviance or eccentricity. The evolutionary explanation of this trait may be the overall adaptiveness of *neophobia:* a fear of the new and unknown (or conversely, a love of the familiar and routine). Charles J. Lumsden and E.O. Wilson note that rats are known to be neophobic: this behavior protects them from going near dangers new in the environment, such as traps set by humans.[52] In hominid times, it may have been adaptive for humans to be conformist or rule-abiding, simply because that is safer than being a pathbreaker.

In any case, there is some evidence that the "order" aspect of human morality has an evolutionary background. No doubt the order aspect and the judgment aspect of morality initially fitted together rather easily: rules of order could be absorbed into the reification of right and wrong. Once language and culture arrived, the rules could become elaborated into such things as "taboos of the ancestors" or "the revealed commandments of God."

Welfare-Provision. The evolutionary origin of the trait which predisposes us to welfare-provision, namely *sympathy*, is less clear. Darwin seemed to believe that it was an extension of animals' "love of their own kind." In *The Descent of Man* he cited much anecdotal evidence such as "Mr Blyth, as he informs me, saw Indian crows feeding two or three of their companions which were blind" and "Brehm states that when a baboon in confinement was pursued to be punished, the others tried to protect him."[53] However, Darwin admitted that there is little *proof* that any animal experiences pity, and indeed it may be that even chimpanzees do not possess this trait.[54] The vicarious suffering of another individual's pain that is so normal in human life, seems virtually absent in other species. There are at least three possibilities as to the evolutionary origin of human sympathy. It could in some way be related to the general ability to role-play, to imagine oneself intellectually in someone else's place. It could be a general extension of the tender maternal care of the young. Or it could be an outgrowth of reciprocal altruism.

I favor the first of these three suggestions, namely that our role-playing ability to see things from another's point of view led to the ability to experience vicarious *feelings*, as well. But probably maternal care and reciprocal altruism were involved also. As noted in the case of the vampire bat, the system of reciprocity required at least a recognition of, but not necessarily a sympathy for, the fact that certain bats were starving. It can also be argued that sympathy is largely learned rather than innate: there is enormous cultural variability in the amount of sympathy displayed among human societies, indeed in the expression of emotion in general.

In any case, if sympathy is even to a small extent "genetic," it must be listed as one of the predispositions that assists the third area of human morality which I have called welfare-provision. Most human societies from primitive to modern have systems of caring for helpless individuals, even individuals who can never be expected to repay society's kindness. Most civilized societies also have religious pronouncements about welfare, about the rightness of giving to those less well-off. This sort of gratuitous altruism is definitely not based on any system of altruism that evolved by natural selection. As noted earlier, *evolved* practices are not directed toward the good of the group: they must benefit the individual who possesses the altruistic trait. Therefore, human welfare systems are not "natural." They could, however, be based on natural traits, the most important of these being sympathy.

Human welfare systems may have been helped along additionally, by the natural human intellectual habit of *universalizing*. Once language had evolved, human ideas had a tendency to move from the particular to the general. That is, it is a feature of language itself to generalize and universalize propositions. Finally, it must be admitted that a large part of the explanation for human welfare systems is enlightened self-interest. People are willing to take out a "social insurance policy" for themselves, paying the price of gratuitous altruism.

Genes and Culture

I shall now attempt to make some distinction between that component of human morality which is most likely genetic, and that which is cultural—

although no fine line can be drawn. I have suggested in this chapter that human morality has some biological basis. Two kinds of *altruism*—kin and reciprocal—evolved genetically in the animal kingdom, but these do not constitute *morality*. One of the hominid species, Trivers argued, took reciprocal altruism to a new level by evolving emotional sensibilities toward "right and wrong." This could be called a *proto-moral* system, and we may assume it was mainly genetic. However, culture soon effloresced in the genus *Homo*, and more so in the species *Homo sapiens*, and it is culture that produced the specific moral rules of early humans and, of course, the advanced ethical ideas of civilized society.

How much of our moral behavior today is based on innate impulses, and how much is culturally induced is open to debate. At least three positions on this have been taken by scholars. The first position is nondeterministic: it holds that our genetic inheritance merely provides us with a conscience and that the conscience can become filled with arbitrary rules. William Ernest Hocking noted, in 1918, "While the totem gods and other gods gave extraordinarily different commands, the tendency of conscience to respect these commands is always there."[55] Hocking defines conscience as "the disposition to find an object of devotion and to set this object up as an authority in details of conduct, finding what one "ought" to do . . . from this source."[56] So, humans will be drawn ("with a blindness that savors of the tropism"[57]) to any cultural system of morality. George Edgin Pugh holds a related view. He believes that the human brain is a value-driven system. It contains both "primary values," which are inborn—such as the value of food and sex—and secondary values. The latter are learned from the culture, although they seep down into the brain in such a way as to seem like innate values.[58]

A second position holds that moral rules are somewhat more genetically determined. Culture is still required here to furnish the individual with the particulars, but his brain is constructed in such a way as to make him open to learning certain things and not others—this is known as "prepared learning," or "directed learning."[59] Charles J. Lumsden and E.O. Wilson, in their theory of gene-culture coevolution, propose that the brain evolved at the same time that culture was evolving and so the brain is *keyed in* to culture.[60] The child's brain, rather than being a blank slate, is more like a template to which certain things readily attach. This theory is deterministic to the extent that it says the child would have difficulty learning any ethical rule of culture that "goes against the grain." For instance, most cultures have a rule "Love thy Mother and thy Father." If, say, in some social engineering experiment a culture adopted the rule "Hate thy Mother and thy Father," children would tend not to obey that rule. (The idea here is that cultures will *invent* only certain rules and not others, because of innate human traits.) Evidence that the moral system is not a completely open one can be seen, for example, in the universal rule of reciprocity. Peter Singer notes that Edward Westermarck in his 1906 book, *The Origin and Development of Moral Ideas*, recorded the fact that "to requite a benefit, or to be grateful to him who bestows it, is probably everywhere, at least under certain circumstances, regarded as a duty."[61]

A third position which is even more deterministic, holds that specific ethical rules are innate. One such rule that has been pointed out by E.O. Wilson[62] and by Richard Alexander and Donald W. Tinkle[63] is the "incest taboo." They believe that there is a natural aversion to sibling-mating which evolved by natural selection, as a protection against the deleterious effects of inbreeding. The natural aversion then gave rise to the official prohibition on incest. Michael Ruse and E.O. Wilson, however, have recently made the broader claim that *all* ethical rules can be explained genetically. They write, "Internal moral premises do exist. . . . They are immanent in the unique programmes of the brain that originated during evolution,"[64] and "We suggest that it will be possible to proceed from a knowledge of the material basis of moral feeling to generally accepted rules of conduct."[65] I think that this statement goes too far. Ethical rules are the products of moral reasoning as well as of moral impulse—and moral reasoning *has its own dynamics*. For example there is a tendency for moral reasoning to become very wide, even universal in its scope; this could not be predicted from the "programmes of the brain"—unless Ruse and Wilson mean to include the programs of reasoning as well as those of "moral feeling."

The Practical Function of Morality

Does all this discussion of the biology of morality yield any worthwhile ideas about the meaning of morality in contemporary human life? I am persuaded that it does. First of all, it shows that morality is no intangible will-o'-the wisp thing, of interest only to "utopians"—as it is sometimes portrayed. Rather, morality is a part of human nature, a part whose antecedent forms emerged through the survival-of-the-fittest mechanisms of natural selection, and whose later forms are so ingrained in culture as to be virtually unremovable therefrom.

What are the practical functions of morality? I believe that the new insights into the biology of animal altruism, and the evolution of moral emotions in hominids, give us a clearer idea of what tasks morality performs in human society. As we saw, in certain highly developed animal societies, such as the social insects, altruism is the thing *that makes society possible*. Society *consists* of the cooperative acts and relationships among its individual members. The human species, of course, does not operate on instinctive acts of kin altruism as do ant species. Rather, humans submit to externalized rules and customs about how to behave toward fellow members. Those rules got there by invention, trial and error, inspiration, reasoning, and other more or less deliberate human activity (humans having been moved to erect those rules by their instinctive moral emotions). But the net effect is the same as for ant society: a system of altruistic or cooperative behavior *makes possible* a complex social life that could never come about if individuals were limited to selfish acts.

In human society, social exchanges can become far more abstract than if they were still tied to the one-to-one exchanges of earlier reciprocal altruists (such as chimpanzees). The externalization of rules and principles of behavior moves the reward and punishment system up from the level of one's neighbor to the level of society as a whole. Cultures provide myths to explain why certain practices are encouraged or forbidden, and thus make it easier for people to be motivated to good behavior.

The two functions that I see for morality, therefore, are that morality makes complex human society possible and morality makes social life emotionally comfortable. Instead of fighting with one's neighbors all day to gain one's just due, one can point to the law, or the custom, as the source of one's rights. Within a given society, everybody knows what is right and wrong (that is, what is considered by that society to be right and wrong). Conceivably, some society could develop a morally nihilistic stance, and thus make it hard for its members to have predictable social relationships with one another. However, in that event, the moral emotions—or, more precisely, our penchant for moralizing—would, I believe, reassert themselves in due course, demanding that some external rules be set up once more.

The foregoing chapter offers some general illumination about morality, though not especially about international morality. Chapter 6 now turns to another topic, that of the evolution of groups. Later, the discussion of morality will be brought up again, with particular reference to international morality.

6

The Evolution of Intergroup Behavior

> *The essence of the group is its distinction from outsiders;*
> *morality consists primarily of right conduct towards the*
> *other members of the group. The kind of violent moral-*
> *ity practiced by the Mafia . . . is the extreme case of a*
> *general rule: that the group comes first . . . and that, if*
> *others suffer, that is too bad.*
>
> *—J.D.B. Miller*

This book asks the question "Is there a moral relationship among states (i.e., nations)?" In order to answer that question, definitions of the major concepts are needed. The preceeding chapter offered a new sociobiological slant on the concept of morality; this chapter inquires into the *relationship among nations*, or among human groups generally. The main sociobiological idea to be presented here is that humans evolved in groups, and that such evolution accounts for two important phenomena: the strong feelings of loyalty and cooperation within a group, and the frequent unfriendliness and lack of "moral restraint" between groups.

In this chapter I shall present both a mild and a strong version of the theory of the evolution of human groups. The mild version, to be presented first, is Pierre van den Berghe's hypothesis that the modern phenomenon of ethnocentrism can be explained by kin altruism. The strong version, first suggested by Darwin and later developed by Arthur Keith, Richard Alexander, and Robert Bigelow, hypothesizes that there was hostile intergroup competition among hominids. This proposition involves the controversial issue of "group selection" that is, the question of whether natural selection can operate on the group as a unit. I shall discuss the current biological thinking on this subject, and also inquire into the reliability of the evidence of warfare in hominid or prehistoric times. Additionally, I shall bring in material from social psychology that supports the argument that group behavior is based on innate traits. Lastly, I shall discuss group morality.

The Social Structure of Hominids

At the outset it should be noted that the social structure of prehuman hominids is unknown. Among living species of primates there is a wide variety of social structures.[1] The orangutan is relatively solitary, the gibbon has only the mated pair as its family structure, while the gorilla has a larger "polygamous" family but no further interaction with a wider group. The chimpanzee has promiscuous mating but lifelong bonds between mother and offspring. Chimpanzees are organized into societies of about 50 members, in which adult males defend the whole group, not just their own kin. Baboons, too, have large troops whose travelling formation consists of females and infants on the inside, and males on the outside for defense against predators.[2] It can be hypothesized that social life in baboons and chimpanzees came about as an adaptation for defense, particularly for protection of the young.

As noted earlier, humans are closely related to chimpanzees, and shared a common ancestor as recently as 5 or 6 million years ago. But this does not mean that hominid social structure was like that of chimpanzees. For one thing, the chimpanzee of today may have diverged greatly from what the common ancestor was like. For another thing, even small changes in ecological circumstance—availability of food, or presence or absence of predators—can cause even very similar species to evolve different social structures. So, for the moment, it is only a "good guess" that prehuman hominids lived in small groups, and that they did so initially as an adaptation for defense.

Before proceeding to the discussion of the evolution of human groups, let me point out again that when I speak of any human trait that evolved via natural selection, I am referring to one which evolved prior to 40,000 years ago—the time at which the human genome was complete. Thus if I mention psychological traits such as xenophobia, I am claiming that these changes in the brain took place prior to the emergence of modern *Homo sapiens*.

Van den Berghe's Theory of Ethnocentrism

Pierre van den Berghe had published widely on the sociology of race relations before he happened to take up the study of evolutionary biology. He had noted the social sciences' lack of any adequate theory to explain the pervasive human phenomenon of ethnocentrism, and when the sociobiological theory of kin selection came along, he recognized it as the likely explanation. He hypothesizes that ethnocentrism, or favoritism to "one's own people" is simply an extended version of *nepotism*, or willingness to help one's kin.[3]

Van den Berghe notes that in small societies of animals, all the members are related to one another, and so altruistic acts are sometimes extended to the whole group. The creatures need have only a simple mechanism to differentiate members from nonmembers, and an instinct for *not* helping nonmembers—or perhaps an instinct for outright hostility to nonmembers. The method most animal species use to identify group members is by odor or by visual recognition. For humans, Van den Berghe notes, tribes always have markers such as costume, facial scarification, or language dialect, which differentiate them from their neighbors.[4]

This theory is built entirely on the positive aspects of kin selection. Thus, Van den Berghe believes that ethnocentric feelings evolved but that racism, as such, did not. For one thing, in evolutionary times, human groups were never contiguous with groups of people who differed greatly from them in color of skin, shape of nose, and so forth. Rather, racist behavior is just a negative aspect of nepotism—a failure of people to extend the umbrella of altruism to cover all. That failure, he says, could explain why alien minorities "are often exterminated without a whisper of protest in the general population."[5]

Van den Berghe's book, *The Ethnic Phenomenon*, is a survey of slavery, massacres, and genocides in the historical and contemporary period. He shows that "in every age since the recorded history of States, nationalism has inspired masses of people to veritable orgies of emotion and violence" and that "nationalist conflicts are among the most intractable and unamenable to reason and compromise." This he attributes to the fact that humans are genetically programmed to favor their own kind, although he admits that the term "one's own kind" can be applied rather arbitrarily.[6]

Gary Johnson, Susan Ratwick, and Timothy Sawyer have conducted a study of the use of kin terms in patriotic speech. They find that "the citizen body may be referred to as a 'family,' those beside whom one fights may be called 'brothers,' and the nation itself may be referred to as 'mother' or 'father'."[7] They note that patriotic behavior, especially sacrifice in battle, is routinely performed for non-kin, and that this would tend to suggest that the biological phenomenon of kin altruism is not at work here. However, they believe this is misleading. "Biological kinship is, paradoxically enough, irrelevant *for the social sciences* in accounting for human behavior that results from kin selection. . . . What evokes altruistic behavior on behalf of kin, for any animal, is not [actual blood relationship] but environmental cues that have typically been highly correlated with kinship."[8] When animals use environmental cues to guess kinship, they usually get it right; humans perhaps do not. Johnson, Ratwick and Sawyer conclude:

> Patriotism, applying as it does to large-scale societies composed predominantly of non-kin, may be viewed under this theory as manipulated altruism. A biologically-based capacity produced by kin selection is called forth by successful manipulation of the cues which evolution has produced for eliciting altruism.[9]

In sum, Van den Berghe's hypothesis is that ethnocentric behavior can be explained as a manifestation of kin altruism, and, as such, it evolved by the mechanism of kin selection. The fact that groups whose members are not really blood relatives now carry out altruism on a wide ethnic scale does not hurt the argument. The original behavior, that is, unselfish acts to help others, had taken place among *real* kin, or the behavior could not have evolved, according to the theory of kin selection. However, once the psychological traits are in place, it is possible that they can be used "erroneously" to motivate altruism toward compatriots.

The Theory of Intergroup Competition

There is an alternative theory to explain such psychological traits as patriotism and tribalism, namely, the theory of intergroup competition. This theory is bolder and more encompassing than Van den Berghe's theory of kin selection, and involves group selection. This theory has the dual effect of explaining the evolution of altruistic traits *within* the group, and of predispositions for violence *between* groups. Darwin first suggested it in 1871:

> When two tribes of primeval man ... came into competition, if (other circumstances being equal) the one tribe included a great number of courageous, sympathetic and faithful members, who were always ready to warn each other of danger, to aid and defend each other, this tribe would succeed better and conquer the other.[10]

Arthur Keith took this up in his 1946 essay and his 1949 book, *A New Theory of Human Evolution*. He noted that "a great number of small competing units favor rapid evolutionary changes" and that "in all stages of human evolution, cooperation has been combined with competition."[11] Approximately two decades later this idea was given a much fuller treatment by Richard Alexander[12] and Robert Bigelow,[13] who particularly see intergroup competition as the best explanation for the high level of human intelligence.

It is known that the hominid brain trebled in size quite rapidly. *Australopithecus*, or "ape-man," dating to 3 million years ago had a brain only the size of a chimpanzee's, namely 450 cc, while *Homo sapiens'* brain size is 1400 cc. It is axiomatic in biology that there must have been some environmental pressure to cause this evolution; the question is: for what was intelligence *adaptive* during the Pleistocene? The commonly assumed answer is that intelligence helped hominids to gain control over neighboring species, for example, by thwarting predators such as leopards, and by capturing prey such as small animals. This indeed is probably the explanation as to how hominids rose to the *Homo* grade. Some *Homo* fossils with skulls of less than 700 cc are associated with primitive tools.[14] The ability to use tools and weapons gave these hominids a radical advantage over other species. Yet this does not explain why the brain then continued to double *after* the neighboring species were conquered. George C. Williams noted in 1966:

> I cannot readily accept the idea that advanced mental capabilities have ever been directly favored by selection. There is no reason for believing that a genius has ever been likely to leave more children than a man of somewhat below average intelligence.[15]

Here then is the question: what *selective force* could account for the continuing evolution of the hominid brain? Robert Bigelow proposes that among hominids that force was "each other," that is, hominids competed, group against group, over resources such as food and shelter. He believes that hominids were already living in groups, for purposes of protection of the young, and so had developed advanced social life and cooperation. That very cooperation gave rise to the situation where one group could be united against another group.[16] By "group" here is meant a large family unit. Richard Alexander and Donald W. Tinkle note that "each family group would have been . . . a gene pool and a microculture of its own."[17] Each group would have varied in average intelligence, in level of cooperation, in skill with weapons, and so forth. Alexander and Tinkle state:

> We visualize a situation in man's early hunting ancestry in which . . . some group, possessing higher frequency of individuals of greater intelligence, were able by intra-group cooperation and communication to exterminate and replace adjacent groups.[18]

Obviously small groups would be at a disadvantage compared to large groups. Alexander has put forth the "Balance-of-Power Hypothesis" to explain why humans band together. No more than a dozen men, he notes, would be needed for a hunting party,[19] but humans even in prehistoric times often lived in groups of 500 or more. They formed alliances for competition, to balance the power of the opposing group. Alexander writes, "And I am suggesting that all other adaptations associated with group living, such as cooperation in agriculture, fishing, or industry, are secondary—that is, they are *responses* to group living . . ."[20]

Robert Carneiro has reconstructed the formation of villages, chiefdoms, and empires in the Mayan and other Meso-American civilizations and found that alliance-formation and conquest of one group by another can also explain post-evolutionary increases in the size and organization of groups. He names scarcity of favored land and resources as the environmental factor leading to war and to the eventual formation of states.[21]

Does the theory of intergroup competition mean that bellicose individuals or groups won out over more pacific types in hominid times and therefore that the final product—us—is innately warlike? Not exactly. Bigelow insists that the success which a given group had in dealing with other groups was largely a function of that group's *communication*, *cooperation*, and intelligent *self-control*.[22] Indeed it is these traits which explain the increase in brain size that accompanied intergroup competition. The group had to respond to external threats *as a unit*, not as a band of aggressive individuals.

> At all stages the effectiveness of aggressive group response . . . was due to self-control within the group. . . . Capacities for self-control are provided . . . particularly by the cerebral cortex. The result of human evolution was not an array of bodiless 'instincts', but a network of physical nerves and endocrine organs. As this physical organization became more complex and efficient, it provided greater capacities for learning from experience, for the repression of emotional drives, and hence for more intelligent self-control.[23]

In intergroup encounters, sheer violence would not always be required. Bigelow writes, "Groups that were easily 'persuaded' to leave favorable territories, and to take up residence in deserts, would have produced fewer offspring."[24] Threats alone were probably adequate in most intergroup confrontations, he believes, and would need to be backed up only occasionally by fights. The winners would win mainly in the sense of greater reproduction, thanks to abundant resources.[25] Finally, the competition would have been technological as well as physical. Alexander notes that the need for better weapons in intergroup competition is the driving force in the invention of most technology—even today.[26]

Summary of the Darwin-Keith-Alexander-Bigelow Theory

The following are the main points discussed so far which support the intergroup competition theory of human evolution: 1. Social life evolves where it is adaptive for defense or predation. (This was discussed in Chapter 5). 2. Most primates are social; our closest relatives, the chimpanzees, are very social, apparently for group defense in protection of the young. 3. Early hominid species probably had some degree of social life as a form of defense. 4. At some point the hominids became group predators; once the use of hand-held weapons was achieved, hominids gained control over neighboring species. 5. The subsequent increase in human intelligence was probably a result of intergroup competition within the human species itself. 6. Small hominid groups were composed of genetically-related individuals; these groups differed in intelligence and cultural skills. 7. Scarcity of food and shelter was a likely cause of competition among groups. 8. Groups started to form alliances to balance the power of large groups. 9. The winners in intergroup encounters were those with the most intelligence, best communication, cooperation, aggression, and best weapons. In Bigelow's words, "Although aggressive behavior is, in a sense, the opposite of cooperative behavior, the two have evolved together as highly interdependent components of a single evolving system."[27] 10. Intergroup competition was a driving force in the invention of technology.

The Question of Warfare

The foregoing hypothesis about intergroup competition and the resultant selection of traits may make sense, but did it really happen that way? Is the prehistory of mankind a violent one? Hard evidence is scarce and is subject to conflicting interpretation. Marilyn Keyes Roper conducted a study of 169 pre-*Homo sapiens* hominids, and found that 56 of them, that is, more than a third, showed evidence of "intrahuman violence."[28] Some anthropologists endorsed her study, while others disagreed, showing for example that a cracked hominid skull could have been damaged after death rather than before.[29] It should also be noted that weapons do not furnish definitive proof of intraspecies killing: arrowheads, for example, could have been shot at animals rather than at other hominids.

Not only is the prehistoric record disputed, but even the record of warfare *during* human history is subject to challenge. Johan van der Dennen correctly notes that many sociobiologists make general statements that war is endemic in all types of human societies, without backing this up.[30] He believes that the idea can be traced to a study popular in the Social Darwinist days, namely M.R. Davie's book *The Evolution of War* (1929). Davie compiled much of the ethnographic literature of the 19th century, concluding that the principal cause of war was competition over scarce resources. Van der Dennen complains:

> Reports from explorers, missionaries, ethnographers [in Africa] had accumulated to such an extent that the Negro was considered to be most 'warlike race' by Davie. One cannot escape the impression however that much of the havoc that befell that poor continent . . . has been caused, directly or indirectly, by European colonial intrusion. . . . Much of [this] literature does not describe original primitive war at all.[31]

From his own inventory of the anthropological literature, Van der Dennen finds that most primitive societies which have ever been described by anthropologists have not had war recorded. This, of course, does not prove that they did *not* have war, but that no anthropologist has mentioned it.[32]

Whilst Van der Dennen believes that theorists are over-eager, for some ideological reason, to find evidence of war, Bigelow and Alexander argue that most writers are ideologically disposed to assume a peaceful ancestry of humans. For instance, Bigelow states that even in the face of evidence, we sometimes go to great lengths to explain it away, saying, for example that "a hole in a fossil skull may have been due to a rock that fell from the roof of the cave while [the individual] was asleep."[33]

As for the lack of *proof* of intergroup aggression in primitive human societies, Alexander notes that even great destructions do not leave a record for the archeologist to trace. He asks "if there were no written records, what evidence would there be to tell us what happened to the Tasmanians and the Tierra del Fuegians?"[34] Moreover, "can we even be sure . . . that what happened in the twentieth century at Buchenwald and Auschwitz, and in Nigeria and Cambodia, will be properly interpreted, say, a million years from now?"[35]

Alexander holds that it is not only unfair to make such demands of the fossil record, but that the "ban" on extrapolating backwards from modern behavior is also needlessly stringent.

> We know that cooperativeness on the grandest scale, and the greatest of all the alliances of history, were in responses to upset in balances of power and the aggression of one nation against another. We know that competition is continuous among the various kinds of political groups, large and small, that exist across the whole earth.[36]

So why presume that early humans were different? He concludes, "I do not believe the burden of proof is upon those of us who see humans as evolving while behaving more or less as they do today."[37]

Finally, in regard to those contemporary hunter-gatherers who are considered to be particularly peaceful, such as Eskimo or Bushmen, Alexander notes that the harsh conditions under which they live *force* them to be unusually cooperative.[38] And Bigelow points out that the reason people live in Arctic or desert areas is that they have been pushed there by others—they were the losers in intergroup competition. "When European and Bantu peoples invaded South Africa . . . Bushmen and Hottentots were living *outside* the Kalahari desert. American Indians, Australian Aborigines . . . were driven forcefully from land that Europeans coveted."[39] In short, the example of these hunter-gatherers' way of life is not helpful in the search for a determination of our pacific or bellicose past.

The Group Selection Controversy

More troublesome than the question of the evidence of warfare, for the theory of intergroup competition, is the theoretical question of whether traits can evolve by means of *group selection*. David S. Wilson remarked recently that group selection "rivalled Lamarckianism as the most thoroughly repudiated idea in evolutionary theory,"[40] while Elliott Sober has said that group selection "now appears to be rising, phoenix-like from its own ashes."[41]

It has been recognized since Darwin's time that natural selection can operate at the level of the individual. An individual with an adaptive trait has high "reproductive fitness:" his trait is passed on to his direct descendants. Likewise, it has been appreciated since 1964 that an individual with an adaptive trait which favors family members will have high "inclusive fitness:" his trait will be passed on to his collateral descendants. This was described in Chapter 5 as "kin selection." But can a member of a group possess an evolved trait that favors the *group's* survival rather than his own or his relatives' survival? For example, can an individual animal possess a genetic trait inclining it to sacrifice itself for the good of the group? How could such a trait be inherited? The few who possessed it would die out, and the trait would disappear. The only way the selection of this trait would be possible would be through intergroup competition. If one group with a high frequency of self-sacrificing or cooperative genes competed with a group possessing fewer of these genes, the first group could win out and displace the second group—either by killing them outright or by controlling essential resources.

Vincent Wynne-Edwards in his 1962 book, *Animal Dispersion in Relation to Social Behaviour*, proposed that group selection is common. He observed that birds of certain species appear to hold down their brood-size altruistically in order not to over-exploit the food resources or nesting sites in a given area. That is, he hypothesized that individuals limit the number of their offspring for the good of the group, and that other groups where the individuals did not do so experienced periodic population crashes.[42] Wynne-Edwards' theory turned out to be wrong, and led to more careful analysis by biologists. George C. Williams demonstrated in his 1966 book, *Adaptation and Natural Selection*, that most apparent instances of "group fitness" are merely statistical summations of the individual fitness of the members. For example, a herd of deer which uniformly runs very fast can escape better from predators than a herd which runs slower, but they simply win out by individual selection, not group selection.[43] Williams and others have also noted that apparent instances of group selection are really instances of kin selection: a bird gives an alarm call to his "neighbors" but the neighbors turn out to be his relatives. Population geneticists agree, according to E.O. Wilson, that group selection is an "improbable event."[44]

Nevertheless, group selection, according to mathematical models, is not impossible. Among those who support the possibility of it are John Maynard Smith, D.S. Wilson,[45] E.O. Wilson (who calls it "interdemic selection")[46] and Richard Alexander. Maynard Smith notes that at least three conditions must be met in order for group selection to occur. First, the groups must be partially isolated from one another.[47] Second, "if group selection is to be responsible for the establishment of an 'altruistic' gene, the groups must be small, or must from time to time be reestablished by a few founders." Third, the group must have both the possibility of going extinct and the possibility of "reproducing" by fissioning into new groups.[48] The problem, he says, is not one of *maintaining* altruism: that can be done even in a large group. Rather, the issue is how an altruistic behavior gets started without its carrier being wiped out.[49] As a separate point, E.O. Wilson notes that group selection "has the interesting property of requiring a selection episode only very occasionally in order to proceed as swiftly as individual-level selection."[50] All-out conquests, he says, "need take place only once every few generations to direct evolution. This alone could push truly altruistic genes to a high frequency within the [hominid] bands."[51]

Richard Alexander and Gerald Borgia believe that "human social groups represent an almost ideal model for potent selection at the group level."[52] This they attribute to two special factors. First, human groups have been able quickly to develop enormous differences in reproductive and competitive ability because of cultural innovation and its cumulative effects.[53] Second, humans "are uniquely able to plan and act as units [and] to look ahead," and can improve the group's position by restricting disruptive behavior within the group.[54] E.O. Wilson summarizes the human or hominid advantage as follows:

> One band would have the capacity to consciously ponder the significance of adjacent social groups and to deal with them in an intelligent, organized fashion. A band might then dispose of a neighboring band, appropriate its territory, and increase its own genetic representation in the meta-population, retaining the tribal memory of this successful episode, repeating it . . .[55]

Supporting Evidence from Social Psychology

The foregoing discussions of the evidence of warfare and the group-selection debate indicate that the important hypothesis of intergroup competition is not proven. However, there is a range of other evidence that suggests that people "instinctively" behave differently toward group members than toward outsiders. Some relevant human-nature traits are: clannishness and a need to belong, a ready response to charismatic leaders who inspire group loyalty, and a sense of superiority felt by locals toward strangers. There are also more complex behaviors connected with group interactions. These include: the scapegoating of internal aliens in order to explain society's troubles, the imagining of worst-case scenarios regarding the enemy's plans, and the demand for internal ideological conformity or "group-think." All of these are easily accounted for if the evolutionary hypothesis of intergroup competition is true.

In 1985, the European Sociobiological Society convened a symposium at Oxford to discuss "the biological bases for in-group/out-group phenomena."[56] The participants were not biologists but political scientists, psychologists, anthropologists, and sociologists. They presented an assortment of evidence and interpretations of behaviors related to xenophobia, racism, and nationalism. The meeting took a particular interest in the paradox, first noted by Herbert Spencer, that the Code of Amity is connected with the Code of Enmity. Spencer had said in 1892, "Rude tribes and civilized societies have had continually to carry on an external defence and an internal cooperation: external antagonism and internal friendship. Hence their members have acquired two different sets of sentiments and ideas, adjusted to these two kinds of activity."[57] At the symposium, Hans van der Dennen provided a background survey of the literature on this subject,[58] of which I shall mention a few examples.

First there are the studies that look at children's behavior to find hints of innate traits. Babies go through a predictable stage of being afraid of strangers, which lasts from about age 7 months to 9 months. No unpleasant experience is needed to trigger this behavior of shyness or fear; Eibl-Eibesfeldt observes that it occurs in blind and deaf children as well.[59] It is thus hypothesized that humans have an innate propensity to feel differently towards strangers, any strangers.[60] Another widely observed phenomenon is that young children of school age are inclined to be cruel to an "odd" child, whether his oddity be in size, shape, speech, or behavior.[61] This irrational reaction to oddness may be similar to a behavior noted in animals: they sometimes mob and attack one of their own members that has accidentally become deformed.[62] A probable interpretation of this is that the animals no longer see the creature as a local, but as a stranger in their midst.

Besides investigating children, social psychologists can conduct experiments in artificial environments in order to isolate the elements of everyday behavior. One such experiment consists of breaking a group arbitrarily up into two groups, A and B. After a very short time, it is found that each group has formed an identity of itself as superior to the other group. Although this does not prove the *innateness* of the behavior, it proves that the belief in one's own group's superiority need not be related to any particular evidence of actual superiority. In a famous experiment, Sherif and Sherif attempted to create the feeling of "we" and "they" among 12-year-old boys at a summer camp, all of whom had come from similar backgrounds and who had no previous friendships with one another. Two groups were created and given suitably aggressive names, the Bulldogs and the Red Devils. Within five days the boys developed strong in-group loyalty to their group and out-group hostility toward the other group, just as though the two groups had genuine separate histories. Indeed violence got out of control and the experiment had to be ended.[63] To my knowledge it has not been repeated.

In a more subtle experiment, the psychologist P.C. Zimbardo asked students to play the role of prison guard. It was found that whilst occupying a legitimate *role* of aggression, the students acted much more brutally than they otherwise would.[64] The guards' *anonymity*, aided by the wearing of uniforms and sunglasses, seemed to help them lose their inhibitions of aggression.[65] R.I. Watson followed up on this experiment by conducting a cross-cultural survey. He found that "killing, torturing, or mutilating the enemy was more prevalent in societies where warriors were 'deindividuated' by putting on body paint, masks, etc., before going into battle."[66]

The behavior of collective violence could perhaps have evolved in hominid times without any need for the individuals to have language. However, it has certainly been *aided* by the arrival of words and ideas. These allow humans to justify violence "for a good cause," rather than merely to compete over scarce resources. As Erik Erikson notes, groups can become so certain of their moral superiority and uniqueness that they engage in "pseudo-speciation" alleging that members of other human groups are veritably of a different species. Man is "indoctrinated with the conviction that his 'species' alone was planned by an all-wise deity, created in a special cosmic event, and appointed by history to guard the only genuine version of humanity."[67]

Ironically, Van der Dennen observes, high ideals are often the cultural cue by which tribal feelings can be aroused.

> The most extensive, quixotic and disgusting violence is justified with the invocation of a utopian ideology, a paradise myth, a superiority doctrine . . . or other highly abstract political/ethical categories, metaphysical values, and quasi-metaphysical mental monstrosities: national security, *raison d'etat*, freedom, democracy, *Gott, Volk und Heimat, Blut und Boden*, peace, progress, empire, historical imperative, sacred order, natural necessity, divine will, and so on and so forth.[68]

It would be senseless to suggest that such *ideas* evolved biologically, but humans could have a predisposition to believe myths that strengthen the group.

In general, it can be said about people's beliefs that they are not rationally chosen according to their accuracy. Cognitive psychologists have shown, for example, that we seem predisposed to believe a consistent story, in order to avoid "cognitive dissonance" and that we typically select information that is socially comfortable for us.[69] Heiner Flohr notes, "The processing of perceived information is not some kind of [disinterested] registration. It is influenced . . . at each important junction by existing emotional and cognitive commitments."[70] This could be an evolved phenomenon, though it need not have evolved for the purpose of group unity: it could be based on some internal requirement of mental processing. Nonetheless, it has the effect of suppressing criticism of the beliefs of one's own group.

Genes and Culture

Ian Vine disapproves of sociobiologists making crude claims that such a large behavioral syndrome as "ethnocentrism" is an evolved trait. What is innate, he says, is probably "little more than apprehension, a somewhat exploitative orientation, and a readiness to react against any apparent threat."[71] Vine believes that "a modest amount of genetic priming" can make the difference in inclining us to a certain direction of behavior. For example, our sense of self is such that we exaggerate our own deservingness and trustworthiness and are "suspicious and jealous of others enough to resist making major unilateral sacrifices for any but our closest kin."[72] This small act of self-deception reinforces any innate tendency we possess for being helpful toward kin and indifferent toward strangers.

As in the previous chapter, which distinguished between the proportion of morality that is attributable to genes and culture respectively, it is important here to note that much in-group/out-group behavior is a matter of cultural training. All I claim is that since groups evolved in competition with one another, they would have developed some psychological tendency to act differently with their fellows than with their opponents. This is not to say that the genes incline a person to identify with a particular ethnic group—indeed it is well-known that loyalties may form along other lines such as those of religion, social class, or even *alma mater*.

W.A. Elliott, in his book *Us and Them* has shown how new recruits from Nepal, of Hindu lower-caste background and Mongol race, are made into soldiers of the Brigade of Gurkhas in the British Army. The famous *esprit de corps* which they eventually develop, he says, is related not to class, religion, or national feelings for either Nepal or Britain, but strictly to membership in the *brigade* and its illustrious history.[73] Elliott concludes that all collective feelings or attitudes of *us* and *them* are capable of transformation, depending on the particular focus.

> This evidence is universal and common to all races and hence combines to point to the inherent probability of a group attachment trait that is shared by all humankind. But no actual identities are ever inborn. They are culturally induced.[74]

Group Morality

In Chapter 5, I identified morality as a cultural activity that arose from certain evolved predispositions which had as their original object the monitoring of inter-individual relations. The later development of that morality had as its practical function the control of social behavior in general. Let me now refer to that kind of morality as "standard morality," and conclude the present chapter by identifying a different phenomenon: "group morality."

The object of group morality, as far as its original evolution is concerned, is cohesion of the in-group in order to attack or defend itself against the out-group. Group morality is roughly equatable with such phenomena as patriotism, ethnocentrism, nationalism, xenophobia, and racism. That is, the human pre-disposition to believe in, and proclaim a group morality is probably based on those same emotions or techniques of perception that help it to identify enemies, rally to support of fellow group members, feel proud of one's own group, and so forth.

Thus, group morality is not "morality" if we limit the definition of morality to the kind of standard morality described in Chapter 5. However, it seems impossible to deny group morality the right to call itself morality since, in fact, the sense of right is one of its central concepts. ("Our group is *right*"; "we *should* conquer the evil enemy," etc.) Indeed, group morality is often considered a higher form of morality than standard morality. This may be owing to two factors: 1. group morality calls on altruism, self-sacrifice, team spirit and loyalty—things which, being anti-selfish, seem automatically to be highly virtuous, and 2. group morality emphasizes the moral superiority of one's own group vis à vis the enemy, the barbarian, the heathen, and so forth. In the latter regard, group morality downgrades the status of the other party, denying its right to be treated with consideration.

It should be mentioned here that even if no outside groups ever existed there could still be a "group morality," in the sense of exhortation for members to contribute to the good of society as a whole. Sociobiologists, however, believe that such a group morality would never have come into being by natural selection. Possibly that kind of morality could be worked out by individuals, with the help of reason, in cultural settings. But if we are to say that *biological* predispositions for group morality exist, then intergroup competition is the only plausible stimulus for their evolution.

The point of interest for our study of international morality, of course, is that we have now succeeded in identifying a dual code of morality. The holding of such a code is problematical—although the very existence of a dual code is not often faced. Arthur Keith has noted that two problems are inherent in the dual code. First, the code of justice practiced within a group is often couched as a universalist justice. Hence, to terminate it at the border is to betray one's principles. Second, group morality lacks any moral accountability by individuals for the group's actions.[75] "Collective responsibility" is the custom, but this does not put pressure on anybody's conscience, and conscience is the central monitor of morality, at least within standard morality. Thus, according to Keith "to the ethically minded the practice of the dual code is anathema."[76]

The contrast between standard morality and group morality will prove helpful in our analysis of international morality beginning in Chapter 8. For now, we turn to Chapter 7 for a brief comment on sociobiology itself.

7

Cautions Regarding the Use of Sociobiology

*Heaving a resigned sigh over the erring tendencies of
human nature, [we have] offered to these standards that
'of course' variety of homage which is the beginning of
mental and moral coma.*
> —*William Ernest Hocking, Jr.*

This chapter concludes Part Two, "The Sociobiological Hypotheses Pertinent to International Morality." Those sociobiological hypotheses were, in brief, that morality is based on an evolved system, and that group behavior—and hence group morality—is based on an evolved system, too. I plan, in Part Three, to use these hypotheses in a critique of the traditional theories of international morality. First, however, in this chapter, it will be appropriate to comment on sociobiology in a general way, since it is often considered to be a controversial discipline. I shall point out the two major methodological cautions to be observed in human sociobiology and will claim that my work has observed these. I shall then briefly discuss the debates which have arisen over the use of sociobiology in connection with ethics. Finally, I shall deal with the question "can there be genuine altruism?"

Methodological Cautions

Sociobiology has received much criticism, especially in the first few years of its development.[1]* Two of the most frequently iterated criticisms are: 1. that sociobiologists (and ethologists) make facile comparisons between human and animal behavior, and 2. that sociobiologists overstate the genetic factor and understate the cultural factor in explaining human behavior. These criticisms result in two valuable methodological cautions for the sociobiologist: 1. "Take care when comparing animals and humans," and 2. "Watch out for the temptation to preach genetic determinism."

---

*For vehement ideological complaints about sociobiology, see Steven Rose, Leon J. Kamin, and R.C. Lewontin, *Not in Our Genes,* and Philip Kitcher, *Vaulting Ambition.*

I have assiduously observed the first caution, in the preceding two chapters. In fact, the raw comparison of human and animal behavior has not been a part of my argument. Rather, I showed that evolution works in a certain way, to bring out adaptive traits in any species, and that this way could explain the evolution of certain human traits. As Niko Tinbergen correctly notes, "The message of ethology is that the methods, rather than the results, of ethology should be used for [the study of man]."[2] It is true that I emphasized the similarity of *genetic mechanisms* in all social species, and I grant that I made one bridging assumption between primates and hominids. Namely, I suggested that since the higher primates tend to be very social, the early hominids would probably have been so, too. Nevertheless, our two main hypotheses did not depend on finding particular animal behaviors that are shared by man. Indeed I underscored the fact that morality is *species-specific* to humans, and I pointed out that group selection is a rare phenomenon—perhaps found only in man.

I likewise observed the second methodological caution, regarding genetic determinism. To begin with, I admitted that the genetic element in both behaviors—morality and intergroup behavior—is unproven. We have no hard evidence that these behaviors *evolved*. The lack of an extant ancestral hominid species is a problem for showing the primitive stage of the alleged moral emotions, and the lack of unambiguous fossil evidence of hominid warfare makes the intergroup hypothesis less than solid. Moreover, even in living humans it is notoriously difficult to show that any behaviors—other than those manifested within hours of birth— are innate rather than learned.

Besides that, even if the behaviors in question *are* partly genetic, the interesting or significant point is not that genes are directly dictating human behavior today. Rather it is that the genes *originally caused certain cultural practices to become institutionalized*. It would be my guess that most moral behavior today and most intergroup behaviors today *are* culturally learned, rather than innate. But the culture in which the young do their learning is a culture that reflects genetic constraints.

The "Evolutionary Ethics" Debate

People, it seems, are always keen to find guidelines for morality. Thus, when Darwin published his theory of evolution in 1859, it was thought by some that he had discovered the moral law of nature. This was the law of "Nature red in tooth and claw" or the law of struggle in which the strongest rightly prevailed. Darwin wrote to his friend Charles Lyell, "I have received in a Manchester newspaper rather a good squib, showing that I have proved "might is right" and therefore that Napoleon is right, and every cheating tradesman is also right."[3] Herbert Spencer, and various theorists who came to be known as Social Darwinists, looked upon the survival of the fittest as the true and good method by which Nature weeds out the weak and degenerate. From evolution they developed an ethics, recommending that policy-makers should follow Nature, for instance by not passing legislation that would ameliorate the conditions of the lower classes. The U.S. Supreme Court, in the case of *Lochner versus New York* in 1905, explicitly used this rationale in deciding against a law that would have limited working hours in a bakery.[4]

The use of a "law of Nature" to guide ethics resulted in a heated debate that went on for many years. Thomas Henry Huxley, a firm supporter of Darwin in the late nineteenth century, took the surprising position that the natural trend of evolution should be actively opposed. "Let us understand once and for all," he said, "that the ethical progress of society depends, not on imitating the cosmic process, still less on running away from it, but in combatting it."[5] On the other hand, Peter Kropotkin, a Russian prince, proposed, in 1903, that in fact a more careful study of Nature showed that cooperative behavior of social species was a strategy that won out over competition.[6] Indeed, the socialist Eduard Bernstein had argued in 1890 that biological evolution had socialism as a natural consequence.[7]

This "evolutionary ethics" debate was revived upon the publication of E.O. Wilson's *Sociobiology* in 1975. Sociobiology is suspected of having a hidden ideological agenda, namely the Social Darwinist agenda of claiming that humans must submit to the inexorable ways of Nature. Thus a Marxist group called "The Science for the People Study Group" accused Wilson of justifying current social practices—say, the inequality of men and women—by holding that these social practices have a natural basis, for example, by mentioning that in most mammal societies the males are dominant over females.[8] Wilson has denied on various occasions that he is equating "is" with "ought," or that he is advocating, say, sexism rather than merely trying to account for it.

There was also a new twist added to the evolutionary ethics debate, since Wilson named his first chapter "The Morality of the Gene." That chapter starts out by saying that Camus was wrong in his assertion that the only serious philosophical question is suicide. After all, Wilson notes, "in evolutionary time the individual organism counts for nothing."[9] Wilson however, was not proclaiming a new morality—that of the gene. Rather, he says, he began his book this way in order to "characterize the essence of sociobiology"[10]—to move attention away from the traditional focus of natural selection, the individual, to the gene. Obviously the phrase "the morality of the gene" is a metaphor, like Richard Dawkins's "selfish gene," meant to indicate that some activities are good "from the gene's point of view."

Heuristic devices of this sort are frequently used in evolutionary biology and are very helpful in reconstructing the history of a species.

Indeed, finding out "what the gene wants" has been the key to understanding kin altruism. It may be tempting to suppose that such a radical new discovery concerning Nature's way would open up new ethical insights, but I believe that this does not follow. It turned out that the nineteenth century discovery of the "survival of the fittest" had no particular relevance to human ethics; so, too, the twentieth century discovery of the "selfish gene" has no particular ethical connotations. That is, it does not advise us what we ought to do.

In short, it is my impression that the structure of Nature does not shed any direct light on what is ethical for humans. Yet, as I have said, the contribution of sociobiology to an understanding of *our ethical nature* has been tremendous. It shows that "right and wrong" are phenomena which sprang from our evolved moralistic nature.

Can There be Genuine Altruism?

Finally, I should mention the controversy over "genuine altruism" since it seems to flavor much of the writing about sociobiology and ethics, and since it may be relevant to a discussion of international morality. The question is whether any acts of human morality or altruism are manifestations of genuine goodness or selflessness, or whether they are always selfish. Various authors seem to think that sociobiology's major discovery in relation to morality is that morality is not genuine. For instance, in Chapter 5 I noted Richard Alexander's claim that all acts of kindness could be motivated by a wish to improve one's reputation, and that an improved reputation enhances the actual welfare of oneself and one's family.

I will go so far as to grant, with Trivers, Alexander, and virtually all sociobiologists, that animal altruism, at the outset, had to be nongenuine altruism. It had to contain a hidden or delayed benefit for Ego and Ego's offspring. Otherwise, the genetic tendency to be altruistic—that is, to do things which help others—could not have got passed on, and would never have become the common behavior of so many animal species. I would also be happy to grant that much of human morality is motivated by a desire on the part of the individual to get something in return for his goodness.

However I do not see any need to reinterpret the general phenomenon of human morality in this light, or to declare that morality is really something other than what it has traditionally appeared to be. To my mind morality *is* what it appears to be. And that, as we have seen, is at least three things: order, welfare-provision, and judgment. People work out rules of social behavior ("law and order"), and ways of helping those who need help (welfare-provision), and are concerned—sometimes obsessively—with right and wrong (judgment). These factors are all major elements in every culture; they thus form the environment in which people live.

Then, *because those things are there in the environment, individuals can easily be trained to take a genuine interest in leading moral lives.* Morever, moral ideas are frequently woven into a culture's stated belief about what forms the best and most desirable life. Indeed the goals toward which a society works typically have to do with improving the society's order, its welfare function, or its ability to produce fair judgment.

Thus, in my opinion, it is pointless to look for some overall "biological" interpretation of present-day moral behavior. The last time biology "had a hand in it" was when natural selection helped to design the moral emotions in hominids. I think it is faulty logic to say "natural selection of altruism requires that the altruism be selfish, and therefore all human altruism today is really selfish." As I have emphasized, humans *moved out of the phase* in which biological imperatives controlled their altruism. They entered a new human-created environment in which morality has different ways of controlling their behavior and influencing their motives. We cannot now reduce human morality back to its "evolutionary essence" by some sociobiological discovery that genetic altruism is really genetic selfishness.

This is not to say that the selfish side of altruism is not worth studying. I believe it is useful, for example, to point up all the areas in which moral advances get achieved largely because they appeal to enlightened self-interest. I think it is worth knowing that, as Alexander says, people perform self-sacrificing deeds to gain reputation. But it would be incorrect to imply that the fully developed cultural-moral system of humans is no more than a game in which Egos try to further their interests.

This chapter concludes the Part Two discussion of sociobiological hypotheses pertinent to international morality. We now turn to a critique and conclusion.

Part III

Critique and Conclusion

8

Critique of the Traditional Arguments concerning International Morality in the Light of the Sociobiological Hypotheses

> *Either* realpolitik *and world community, or no world community.*
>
> —R.J. Vincent

Introduction to Part Three

We can now return, in Part Three, to the subject of international morality. Recall that at the end of Part One's discussion we had reached an impasse. The traditional arguments of international morality were polarized into a negative and a positive position, each seemingly very persuasive. Then, in Part Two, we took an excursion into the realm of sociobiology to find new ideas bearing on our subject matter, particularly, evolutionary ideas about morality and group behavior.

The format of Part Three "Critique and Conclusions" will be as follows. Chapter 8 will apply the pertinent sociobiological hypotheses from Part Two to the traditional theories of international morality from Part One. It will be seen that with benefit of sociobiological ideas, the classical contradiction between the negative and positive positions on international morality can be explained. The central point of this chapter will be the identification of two separate kinds of morality—standard morality and group morality. Chapter 9 will then attempt to find a more conclusive, sociobiologically-informed answer to the question. "Is there a moral relationship among states?"

Recapitulation of the Sociobiological Hypotheses

Before proceeding to analyze the twelve traditional arguments, it will be useful to recapitulate the two sociobiological hypotheses from Chapters 5 and 6 respectively, highlighting the points they make that are relevant to our task here.

Hypothesis One. Humans have some sort of moral sensibility, owing to certain evolved predispositions. These include a predisposition for judging and moralizing, a predisposition for obeying and conforming, and a predisposition for sympathizing with others. Because humans are equipped with these predispositions, cultures everywhere engage in the development of ethical principles, in lawmaking, and in the provision of social welfare.

Hypothesis Two. Humans often behave differently toward members of their own group than toward nonmembers, owing to predispositions that evolved during intergroup competition. Within the group, people tend to be altruistic, cooperative, and willing to make sacrifices for others. In their behavior toward individuals who are nonmembers of the group, people often experience fear and mistrust of strangers, and lack of compassion for persons of an alien culture. When two groups come into hostile or competitive contact with each other, additional behaviors are triggered within each group. These include a manifestation of greater patriotic loyalty and belief in the group's superiority, suspicion of and aggressiveness toward the enemy, and activities directed at winning, such as alliance-formation and improvements in technology.

The "Accuracy" of the Twelve Arguments' Observations

In this section, the twelve traditional arguments concerning international morality will be paraded out once more. I shall subject each of them to a test of accuracy concerning their observations, particularly their observations on human nature, morality, and group behavior. That "test of accuracy" will simply be a measure of how well their observations accord with the sociobiological hypotheses. Of course, the sociobiological hypotheses contain many ordinary statements, such as that "groups form enmities," which people have observed for ages. But here I shall proceed as though the *evolutionary explanation* of these claims gives them new validity — which I believe to be so.

I begin by reviewing the six negative arguments as to the accuracy of their observations.

1. The *national interest* argument observes that the relationship among states is mainly one of competition and self-help, and that members of a group expect their leader to act on their behalf. That is certainly accurate according to Hypothesis Two. Some of the national-interest theorists also claim that moral discussion of foreign policy issues is "irrelevant." To the extent that this is mere advocacy, these hypotheses cannot yield a judgment of accuracy. To the extent that it is meant as a historical fact, however, it is accurate under Hypothesis Two: groups have traditionally acted on strategic principles, more than on moral principles, in their dealings with one another.

2. The *international anarchy* argument observes that nations are routinely suspicious of other nations, concerned with their own security, and cautious

about participation in international affairs. That is perfectly accurate under Hypothesis Two. Hobbes' international-anarchy theory claims, also, that nations are in a pre-contract state of Nature. According to Hypothesis Two that is an accurate description of the past; regarding the present, however, its accuracy is limited since there are thousands of international treaties in force.

3. The *national sovereignty* argument does not make any observations about human nature, morality, or group behavior. It makes only statements about the rights of nations, such as the right to privacy, as will be mentioned below. (To the extent that national sovereignty's claim that "states are equal" could be called an observation rather than a legal fiction, it is of course inaccurate: Hypothesis Two implies that nations differ in power according to their size, their internal solidarity, their weapons technology, and their skill in dealing with opponents.)

4. The *nationalist* argument observes, firstly, that the group transcends or is "greater than" the individual. That is accurate under Hypothesis Two to the extent that individuals need their group for survival, and are prone to subordinate their selfish interests, in some cases, to the good of all. Secondly, the romantic form of nationalism claims that the history of culture is made up of separate group achievements. That is inaccurate of today, but under Hypothesis Two it is probably an accurate account of the past, since cultural achievements could have best come about in cooperating, self-contained societies. The nationalist argument claims, thirdly, that ethnic groups compulsively seek self-determination. Observation shows this to be inaccurate: people accept political systems that benefit them, regardless of ethnic "match." However, according to Hypothesis Two it is accurate to say that ethnic solidarity may be called upon as a means of uniting people, for instance against an alien ruler with whom they are dissatisfied.

5. The *immorality of groups* argument observes that the practice of morality between groups is different than between individuals. That is one of the main conclusions of Hypothesis Two. Niebuhr's observation that patriotism paradoxically transmutes individual altruism into national egoism also accords perfectly with Hypothesis Two. Group immorality theory is also accurate, according to Hypothesis Two, in its claim that the group's immorality is partly explained by the suppression of self-criticism within the group, and the tendency of a group to indulge in exaggerated righteousness and hypocrisy.

6. The *cultural pluralism* argument observes that each group has a morality peculiar to its history and world view. That is accurate under Hypothesis One to the extent that *some* areas of cultural morality are flexible, such as those related to a culture's understanding of contract, or its sense of

the importance of the individual. Cultural pluralism also claims that no international morality exists. According to Hypothesis Two, that is accurate as a statement about the distant past. Observation suggests that it is fairly accurate about the present as well.

I shall now review the six positive arguments concerning international morality as to the "accuracy" of their observations about human nature, morality, and group behavior.

1. The *natural law* argument observes, firstly, that all human beings have a sense of right and wrong, a conscience. That is perfectly accurate under Hypothesis One. Natural law claims, secondly, that certain basic moral practices, such as the keeping of promises and refraining from assault, are natural to man's social existence. According to Hypothesis One that is accurate, insofar as the cultural invention of certain ethics is predicted by the necessities of social living. Natural law theory claims, thirdly, that a general moral law constrains rulers and nations. According to Hypothesis Two that is inaccurate: groups have a double standard of morality for their domestic and international behavior. They may hold their leader to high standards at home, while condoning his "unprincipled" behavior abroad.

2. The *cosmopolitan morality* argument observes that all humans are similar because they have the use of reason, and that any two human beings are potentially capable of treating each other with justice and sympathy. That is accurate according to Hypothesis One as long as the word "potentially" is used. As far as statistical trends are concerned, however, generosity is found much more among friends than strangers—as would be predicted under Hypothesis Two. Moreover, once interacting groups exhibit enmity, according to Hypothesis Two, individuals of one group may be disinclined to act sympathetically towards individuals of other groups.

3. The *society of states* argument observes that groups can overcome their hostility when this is of mutual benefit, especially in an emergency, and in regard to forming alliances for a balance-of-power. That is completely accurate under Hypothesis Two. The theory of the society of states also claims that social order is a prerequisite for the formulation of morality and justice. That is accurate according to Hypothesis One, insofar as people's willingness to participate in reciprocal exchanges seems to require an atmosphere of predictability.

4. The *just war* argument offers no observations, only ethical recommendations; these will be mentioned below.

5. The *human rights* argument observes that human individuals are equal and are entitled to certain rights. The only way we could register "accuracy"

for this claim would be to note that, under Hypothesis One, a culture can make specific rules about how individuals may treat each other morally, and perhaps even determine how they view each other—as equals, for example.

6. The *world order* argument observes that problems which impinge on the world as a whole, rather than on a particular group, require rational decision-making by parties acting not strictly in the capacity of national leaders. That is accurate according to Hypothesis Two. World-order theory also maintains that humans construct moralities in accordance with their values, and with special reference to social relations. That is perfectly accurate under Hypothesis One.

So far, then, it appears that all twelve arguments concerning international morality, or at least the ten that offer some observation about human nature, morality, or group behavior, rate high in accuracy according to the "standard" offered by the sociobiological hypotheses. That should not surprise us, since presumably these arguments become well-established in the first place by virtue of their accord with the obvious facts of life. However, while each may be accurate in regard to the particular observation it makes about human nature, each is inaccurate in its claim to state the whole truth. As alluded to in Part One, the student of international relations faces a *potpourri* of explanations for international moral behavior. The reason for this, we see now, is that each of the twelve dwells on only one facet of a very complicated behavior. Even when the six arguments of the positive position are taken as a whole they defend Hypothesis One almost exclusively, while the six arguments of the negative position defend Hypothesis Two almost exclusively. Hence none of the traditional theories of international morality is "balanced."

The Prescriptive Content of the Traditional Arguments

Besides determining the accuracy of the twelve arguments' observations about human nature, morality, and group behavior, the above exercise has another value. Namely, it assists us in seeing what is left within each argument after these descriptive observations have been separated out. For the most part, what remains is a set of prescriptions. Rather predictably, the prescriptions of the negative arguments are political in tone while the prescriptions of the positive arguments are normative. This can best be demonstrated by paraphrasing each of them in simple language.

I offer the following paraphrases of the prescriptive content of the six negative arguments:

1. *National interest:* We want what is best for our nation, or certain groups in our nation; we should seek it aggressively, as no-one else will help us.

2. *International anarchy:* We should carefully protect our nation against the likely aggression of others. There is no need to be hampered by international morality since there is no global social contract—and one-sided morality would put us at a disadvantage.

3. *National sovereignty:* We want independence and privacy for our nation and, as the price of that, we agree to extend the same to our equals—that is, other large powers. Small powers will be allowed independence if the politics of the day permit.

4. *Nationalism:* Our nation is important and citizens must cooperate to make the nation strong; our cultural heritage is superior and should be allowed to flourish.

5. *Group immorality:* We know we should be more generous with other nations, but this is almost impossible owing to our moral weakness when behaving in groups.

6. *Cultural pluralism:* Our Western culture is advanced and civilized; the others are not up to performing morally in the international arena, and so this excuses us Westerners from needing to try.

I offer the following paraphrases of the prescriptive content of the six positive arguments:

1. *Natural law:* We know we should do good and avoid evil. The particulars of morally right behavior should be codified in law and should apply internationally.

2. *Cosmopolitan morality:* Decency to fellow human beings, especially the suffering or the persecuted, is a paramount consideration; we must not let the complex institutions of advanced society, such as the corporation, conceal the moral relationships among people.

3. *Society of states:* We should look for areas in which we can do good, especially where our rights as powerful nations will not be impinged upon; we should even sacrifice some of our privileges and sovereignty in urgent situations.

4. *The just war:* We should avoid waging war, except for certain causes, since war is evil; once engaged in war, we should not be cruel to individuals or do more damage than is necessary.

5. *Human rights:* We are modern people who understand that governments must be made accountable to the governed. We have culturally developed the idea that our dignity as human beings rests on our having certain rights, and so we should act on that principle to help others.

6. *World order:* The rules which guide the morality of individuals cannot effectively reach up into the more complex areas of political and economic institutions; we should restructure these institutions in line with the rational pursuit of human values.

As was so in the preceding list of the twelve arguments' observations about human nature, morality, and group behavior, these paraphrases of prescriptive content show a certain pattern. Namely, the positive arguments align with Hypothesis One and the negative arguments align with Hypothesis Two. For example, the prescriptive content of three of the positive arguments—natural law, cosmopolitan morality, and the just war—emphasize *conscience, conformity to law,* and the *dictates of human decency,* while two others—human rights and world order—stress the *cultural creation of values.* These constitute a veritable roundup of the elements contained in evolution-of-morality theory, as described in Chapter 5. Among the prescriptions of the negative arguments, national interest stresses *competition;* international anarchy, *defense;* and nationalism, *group solidarity.* Two others, group immorality and cultural pluralism, speak of the *nonextension of the group's domestic morals* to include other groups. These, likewise, are the very features emphasized in group-evolution theory, as presented in Chapter 6.

From the foregoing sorting-out process, it can now be seen that the twelve arguments are not just so many disparate approaches to the philosophical mystery of international morality. In fact the negative and positive positions are not, as they first seemed to be, direct confrontations on the same "ethical" issue. Rather, they are talking about apples and oranges. The negative position is talking about the "apples" of intergroup competition. The statement, "There is not and cannot be a moral relationship among states," reflects the evolutionary fact that the relationship between groups indeed had no moral dimension to it. It was characterized by competition, conquest, and mutual suspicion—as Hobbes, Machiavelli, Treitschke, and others saw. The positive position is talking about the "oranges" of moral principle. The statement, "Rules of morality apply to all transactions whether the actors be individuals or states," reflects the fact that the human mind perceives the right and wrong of any situation, including international situations. This view appears in the writings of Falk, Shue, Donelan, Beitz, and others.

Another issue that may be clarified here is the confusing attempt by many of the negative theorists to engage in moral talk. As was mentioned in Chapter 4, part of this is simply propaganda, but now we also see that defenders of state selfishness have the sentiments associated with group morality at their disposal. Indeed much of the more sophisticated realist writing, such as that of Morgenthau or Kissinger, emphasizes the statesman's moral duty to be amoral. Morgenthau declared:

> The individual may say for himself *Fiat justica, pereat mundus*, but the statesman has no right to say so in the name of those who are in his care.... While the individual has a moral right to sacrifice himself in defense of ... a moral principle, the state has no right to let its moral disapprobation ... get in the way of successful political action.[1]

Thus some realist writers want to have it both ways—to stress both the statesman's wrong behavior (his "dirty hands" behavior) and his right behavior (his protect-the-nation behavior), simultaneously. I believe it makes more sense to separate the two, and to admit that the statesman is being judged according to two separate types of morality: standard morality and group morality.

I suggest that one of the principal benefits of the sociobiological critique of the theories of international morality is the revelation of the contradiction—I shall call it The Contradiction—between these two moralities.

Why Is There No International Theory?

I believe that the very existence of The Contradiction can explain the general lack of development of an ethical theory of international relations. Standard morality, which arose out of our moralistic nature, has given rise to abstract principles and tends toward universal application. Group morality, being limited to the one role of protecting the group, does not lead to further ethical development. It seems that this situation is largely responsible for the fact, noted by Martin Wight, that "international theory is marked not only by paucity but also by intellectual and moral poverty."[2]

In 1966, Wight published a famous essay entitled "Why Is There No International Theory?" By "international theory" he meant "a tradition of speculation about relations between states, a tradition imagined as the twin of speculation about the state to which the name "political theory" is appropriated."[3] Wight proposed two reasons for the lack of such theory. The first reason is that international society has been organized since the sixteenth century in such a way that only sovereign states, or their "princes," can belong to it. "The principle that every individual requires the protection of a state, which represents him in the international community ... has absorbed almost all the intellectual energy devoted to political study."[4]

The second reason why there is no international theory, according to Wight, is that international politics, being recurrent and repetitious, is incompatible with the all-important belief in progress. Wight noted that if Sir Thomas More or Henry IV returned to England and France in 1960, they would see that their countries had changed *domestically* along certain lines.

> But if they contemplated the international scene it is more likely that they would be struck by resemblances to what they remembered: a state-system apportioned between two Great Powers each with its associates and satellites . . . universal doctrines contending against local patriotism . . . the empty professions of peaceful purpose and common interest, the general preference for going down to defeat fighting rather than consenting to unresisted subjugation.[5]

I must agree with Wight's two points. The fact that the actors are states rather than individuals—that is, the fact that the actors are entities which do not have a mind, a will, a conscience in the way that a human being does—removes the topic of interstate relations from discussion in the tradition of political philosophy and theory. The fact that the system of competing groups is not very "progressive" has, likewise, an inhibiting effect on intellectual exercise.

Wight further accounted for "the recalcitrance of international politics to be theorized about" by citing the difficulties of language. He showed that the only language we have in which to conduct such theorizing is the language of political theory and law. But this, he says,

> is the language appropriate to man's control of his social life. Political theory and law are maps of experience . . . within the realm of normal relationships and calculable results. They are the theory of the good life. International theory is the theory of survival. What for political theory is the extreme case (as revolution, or civil war) is for international theory the regular case.[6]

According to Wight, international theory contains talk about strange things. Examples are "the traditional effort of international lawyers to define the right of devastation and pillage in war," and "the long diplomatic debate in the nineteenth century about the right of intervention in aid of oppressed nationalities."[7]

Wight concludes that "all this is the stuff of international theory, and it is constantly bursting the bounds of the language in which we try to handle it. For it all involves the ultimate experience of life and death, national existence and national extinction."[8] By contrast, I believe that the reason why it bursts the bounds of our language is not that it has to do with life and death but that the words and concepts of group morality get in the way of our applying standard moral terminology to the subject matter of international relations.

Summary. To summarize this chapter, the sociobiological ideas of Part Two were brought to bear against the traditional arguments concerning international morality discussed in Part One. I analyzed the twelve arguments and found that, for the most part, the six that constitute the *positive* position make observations that correlate with sociobiology's portrayal of the *evolutionary function of morality* (Hypothesis One). The six that constitute the *negative* position make observations that correlate with sociobiology's description of the *evolution of groups* (Hypothesis Two). Then, having removed the descriptive observations from all twelve arguments, I exposed their prescriptive content. It was seen that the positive position talks in the language of standard morality, while the negative position either talks frankly in the language of group morality or conceals its purpose by borrowing language, inappropriately, from standard morality. I proposed that the identification of The Contradiction between the two moralities is the key to understanding the impasse between the two positions. Moreover, The Contradiction sheds light on the apparent lack of development of an ethical theory of international relations.

9

International Morality and Its Obstacles

> *War appears to me, here, now, something evil, in which*
> *any kind of acquiescence is, in some measure, morally*
> *degrading. Organized violence itself, and the habits and*
> *attitudes associated with threatening it and preparing*
> *for it, are ugly and alien.*
>
> — *Hedley Bull*

It is now appropriate for us to reconsider the main question of this book, "Is there a moral relationship among states?" Of course, there are two ways to interpret that question. On the one hand it can be interpreted as an abstract, philosophical question, meaning "do the relations between states have some intrinsic characteristic that makes them subject to a moral law?" On the other hand it can be interpreted as an empirical question about the contemporary world.

The Empirical Question

Let us deal briefly with this second interpretation first. If we ask empirically, "Is there a moral relationship among states?" I believe that the either the answer "Yes" or "No" could reasonably be defended. Many states have a moral relationship with one another because they choose to do so. Typical examples are: close neighbors, long-term trading partners, and nations which share a language, religion or a past colonial relationship. When I say these states have a "moral" relationship I mean roughly that the relationship is characterized by trust, cooperation, sense of obligation, and so forth: they treat each other as friends, not enemies. The existence of such moral relationships among states, however few in number they be, belies any claim about the absolute impossibility of such relationships.

Even among enemies there is apparent moral restraint. Marshall Cohen writes, "Washington often acts in conformity with moral requirements, even in its conflicts with Moscow. After all, Washington refrained from attacking Moscow at a time when the United States enjoyed a monopoly of nuclear weapons."[1] Raymond Aron observes:

The Spenglerian realist who asserts that man is a beast of prey and urges him to behave as such, ignores a whole side of human nature. Even in the relations between states, respect for ideas, aspirations to higher values and concern for obligations have been manifested. Rarely have collectivities acted as if they would stop at nothing with regard to one another.[2]

Nevertheless it would be going too far to say that a moral relationship among states is either the express historical norm, or that it is an accepted legal principle. Contemporary states agree to be bound by a few rules of order, such as the immunity of ambassadors, but they generally disavow moral responsibility for the welfare of other nations and, as we have seen, emphasize their own sovereign rights as paramount. So there is no definitive answer to the *empirical* question, "Is there a moral relationship among states?"

The Philosophical Question

In regard to the philosophical interpretation of the question, many persons have tackled it, as we saw in Part One. When philosophers ask "Is there a moral relationship among states?" they mean to investigate whether states have moral obligations to one another. Hobbes' reply to this question was No: there is no contract, and no supreme authority, so no obligations follow. Bozeman says No: cultures have different values which they cannot impose on one another and so international morality is impossible. The national-sovereignty writers say No: the only moral obligation among states is the liberal one of noninterference. Cosmopolitan moralists, such as Beitz, say Yes: there are obvious obligations of economic justice which apply internationally. Just-war theorists say Yes: states must refrain from arbitrary attacks on one another, and must behave as humanely as possible in war. World-order theorists such as Johansen say Yes: states are morally bound to submit to the global human interest in such matters as ecological protection.

At the end of the presentations of the negative and positive positions in Part One, I did not find it possible to determine that one or the other was correct, since both sides were persuasive. However, after Part Two's discussion of the biological function of morality and the evolution of intergroup behavior, I believe it is now possible to give an answer to the *philosophical* question "Is there a moral relationship among states?" That answer is *Yes*. My reasoning is as follows.

Morality, as we saw, has to do with judging the actions of oneself and others according to some rules which were originally based on reciprocity or fair play. Morality was entrenched in human nature from the start, and subsequently became an artifact of culture. As soon as articulation of rules was possible, societies were able to elaborate these into abstract principle. Such laws and principles are now a major feature of the human environment; it would be hard to imagine either the socialization of children, or the sorting out of conflicting interests among adults, in a context where morality was somehow not present. Morality, it seems to me, is ubiquitous. As the natural lawyers say, "Everyone knows right from wrong." I do not for a moment suggest that everyone *does* right and abstains from wrong, but just that everyone is a moralizer. When we see actions around us in which one party affects another—say, when Party X hurts, helps, or deceives Party Y, we automatically have some moralistic opinion about it: our judgmental sentiments are aroused.

It is for this reason that I believe the positive position on international morality is correct. *Rules of morality apply to all human transactions* whether the actors be individuals or states. To put it another way, no actor, making a human transaction, is exempt from rules of morality. The actor may make a loud statement about his right to be exempted from moral rules (for example, because he is a state) but that will be ignored by most observers of his deeds. I claim that the subjection of the actor's acts to moral rules is a function of *our moral nature*, our habit of "noticing" the rightness and wrongness of transactions between humans. In short, my philosophical assertion that a moral relationship "exists" among states is not based on any observation about states or their characteristic behavior toward one another. It is based on a theory of ethics which simply says that morality arises from our penchant for judging. *What goes on between states is "moral" because we have a moral reaction to it and want to apply rules to it.*

Two Disclaimers

My endorsement of the positive position, that rules of morality apply to all human transactions whether the actors be individuals or states, may give two false impressions. First, it may seem that I am now bound to leap to a description of some specific rules or "moral imperatives" that can be derived from the alleged moral relationship of states. Second, it may seem that I must predict that states will in fact be restrained by this morality. But in fact my claim is a much more modest one than that. Let me disclaim specifically any intention of making the two aforementioned leaps.

First, I claim only to defend in a general way the underlying theme of those six arguments which I labelled collectively "the positive position." Namely, I defend their belief that it is appropriate to discuss international relations in ethical terms (and I conversely reject the claim of the negative writers that moral discussion of international affairs should be in any way off limits). I do not—or at least do not necessarily—support any particular program of international morality. I certainly do not claim to have found, sociobiologically, any ethical truth which shows that we should engage in cosmopolitan economic justice, or that we must pursue human rights for all members of the human population. If anything, I argued that we will *never* find "ethical truth" since it does not exist as such. All that exists, according to my evolution-based scheme, is the combination of our moral nature and our cultural history of ethical invention. Such schemes as human rights, economic justice, or proscriptions against deterrent nuclear weapons on the grounds of disproportionality are probably worthwhile ethical inventions—but they have no special ontological status as discoverable truths.

In order to turn ethical ideas into compelling laws or moral imperatives, the creators of these ideas would, no doubt, have to exhort, cajole, terrify, mythologize, reason with, inspire, reprimand, propagandize, shame, bribe, or otherwise act upon the population in the same way that moral leaders have done in the past. Most likely in the very early days of human society it was quite easy for a group to establish a unified moral myth and obtain compliance with the law. Even in modern times, following the major social disruptions of the Industrial Revolution, it seems to have been remarkably easy to unify large societies around a moral myth, such as liberalism or socialism, and obtain widespread compliance with the law. So it is obviously *possible* that a new set of beliefs—even if they concern international relations—could be turned into the ethical norm of the future. But that is not part of my claim, which, to repeat, is merely a modest claim about the appropriateness of our bringing international matters under moral scrutiny.

The second leap I must disclaim is the related one of predicting the future good behavior of states. I have no particular grounds on which to claim that the behaviors which have always been characteristic of groups will disappear. There is, in fact, much to suggest that such things as nationalism and racism are on the increase, and owing to the multiplication of sheer military hardware, states are more fortified today than ever. The only prediction I could make for an increase in the moral restraint of states—and I make it diffidently—is that states could conceivably come around to the notion that the world has changed and that group selfishness is a fairly dangerous and self-defeating strategy.

In this regard, I cite the recent writings of George Kennan. Although he has famously held that morality is not relevant in international affairs, Kennan changes his approach when it comes to two issues, nuclear war and ecological protection. He notes the following in regard to the danger of war and what he calls the "devastating effect of modern industrialization and overpopulation on the world's natural environment":[3]

> The one threatens the destruction of civilization through the recklessness and selfishness of its military rivalries, the other through the massive abuse of its natural habitat. *Both are relatively new problems, for the*

solution of which past experience affords little guidance. Both are urgent. The problems of political misgovernment is as old as the human species itself. It is a problem that will not be solved in our time, and need not be. But the environmental and nuclear crisis *will brook no delay.*[4] (emphasis added)

He goes on to describe as sacriligious the endangering of the planet for "the sake of the comforts, the fears and the national rivalries of a single generation."[5] He asks: "Is there not a *moral obligation* to recognize in this very uniqueness of the habitat and nature of man the greatest of our *moral responsibilities,* and to make of ourselves, in our national personification, its guardians and protectors rather than its destroyers?"[6] (emphasis added).

In other words, it seems that the logical place to turn for solutions to social problems is morality. Other guidance systems, for example, power politics, have little to contribute; indeed, in the case of nuclear dangers and ecological destruction, power politics is more the cause than the remedy. When things go wrong, when people are dissatisfied, they inexorably turn to moral principle to see what should be done. This is entirely appropriate, since, I claim, the externalization of moral rules in the first place made complex social life possible in the human species. The latter remains dependent on the former.

Obstacles to International Morality

So far in this chapter I have declared that international morality does exist; there is a moral relationship among states. (I said "What goes on between states is 'moral' because we have a moral reaction to it and want to apply rules to it.") Then, it may seem, I took the steam out of this by adding two disclaimers. I disclaimed any intuition about what the rules of international morality might be, and I disclaimed any assurance that the international moral behavior of nations would improve.

The reader may feel disappointed by this. Since the title of this book is *Morality among Nations,* it can be assumed that most readers who were attracted to read it in the first place were looking to find some positive guidance about international morality. The degree to which my thesis is "positive," however, is not inconsiderable. Its main point is that there *is* plenty of scope for the creation of rules of international morality, and at least some reasonable chance of adherence to such rules. I clearly do not support the "bottom line" of the negative theories which is that it is not worthwhile to work at international morality. Nonetheless, I think there are many obstacles to international morality and I shall spend the remainder of this chapter describing them.

The obstacles to be listed here are: group morality, the self-aggrandizement of groups, the weakness of altruism toward strangers, the lack of visible struggle of the powerless, the "acceptability of evil," and the slipperiness of moral language. I do not deny that some important obstacles to international morality have already been identified in Chapter 2, "The Negative Position," namely the obstacles related to national interest, international anarchy, national sovereignty, nationalism, the immorality of groups, and cultural pluralism. Each of them is in some way incorporated into my new categories. I differ from those theorists however, in not offering *one item* as the major explanation for the lack of development of international morality. The picture is, I believe, far more complicated.

Before turning to my list of "obstacles to international morality" I should call attention to the fact that, from here on, my usage of the word "international morality" will change. At the beginning of this book I set a very restricted definition; I was interested only in finding whether international morality "exists." There the phrase was meant to conjure up some abstract idea of a moral relationship among nations. Having argued that such a moral relationship does exist, I now revert to the more common usage of the term "international morality." I now mean something closer to "the actual practice of morality." Thus, "obstacles to international morality" will mean obstacles which deter nations from behaving in a restrained manner, or which prevent them from honoring the law, or which diminish their generosity toward other nations. In short, I mean to invoke the layman's understanding of the word "morality" in my phrase "international morality."

Group Morality

The most salient obstacle to international morality, is the one that was pointed out in Chapter 8, namely a second type of morality that competes with, or contradicts, standard ethical morality. I refer, of course, to group morality—that special set of prescriptions for loyalty and self-sacrifice toward the in-group and ruthlessness toward the out-group. Group morality causes us to see mostly righteousness in our group's cause and takes away our rational ability to review a state's behavior objectively, when the state in question is our own or that of our enemy.

This single-minded moral vision originally evolved in a setting of actual combat between groups; it was part of the struggle for survival. However, group morality carries over, in human psychology, to almost any instance in which an enemy challenge can be cited, and self-defense can be invoked. Consider, as an extreme example, the case of a huge and powerful nation, the United States, construing as its enemy a tiny and defenseless nation, East Timor. In 1974 the Left won power in Portugal, as a result of which many Portugese colonies, such as the island of East

Timor in the Pacific, became independent. In 1975, Indonesia, a large neighboring country, seized East Timor. This required, according to Leo Kuper, a "genocidal campaign."

> In mid 1977 . . . Indonesia, confronted by continued resistance, launched massive aerial bombardment of villages throughout the mountainous interior. This had the effect of destroying the social and economic infrastructure of the society and of driving hundreds of thousands of the inhabitants into the coastal plains, where they were corralled into strategic camps. Here, many died under the harsh conditions. . . .[7]

Americans, one might guess, would react to this blatant injustice by showing some moral indignation. The United States is, after all, a reasonably conscience-bound nation, and the innocence of the East Timorese people in this case was fairly obvious. However, there was a complicating factor. President Gerald Ford and Secretary of State Henry Kissinger were in Indonesia a few days before the takeover, and did not object to Indonesia's plan to seize East Timor.[8] The geopolitical calculation here is not hard to see. Timor, being a weak nation in the Pacific, could probably be coaxed or coerced by the Soviet Union into providing, let us say, a military base. Thus, Americans had to protect *themselves* from the *main* enemy, by allowing the people of East Timor to be sacrificed.

It is not clear how much of a moral opinion the American people ever formed regarding the seizure of East Timor, since the whole event was kept rather quiet. Edward Herman has argued persuasively that U.S. interests were able to censor or "manage" the media in such a way as to prevent information about Indonesia's actions from reaching the American public.[9] But if the matter *had* become known, what would Americans have perceived their options to be? I presume that they would not have perceived any "options". Self-defense would be seen as a necessity, cancelling out the possibility of other approaches. Even criticism of the U.S.'s role in providing military aid to Indonesia would be considered unpatriotic. In short, group morality has a remarkable ability to stifle standard morality, even when the heat of the battle is pretty far away.

E.F. Carritt once noted that a difficulty in judging the ethical content of politics arises out of the vague assumption that politics is either below or above morality: either "a trick below the notice of conscience [or] a kingdom of heaven where morality has vanished."[10] I believe that this is a fair description of the way that states' international behavior escapes ethical judgment. It is either thought to be so inexorably bad that it would be pointless to condemn it, or so "good," that is, cloaked in the righteousness of the cause, that again there is no place for criticism. My impression of group morality is that it shuts down certain mental processes and hence is an almost insuperable obstacle to international morality, at least so long as intergroup enmities remain in force or can be trumped up.

The Self-Aggrandizement of Groups

Quite distinct from the foregoing matter of group morality, although probably related to it in origin, is the second obstacle to international morality, namely, the practice of self-aggrandizement by groups. Here I am not interested in the phenomenon of enmity between groups, and the justification of self-defense, but simply the fact that a group is allowed by its members to pursue its interests in a fairly uninhibited way. Reinhold Niebuhr pointed out that groups act more selfishly than do their individual members. I assume that there are at least two psychological factors operating here. First, the members of the group see the group as a good thing in itself, hence its actions are nearly always considered acceptable. Second, as noted by Arthur Keith, actions performed by the group are not seen to be performed by any one person in particular. Collective responsibility rather than individual responsibility applies—that means *no* responsibility, since a "group" is not an entity that can experience guilt or remorse or the demands of moral rectitude.

The groups under discussion here are not necessarily states: they can be small groups within the state, such as neighborhoods, interest groups, or political parties. However, the *state* and the *multinational corporation* are no doubt the best examples of groups whose penchant for self-aggrandizement is an obstacle to international morality or responsibility. Moreover, these two entities possess internal dynamics of expansion: they seem generally to act on the notion that their aggrandizement is necessary since others like them are pursuing the same advantages in a "zero-sum" world. Indeed the zero-sum notion is *itself* an excuse from moral restraint: unselfishness by states is thought to be peculiar behavior, and unselfishness by business corporations, that is, consideration for the rights of competitors, is considered positively bizarre.

In an essay entitled "Morality, Interests and Rationalization," J.D.B. Miller notes:

> States are, so far, the biggest and most utilitarian groups to which people belong. Because they can exercise force and pressure . . . they can be used to procure advantage, through governmental means, by particular groups within a society. . . . These interests are assumed—rightly—to be pursued in a world of comparative scarcity and insecurity, within which the state provides advantages through such means as tariffs, trade agreements . . . currency manipulation. . . .[11]

For this reason, Miller says, it is not surprising that cosmopolitan morality "which either invites or commands people to treat as equals those who are worse off than themselves, makes so little headway. It is an invitation to be worse off oneself."[12]

In the preceding section I portrayed *group morality* as an obstacle to international morality because it shuts down our ethical faculties. Here, the phenomenon is less absolute. It is a *relative* forgiveness granted to groups which act for their own aggrandizement—on the grounds that they "can do no other." Just as "boys will be boys," states will be states.

The Weakness of Altruism toward Strangers

The two aforementioned phenomena—group morality and the self-aggrandizement of groups—create obstacles to international morality. As we have seen, the practice of moral restraint or general submission to moral rules by large entities such as states is difficult. But it is possible that there are additional obstacles to international morality *within the individual.* Here I mean to convey by "international morality" the idea of people behaving morally toward strangers or foreigners, the same as they behave morally toward their compatriots or neighbors. The obstacles to this practice could be dislike for, mistrust of, or contempt for persons of an alien culture. Such dislike, mistrust, or contempt may either be well-founded or be based on prejudice and ignorance. Another obstacle to moral behavior may simply be lack of motivation to feel empathy for persons who are so far away as to seem nonexistent.

From my description of altruism in Chapter 5 it may have appeared that feelings of altruism or generosity are limited to one's kin or to one's partners in reciprocity. True, in its origins altruism was limited to a few categories of people, but, as we have seen, the principles of morality and the feelings of sympathy are potentially extendable to all human beings. This is because it is in the nature of articulated, cultural morality to attach itself in some way to our faculties of reason. Charles Darwin put it this way:

> I have . . . endeavored to shew that the social instincts—the prime principle of man's moral constitution—with the aid of active intellectual powers and the effects of habit, naturally lead to the golden rule: 'As ye would that men should do to you, do ye to them likewise.'[13]

The Golden Rule is incorporated into the tenets of every major religion; it seems that this is the only direction in which social morality can move. Peter Singer notes, further, that the notion of a moral judgment implies that there is a *standard* or basis of comparison against which the judging is done. Gradually, rules become less and less related to particular people in particular circumstances and become universal and abstract. Singer writes,

If someone tells us that she may take the nuts another member of the tribe has gathered, but no one may take her nuts, she can be asked why the two cases are different. . . . The reason offered must be disinterested, at least to the extent of being equally acceptable to all. As David Hume put it, a person offering a moral justification must 'depart from his private and particular situation and must choose a point of view common to him with others.'[14]

Owing to this characteristic of morality, it may be that efforts to enjoin individuals in the practice of international morality are better made along the lines of reason rather than of "love." Karl Popper notes that humanitarianism is linked to impartiality and rationalism. "We cannot feel the same emotions towards everybody," he says—even the best Christian cannot feel equal love for all men.[15] "We can love mankind only in certain concrete individuals. But by the use of thought and imagination [putting ourselves in the other person's shoes] we may become ready to help all who need our help."[16]

The weakness of altruism toward strangers, as an obstacle to the practice of international morality by individuals, is compounded by the problem of *bigness.* Thousands, millions of people may be suffering, but we would not realistically be able to help them as individuals. The ethical philosopher James Fishkin believes that we need to "rethink, in a radical way, the obligations of individuals for the solution of large-scale problems,"[17] but he declines to suggest a resolution.[18] Peter Singer offers the unpalatable suggestion that in cases of famine, no matter how far away, the affluent must give until it hurts. "This would mean" he says, "that one would reduce oneself to very near the material circumstances of a Bengali refugee."[19] Henry Shue has a more satisfactory idea. He requires that institutions be designed for justice in such a way that no unreasonable demands are made on the moral restraint or altruism of individuals.[20] That, I think, is a more appropriate "design" for international morality. In the demographic transition from small-scale societies to large ones, the demands for contributions by individuals were made specific and were— more or less—applicable to all, for example, the laws of taxation. When coordinating the effort and goodwill of the vast majority, it is necessary that free-riders be seen to be punished or discouraged, and that the demands for sacrifice be imposed on all.

Lack of Visible Struggle of the Powerless

There is another obstacle to the practice of morality among nations which is harder to describe than some of the obstacles listed above. Let me label it "the lack of visible struggle of the powerless." What I have in mind is the fact that in history a weak group has often struggled against a stronger group, and onlookers have come to take up the case of the weak on grounds of some broad moral principle such as justice. The first step is that the aggrieved party makes some visible protest against maltreatment, and articulates its cause. Such struggles usually involve bloodshed and willingness to fight to the death for one's cause.

It is my first contention in this section that contemporary instances of "international injustice" tend to be hard to identify. The party to be blamed may be fairly unidentifiable, the victims may be a very large and unorganized lot, and the specific issue may not have a name. My second contention is that since there is no clear issue, there is no visible struggle, and thus onlookers cannot join in, adding the weight of their moral opinion in support of the cause. As a contrast to these cases which lack a visible struggle, it is easy to think of successful instances in which "international injustice" was successfully opposed. In Poland, throughout the 1970s, opposition to Soviet control took the form of a highly organized protest through the Solidarity labor movement. This cause had a name, a leader, and an obvious ethical tie-in with historical causes such as labor rights, national self-determination, and so forth.

Many other instances of imperial control over small nations have not met with a compelling protest. And "economic imperialism," as a contributor to much gross injustice today, seldom confronts any organized opposition.[21] The economic exploitation of some underdeveloped countries by advanced nations may be widely accepted as fact, but it is still "hard to get at" since it is so diffuse, involving whole systems of trade, manufacture, and finance. Sometimes a focus on a localized problem is effective in arousing public opinion, as when worldwide church groups have sponsored legal action against the murderers of union leaders in South America. Sometimes a visually arresting scene can be produced by an aggrieved party, as when the Mothers of the Plaza de Mayo stand silently to protest the disappearance of their sons. Nonetheless, as a rule today, it is the powerful who are organized, sometimes in extremely sophisticated ways, while the powerless are unorganized, amorphous, and thus invisible.

In short, the traditional avenue of public struggle against cruel or unfair practices is largely unavailable in regard to many of today's international matters. Often the struggle is taken up by better-placed proxies. For instance much academic writing about "international ethics" is a form of moral struggle on behalf of the poor and the oppressed. And thousands of human rights organizations (there are literally thousands) in the West have members who are not themselves the subjects of human rights violations. But because these people are *not* involved in a personal struggle for survival they are not usually willing to put their life on the line—which has perhaps been a decisive factor in important struggles of the past.

The Acceptability of Evil

Another obstacle to international morality is simply the acceptability of evil. My claim bas been that morality is an important feature both of human nature and of culture. Thus I must ask: how is it that there is not greater moral revulsion from international social evils—such as the evils of starvation and torture? In regard to starvation, Michael Donelan has written

> Upwards of 500 million people in the world are sick for lack of food. . . . All newspapers and all news broadcasts, even those that delude themselves that they discuss important world affairs, are filled with trivia compared with this one fact. . . . This great number of men live day in, day out, what would seem to others a living death.[22]

In regard to torture and killing, Amnesty International states, for example, that "There have been consistent reports of massive extrajudicial executions in Guatemala since General Efrain Rios Montt took power in March 1982."[23] A typical example of such a report, from a Kekechi Indian girl, is as follows:

> The soldiers came; we went to the mountains. They seized three of us; they tied them up and killed them with machetes and knives. . . . The army also seized my 13-year-old brother Ramos and shot him in the foot. . . . The soldiers said "They are guerillas, and they must be killed". . . . They killed my mother . . . my sisters and my little one-year-old brother.[24]

Amnesty International has filled hundreds of volumes with such reports, many of them being more gruesome in detail.

Stanley Hoffman refers to the "institutionalization of cruelty;"[25] Hannah Arendt to the "banality of evil"[26] and Bhikku Parekh and R.E. Berki to the "spectacle of inhumanity" in the contemporary politics.[27] I am concerned here with both the acceptance and the acceptability of evil, as obstacles to international morality. By *acceptance* I mean to imply that a decision seems to have been made, a cultural view established, that such evil is "okay." This may be adduced from the fact that the solving of international social problems is generally not an item on the agenda, not even the academic agenda. Parekh and Berki note,

> Indifference can take many forms. It is there, most painfully perhaps, in the self-engineered abdication of philosophers, intellectuals, and social and political scientists, in the face of evil, and their refusal to comment seriously and substantively on the morality of politics.[28]

Of course, the refusal to comment on the "morality of politics" would be defended by many political scientists, as we have seen, as being a matter of professional integrity, or as a matter of not engaging in absurdities.

Nonetheless it is undeniable that moral skepticism and cynicism enjoy a certain fashion among intellectuals.

By the *acceptability* of evil I mean to point to a slightly different phenomenon, namely the equanimity with which the suffering of fellow human beings is countenanced by most people. I shall try to account for this in three ways. First and most obviously, the scale of society has changed since the days in which moral feelings evolved in us. Presumably our moral sentiments are adapted to small communities; our sympathies can be engaged toward individuals whom we actually see suffering, not toward statistical figures that we read about. Indeed the human moral system evolved in closed societies in which all the members knew one another personally, saw the direct effects of their actions on others, and apportioned praise and blame more or less on the spot. Wrong acts were clearly labelled by words such as "sin" or "taboo." Today, wrong acts are more likely to be called sociological trends, or just "the facts of life."

A second, related explanation for the acceptability of evil is the moral immunity of officeholders. Much action taken today that affects human welfare is action taken by large institutions such as states or corporations. Yet it seems psychologically difficult for people to apportion blame to a corporate body. Thomas Nagel observes that this is extended to officeholders as well.

> Public crimes are committed by individuals who play roles in political, military, and economic institutions. . . . Not only are ordinary soldiers, executioners, secret policemen, and bombardiers morally encapsulated in their roles, but so are most secretaries of defense . . . or even many presidents. . . . They act as officeholders or functionaries, and thereby as individuals they are insulated in a puzzling way from what they do: insulated both in their own view and in the view of most observers.[29]

From our discussion of intergroup behavior in Chapter 6 it might be suggested that the moral immunity of role-players is related to the "deindividuation" of warriors. That is, when the warrior goes abroad to fight for his country he overcomes his inhibitions aginst killing by encapsulating himself in this role, while literally encapsulating himself in his war costume. Such a psychological strategy may be involved in modern immunity, but it is also no doubt a cultural phenomenon: the expectation of the public is simply that a person acting in his role should not be held morally accountable for his actions.

A case could be made that this generosity by the public has become too indiscriminate. Morton Mintz commented, concerning a famous lawsuit against a manufacturer of a harmful product, "The human who would not harm you on an individual face-to-face basis, who is charitable, civic-minded, loving and devout will wound or kill you from behind the corporate veil."[30] We have no doubt removed inhibitions from acts that society at large should want inhibited. A possible explanation for the generosity of the public here is simply that it is a *quid pro quo*: it allows each group member to "submerge private moral decision-making within a reassuring consensus."[31] As Lionel Tiger asks, does not the modern industrial system "provide a uniquely efficient lubricant for moral evasiveness?"[32]

A third possible explanation for the acceptability of evil is a cognitive tactic which I might call the zero-sum view of values. We are able to default on certain moral obligations, in a respectable manner, by emphasizing our attention to others. For example, as mentioned in the case of East Timor, Americans can emphasize the value of fighting the evil of Communism, at the expense of other values such as justice. One value crowds out another; there is no discussion of how the two might be accommodated simultaneously. This zero-sum theory of values can also be seen in the fact that a high social value is placed today on "economic growth" and "standard of living" to the virtual exclusion of other political goals. Parekh and Berki show that the concern with private gain

> has become one of the most enduring political fetishes especially in advanced industrial society. The standard of living has been elevated to the status of the highest moral and political value . . . poverty, disease, and starvation of millions are facts apparently easily coexisting with the frenzied pursuit of material prosperity in the more affluent reaches of human society.[33]

The Slipperiness of Moral Language

The final obstacle to international morality in my list has to do with language. For a society to organize the relations of its members in accordance with some moral scheme, it is necessary that the scheme be publicly enunciated. Both the law and the theories justifying the law must be known to all. In primitive society the myth substitutes for theory; in later society religion provides the theory; and in modern society there are secular explanations for the law—for example, liberalist ideology with its emphasis on rights and contract. "International society" obviously lacks a publicly articulated moral program. Earlier, we discussed the natural-law tenet that "people know right from wrong," but the conscience of individuals is no substitute for a culturally-promulgated positive law and supporting myth or theory. Thus, a major language-related problem for international morality is simply: the lack of cultural consensus about international morality, stemming from a dearth of articulation on the subject. That lack, of course, occurs *among* nations, but it also exists *within* the various nations.

Paradoxically, at the same time, there is the problem of an oversupply as well as an undersupply of moral language in international affairs. For example, as shown in Chapter 4, the negative theorists of international morality often use moral terms inappropriately. Or, as Hare and Joynt observe, they "smuggle in" real moral values while they are ostensibly arguing for the irrelevance of these.[34] Let me identify two broad reasons for these language problems. The first is the fact that there are often conflicting moralities involved. The proponents, rather than admit this, usually diminish the moral merits of one system by inflating the merits of the other. Nationalist language, for example, brings in such terms as "holy" or "sacred" to establish the absolute priority of the nation's cause. Indeed, an either-or dichotomy is always implicit in the arguments of conflicting or competing moralities; there is no language of compromise here.

Another factor encouraging the overuse or misuse of moral language is simply that it is an aid to power. As E.H. Carr said, "Power goes far to create the morality convenient to itself."[35] One way that the powerful can manipulate public sentiment is by labelling things moral when they are not. Niebuhr cited the hypocritical rationalizations given for government policy in the Preamble to the Holy Alliance; almost any television broadcast by contemporary political leaders contains transparently false remarks about the motivation for political action. Consider, as an almost satirical example, the following language invoked by the U.S. OPS—Office of Public Safety. This is an American organization which trains police for other countries. Barry, Wood, and Preusch write, in regard to Guatemala in the early 1970s,

> OPS paid for pistols . . . shotguns, ammunition, vehicles, tear gas grenades . . . helmets and safety shields, with the explanation that this aid "provided essential riot control equipment as an interim measure to establish the predicate for more humane treatment of persons involved in civil disturbances."[36]

There is something about moral language that is persuasive even when one knows rationally, as in the above case, that it is self-serving nonsense. I refer to this problem as "the slipperiness of moral language."

This slipperiness—or adaptability—of moral language may help explain how certain ideas concerning group morality have become compelling arguments in the academic theory of international relations. J.N. Figgis said of Machiavelli, "Social justice had no meaning to him apart from the one great end of the salvation of his country. He had the limited horizon and unlimited influences which always come of narrowing the problem."[37] While everyone would agree, Figgis says, that there are times when a government must proclaim a state of siege and allow the supersession of the common rules, Machiavelli—or his follower—have elevated this principle into a norm for statesmen's actions.

When Machiavelli's writings "are made into a system they must result in a perpetual suspension of the *habeas corpus* acts of the whole human race."[38]

I am suggesting here that the absorption of Machiavelli's ideas into academic theory was assisted by the fact that he made a positive moral case for self-defense and ruthlessness. It is always comforting to know *why* we *must* act immorally or amorally—in this case, for the *salus populi*. Even Morgenthau's more complex, more Weberian explanation of the national interest has the comfort of being a sort of law of nature: nations must follow what he calls their "one shining star—the national interest"[39]—it is their *duty* to do so.

The language of realism and national interest has succeeded to an impressive degree in directing our attention away from moral *choice*. Thus, it is interesting to note that a trend in very recent international relations theory has been the reassertion of choice. Michael Joseph Smith, for example, comments,

> The national interest is not an objective datum, an amoral law of interstate existence. Rather, it is defined according to a particular hierarchy of values. Even the Athenians had to *choose* to kill the Melians; and their choice, their definition of the national interest, reflected a hard and murderous morality.[40]

Joseph Nye points out similarly that "the fact that states must act to defend their interests if they wish to survive . . . in the long run does not mean that only selfish acts are possible"[41]—some degree of altruism or consideration of others, he says, *can* motivate foreign policy. Furthermore, cultural pluralism or the existence of different national moral standards does not entirely limit our options. "Just because others may execute prisoners of war . . . does not make it right for us to do so. Two wrongs don't make us right."[42] According to Nye, "no domain of human activity can be categorized *a priori* as amoral when choices exist."[43]

I believe that of all the obstacles to international morality which I have listed in this chapter, the slipperiness of moral language—or the related sloppiness of moral thinking—is the one most amenable to change. At least it is a place where intellectuals could begin, in the creation of an ethics of international relations, if they wished to do so. If a thing is slippery we can try to make it hold still while we inspect it. And it turns out—as I have been arguing—that there is a lot in morality to inspect. There is both a genetic history, that is, our human nature of moralizing, and a cultural history which has produced many useful ideas. Joseph Nye contends that the way to revitalize moral reasoning about foreign policy is to consult our rich heritage—for example the idea of impartiality and integrity. Reflecting his experience in the U.S. State Department, he writes,

When it becomes known that integrity plays no role ... one opens [one's nation] to blackmail by those who play dirty games. . . . Once one allows departure from rules and integrity, is one not on a slippery slope to rationalizing anything? Particularly in complex organizations like governments a widespread permission to waive rules and think only of consequences can lead to a rapid erosion of moral standards.[44]

Nye recommends two handholds that can be introduced on the "slippery slope." One consists of starting with a *strong presumption in favor of rules,* and placing the burden of proof on those who wish to turn to consequentialist arguments. The other consists of the *developing of procedures, related to impartiality,* which, he says, is at the core of moral reasoning—"for example, structuring justification from the perspective of the victim or the deceived, and developing ways to consult or inform third parties. . . . The practice of consulting courts, Congressional committees, allies and other countries can all serve as means to protect impartiality."[45]

These suggestions for handholds on the slippery slope are intended by Nye as guidelines for the formulation of foreign policy in a Western country. They remind the "advanced nations" to live up to their own moral standards. That, of course, cannot guarantee that other nations will be interested in practicing international morality, but it is a place to start. Other theorists also make important contributions to moral language by constructing cosmopolitan theories and utopias. Such endeavors help to show the many dimensions of the problem. In particular, as we have seen, world-order theories and human-rights theories emphasize the needs of entities both above and below the state, namely, the human race and the human individual. I conclude this section on the slipperiness of moral language by reiterating that this is perhaps the one obstacle to international morality which is most within the power of reflective persons to remove.

Conclusion

The object of this book has been to use ideas about human evolution to illuminate the traditional theories of international relations concerning the moral relationship among nations or states. In Part Three I showed that the evolution-of-morality hypothesis together with the intergroup-competition hypothesis helps to explain the existence of the conflicting negative and positive positions concerning international morality. Moreover I have hinted that the sociobiological view offers a "resolution" of the impasse between those two arguments.

That resolution is as follows. Ethics is a cultural invention (reflecting our moral nature) that is constantly developed and refined over time, particularly in the service of organizing human relationships and making social life in some sense satisfactory. The drive for moral judgment is unstoppable: it applies itself to any human transactions "whether the actors be individuals or states." For this reason, I have claimed that there is a moral relationship among states, that is, that international transactions are the proper and logical subject of ethical inquiry. Granted, there is another morality on the scene, and a very powerful one at that—group morality—which also goes by such names as national interest or *raison d'etat*. But this morality has not been accounted for in major ethical systems. It has been either overlooked or excused—or perhaps its presence has been too daunting for ethical philosophers to deal with. The resolution which I offer to this impasse between the two moralities is *in favor of* the standard ethical morality. The behavior of states *should* come under moral scrutiny. This seems to be already realized by most serious thinkers in light of problems which affect the world as a whole, rather than just one group or another. I referred, for example, to George Kennan's reaching toward moral concepts when nuclear or ecological matters are at issue.

In this final chapter I have listed a variety of obstacles to international morality—facts of the world, or of human nature, that have made it difficult for people to impose their ethical concepts on matters of interstate relations. I believe that identifying such obstacles is a step, even if a tiny step, in the direction of overcoming them. The obstacle which seemed most conducive to change was the one concerning moral language. Indeed moral reasoning and articulation are the keys to the establishment of laws and ethical principles. "Public opinion," of an ethical kind does to some extent control social and political forces, but such opinion needs clear articulation. This is, of course, no *deus ex machina* solution to the great problem of international morality. But language is a beginning from which other developments would be likely to follow.

As Michael Walzer says, "Moral talk is coercive; one thing leads to another. . . ."[46]

10

An Afterword concerning Context

> *Few things are permanent in history and it would be*
> *rash to suppose that the territorial political unit is one*
> *of them.*
> — *E.H. Carr*

For the preceding nine chapters, I have been dealing with a certain universe of ideas. I would now like to place that universe against other universes of ideas. That is, I shall attempt in this Afterword to describe the intellectual background of my international-morality thesis.

I believe I can best accomplish that by stating what my book is *not*, and what it *is*. It is not any of the following things: an introduction to international relations theory, a complete catalogue of ideas concerning international morality, or an empirical study of the practice of morality among nations. My work, is, however, all of the following: a participation in the current critique of realism, a commentary on the academic fact/value rule, and a venture into the sociobiology of ethics. If I may be permitted now, I should like to describe each of these briefly.

Not an Introduction to International Relations Theory

A reader who has absorbed all the material about international relations theory in this book, and who has done no other reading in that academic area, could perchance be misled into thinking that he has been given an outline of the field. This is not true at all, as I must now confess.

University departments of international relations teach a wide range of courses, of which typical headings are Power Politics, Strategic Studies, Political Economy, Interdependence Theory, Integration Theory, Issue Areas, and Peace Research. The subject of international relations *theory* may be taught within some of these courses, or may be taught as a separate course. Such theory forms a fairly minor part of the total subject matter. Even among the studies which are devoted to international relations theory, as distinct from international relations in general, the sources that I used—being skewed toward international morality—represent only a small section. Within the Dewey decimal library classification system, "327" is the number of the section on international relations theory. If a

145

given library has a meter-wide shelf of "327" books, the works that I have drawn on would occupy perhaps ten centimeters. (Of course, I drew also from books elsewhere in the library, such as the "171" section on Ethics.)

In other words, the subject matter in this book is a small part of international relations theory. Moreover, as I hinted in Chapters 1 and 2, my presentation of the negative and positive "debate" on international morality is but a heuristic device. I needed to set up a framework so I could examine what was going on in detail both within and among the twelve arguments. The fact is, though, that the defenders of the positive and negative positions do not usually debate each other head-on.

Not a Complete Catalogue of Ideas on International Morality

Even *within* the topic of international morality, my work set itself a very narrow brief. I chose only academic ideas, and only those which grappled with the question of the *existence* of a moral relationship among nations. But these ideas hardly constitute the universe of ideas on the subject of international morality. (And as I noted, many of my theorists were not even particularly interested in international morality. Hobbes, Niebuhr, the Stoics—to name just three—were more interested in other problems.)

The actual universe of ideas on international morality—and it is hardly one that is organized into a library section—includes ideas from religious leaders, humanists, legal thinkers, statesmen, and many others. There is a huge store of opinion about morality among nations. Such opinions change constantly to reflect new sensibilities, new sympathies, new fears, new prejudices, new enlightenments, new models of the future, new views on what constitutes a nation or an ethnic group, and so on. Consider, for example, that the biblical Old Testament is replete with exhortations to smite the enemy—for righteous reasons such as their idolatry, or in self-defense—while the New Testament, written several centuries later, preaches the peculiar rule "Love thine enemy." I have made no attempt to inventory these ideas, nor to trace the causes of their emergence.

Probably the main source of ideas about international morality is simply a nation's cultural belief system. That is bound to influence its approach to the practice of international morality. It is often remarked, for example, that the United States' concern with finding legal solutions to international conflicts is a reflection of the importance of law in that country, domestically. National self-image, too, gives people an idea of the role their country is supposed to play in the world. As Walter S. Jones notes,

> Ideas, even when perverse, govern foreign policy in large measure. Such slogans, for example, as "White Man's Burden," "Manifest Destiny," and "World Policeman" not only express a mood about national expectation but also form a social framework in which national policy is set. Such policies may be a manifestation more of mood than of rational choice.[1]

Of course, I do not mean that we must always look to such an amorphous thing as "culture" or "national self-image" for the source of ideas. Many ideas about international morality are contributed directly by individuals. In the case of statesmen, this is easy to see: the personal beliefs of Woodrow Wilson, Benito Mussolini, or Olaf Palme influenced their nation's foreign policy. Ideas have also come from the experience of ordinary people, at the individual level. The Geneva Conventions, discussed in Chapter 3, developed out of the work of the Red Cross, whose origin can be precisely traced to the personal humanitarian ideas of one Swiss citizen, Jean Henri Dunant.

In any case, the point here is that I have made no effort to trace ideas about international morality outside of the rather limited body of academic ideas. That would be a daunting project indeed.

Not an Empirical Study of the Practice of Morality among Nations

Quite apart from looking at what people have *said*, over the ages, about international morality, one could study what nations have actually *done* — but here again I do not claim to have attempted this. I suspect that in conducting such a study one would find a great variety of behavior. In Chapter 6, I conveyed a picture of the earliest human or hominid groups in a very competitive mode, but in fact there must have been many occasions on which such groups cooperated or simply coexisted peacefully. Among extant primitive societies there are numerous styles of intergroup interaction. For example, feuding is common, as is raiding other tribes for goods or for women. Yet the need to obtain wives from other groups may cause two potential enemy groups to form friendship bonds instead. Interestingly, also, the conquest of one group by another often means the killing off of males but the absorption of females and children into the conquering group — which would not happen if enemies blindly hated each other.

Of all the statistical sum of contacts made between nations, it may be that the most frequent contact is for the activity of *trade*. This sets up some mutual dependence of the parties, and often leads to concern with fair play. Another common activity in which two nations deal is the transfer of laborers — either permanently or for seasonal work. This tends to encourage neighborly behavior among the respective nations. In fact, any time that Nation A has many members of Nation B living within its borders, this could be the stimulus for "moral" consideration of Group B — although it sometimes occasions hostility instead. In short, the picture of nations as exploiters or conquerors of other nations is not a complete one: there is a wide range of international-relations behavior.

In the twentieth century, it has become common for nations to subscribe to membership in international organizations, both at a regional and worldwide level. Here, as mentioned earlier, their "good" behavior is considered unremarkable. Most nations, for instance, give courteous attention to international postal regulations, the scheduling of air traffic, meteorological information-collection, and so forth. There are also constant transfers of aid from one nation to another in the form of wealth or training, not only by private charities but by governments. Although it is usually possible to identify some "political motive"—meaning a selfish national motive—for aid-giving, I have no doubt plenty of such generosity is just plain generosity among nations. In times of particular difficulty it is normal even for sworn enemies to help each other.

In conclusion, I do not claim to have conducted any research into whether or not nations actually do behave with moral restraint toward one another. No doubt it would be useful to have such an empirical study to use as a check on the flights of fancy of some theorists of international morality—one way or the other!

Having now said what this thesis is *not*, I dare to say what it *is*. Again, placing this study in a wider context—this time, the context of other academic works—I believe I can identify three areas in which it makes an original contribution. These concern realist theory, the fact/value debate, and the sociobiology of ethics.

A Participation in the Current Critique of Realism

In a mostly unintended way, my study fits into the contemporary critique of realism. As noted in Chapter 2, realist theory arose in the 1940s and has maintained a prominent position since then. There are many nuances to realist theory, but a range of writers concur on certain points. John Garnett describes that concurrence as follows with regard to the writings of Carr, Kennan, Morgenthau, Wight, Bull, Thompson, and Kissinger:

> Realist thinking . . . tends to be conservative. Its disciples tend to believe in the permanence of the society of sovereign states. They are pessimistic about the chances of improving the human conditon, and obsessed by the ubiquity of the power struggle and the primacy of national interests.[2]

For purposes of the point I wish to make below, concerning my work, let us note that realists initially provided a focus for the discipline of international relations by answering, concisely, the question *who* does *what*, and *why*. They said: *states* pursue *power* (or interest) because of *human nature*. It turns out now, however, that all three parts of their claim are open to attack. To date most such attacks have come not from hostile critics, but from those who tried to apply realist theory and found that its concepts were too loose. Let me briefly outline what I see as the "unravelling" of the three once-accepted premises of realism—the who, the what, and the why.

As far as the *who* is concerned, realists talk mainly of *states* as though states were unitary rational actors.[3] In the case of Hitler's Germany, the state was almost certainly acting as a unit and was "rationally" plotting its conquests. But we can see that there are problems with assuming that states typically act as unitary actors on the international scene. Firstly, there are activities going on all the time that affect international relations but which hardly involve governments. James Dougherty and Robert Pfaltzgraff note that, "loosely defined, international relations could encompass: international communication, business transactions, athletic contests, tourism, scientific conferences, educational exchange programs . . . and religious missionary activities."[4]

Secondly, even within the more usual definition of international relations or international politics where the actors *are* states, their actions may not be unitary. Chadwick Alger commented in 1968:

> As more national goverment departments have become involved in international relations and as participation in international organizations has increased, the number of sites at which a nation's representatives simultaneously interact with their counterparts from other nations has greatly increased. The ability of foreign offices to control or even to coordinate foreign policy seems to be declining.[5]

Thirdly, to say that a *state* can be counted on to perform predictably (such as "states will pursue power") is to say that the state has a desire of its own. This ignores the political processes going on within that state that lead to certain foreign policies. The "systems" approach in particular, emphasizes the forces in the international environment. For the systems theorist, state behavior is explained largely as a reaction to the behavior of *other* states—hence, attention is directed away from internal state politics. John Spanier notes by contrast that "International politics must be analyzed . . . also in terms of how the purposes of nations and their general behavior is shaped by the nature of their societies and the specific policy makers who conduct foreign policy at a particular time."[6] Along this line, Michael Joseph Smith blames the realists for contributing "perhaps unwittingly . . . to an unfortunate compartmentalization of domestic and international history and theory."[7] Realists, he says follow in the footsteps of Max Weber; thus they tend "to regard domestic politics and institutions merely as (somewhat irritating) variables that affect a state's ability to compete effectively in the international milieu."[8]

Fourthly, classical realist theory considers states to be the actors with the most power on the international stage. But even this is troublesome.

As Arnold Wolfers has pointed out, the trend now is to focus on *other corporate actors*.[9] Indeed, for Robert Keohane and Joseph Nye, the importance of nonstate actors by the 1970s called for a new paradigm in international relations theory—one that would account for the various types of transnationalism.[10] The problem suggested by the title of Raymond Vernon's book, *Sovereignty at Bay*,[11] is that a nation's sovereignty may be held at bay by powerful corporations, and as suggested by the title of Richard Barnet and Ronald Muller's book, *Global Reach*,[12] multinational corporations are global in their reach. This is not to say that corporations and the state necessarily diminish each other's power—they may enhance it. (As Spanier says "they need each other."[13]) Nevertheless, it shows that states are not the only, or even the most important actors on the world stage.

In short, the "who" in international relations is a problem. So also is the "what." The major premise of the realists has been that states pursue *interest* (which, Morgenthau says, is to be defined in terms of *power*[14]). It *is* true that the superpowers often appear to pursue power abroad, single-mindedly. They believe that geopolitics in a zero-sum game in which any loss of power by one side is a gain for the other. Their pursuit of national interest includes purchasing advanced weapons, putting out propaganda against each other, buying the friendship of small nations, and keeping an eye on strategic economic resources. However, this game of power politics is not necessarily the major activity in international relations.

A weakness of realist theory here is simply its lack of a good definition of *national interest*. As John Vasquez notes, the concept of national interest became central in American foreign policy—"It quickly dominated both public and scholarly discusssion."[15] But, he believes, the concept was ambiguous.[16] Wolfers has pointed out that the concept of national interest could include just about anything. Moreover, he says, "survival may be the most important goal of states when they are directly threatened, but it may not guide their daily activities as much as other goals."[17]

As to the concept of *power*, Werner Feld notes that "it may not always be sufficient to give you a full insight into the motivation and causes of international action."[18] Alger points out:

> As power tended to become the central concept in the international relations literature, concern developed about the analytic effectiveness of subsuming so much under one concept. There was particular difficulty in accounting for occasions when smaller nations influenced the behavior of larger nations, thus revealing the limitations of a single measure of national power.[19]

He adds that there was "a tendency for the concept to become a fad rather than a useful analytic tool."[20] Smith has ably identified a deficiency in the realist writings of Carr and Morgenthau by noting that they treat power *both as a means and as an end.*[21]

Besides the conceptual difficulties there are, of course, *real-world changes* in national interest that have taken place since the 1950s. At least since the emergence of OPEC in 1973, some analysts have argued for international economics as the new international politics. This no longer focuses on security and territorial issues, but revolves around social and economic issues.[22] In regard to this New Agenda, Kissinger stated in 1975, "A new and unprecedented kind of issue has emerged. The problems of energy, resources, environment, population, the uses of space and the seas now rank with questions of military security, ideology, and territorial rivalry which have traditionally made up the diplomatic agenda."[23] Moreover, today, as Spanier observes, "the great-power hierarchy is being weakened by the rise of newly assertive regional powers,"[24] and the sheer number of new states would make it unlikely that all their interactions are of the power-politics kind. The new academic approach to Issues Areas in international politics gives a more balanced view—showing that there is a series of problem areas that create both competition and cooperation among states. William Coplin observes, "Problems such as preventing oil spills, stimulating international trade, finding a homeland for displaced ethnic groups, avoiding worldwide inflations, solving racism . . . create situations that lead to conflict and cooperation among nation-states."[25]

Finally, I come to the third element—the "why" in "who does what, why?" Realists hold that the underlying cause of states' pursuit of power is *human nature.* They do sometimes suggest that it is the structure of the world that demands this behavior, but Morgenthau explicitly traces the problem to biological human nature, which he says is "the same everywhere and at all times."[26] That nature is destructive, aggressive, selfish, and power-seeking.

I am unaware of any detailed criticism of the realists' attribution of power-seeking to human nature, but am myself entirely dissatisfied with it—on evolutionary grounds. As described in Part Two of this book, sociobiology shows us that there are two quite separate explanations for certain human behaviors. The first explanation concerns the evolution of the individual human being. Here it is logical to suggest an instinct for selfishness, since mammals are predominantly selfish. (I stated that humans and other social species also have evolved tendencies for cooperative social behavior, but this is a modification of their basic selfishness.) The second explanation for certain human behaviors concentrates on the fact that they probably evolved in groups, and hence developed behaviors *as members of groups.*

The kind of power-seeking behavior that international relations theorists are really interested in has to do with the behavior of groups, not the behavior of individuals within domestic society. Morgenthau can hardly be blamed for having failed to anticipate the two separate evolutionary explanations, but in any case his explanation is wrong. States do not act violently toward one another because of some behavioral feature traceable to individuals (such as a "will to power") but because of a behavioral feature traceable to *groups* (even if, of course, the group behavior requires participation by individuals). I believe that sociobiology's main potential contribution to international relations theory—and not just to international morality theory—lies in its emphasis on the evolution of group behavior.

It is for this reason that I see my book as fitting into the overall critique of realism. I should acknowledge that a dissatisfaction with real-ism aided me somewhat in organizing this study. To be more precise, I was dissatisfied with "vulgar realism"—that easy tactic of declaring that international behavior is exempt from moral scrutiny because moralizing here is futile, dangerous and irrelevant—"as all the experts know." This led me to look more deeply into the concepts at hand. The resulting contribution I have made to the critique of realism (particularly to the refutation of vulgar realism) is to confirm the observation—which has been made by others—that realist theory is, in some large part, a justifi-cation of certain policies. It is a polemical argument in favor of a certain mode of intergroup behavior.

As I demonstrated in Chapter 8, the "negative argument"—that there is not and cannot be a moral relationship among states—is a restatement of group morality. As such it *favors* the group as an entity, both over the individuals who comprise it, and over some wider body such as humanity. Realism is a pro-group or pro-state position, just as, say, human rights is a pro-individual position and world order is a pro-humanity position. Garnett acknowledges this when he says "The national interest is a com-pelling constraint only because governments accept a pattern of values in which national security and prosperity enjoy high priority."[27]

I do not mean that I *set out* to prove that realism is a justification of certain policies. In fact I had no idea of the outcome of my research until it was nearly finished. (What I *set out* to do was investigate the concept of international morality.) I also do not mean that the main thrust of my work is a critique of realism. Rather, the main thrust of my work is an evolutionary account of the two types of morality. All I wish to propose is that one obvious way in which my work finds association with a major trend in the academic field of international relations is that it accords with the contemporary critique of realism.

A Commentary on the Academic Fact/Value Rule

Another position arrived at in a more or less incidental way in the course of my study, concerns the academic fact/value rule. For decades it has been the rule in the social sciences that topics dealing with human behavior should be taught in a way that emphasizes how people *do* act, not how they *should* act. That certainly seems like a reasonable restriction, as one would never be able to study behavior in a scientific way, if one were applying moral evaluation to it all the time.

In my research into the biological evolution of human morality I believe I study how people do act, in the moral sphere of their lives, not how they should act. Moreover, I explain in a particularly "scientific" way how this came about—through the law of natural selection. Nevertheless, I have been aware of some opposition from my colleagues. In fact, as soon as I broached the idea that I would be writing about international morality, a few of them took me aside to let me know that this was not considered an appropriate topic in political science. (To be fair, they probably assumed that I believed the behavior or intentions of nations to be basically good. This is considered to be the ultimate sign of naiveté in a student—and rightly so.) In any case, owing to the constant need to defend my choice of research area I became quite conscious of the fact/value debate, or non-debate as the case may be. Thus I delved into this matter, in Chapter 4, more than I otherwise might have done.

The main conclusion which I draw about the fact/value rule, from my investigation in Chapter 4, is that it is wrong-headed, at least in the area of international relations. First, it has the effect of ridiculing the study of morality itself. *Power* is seen to be the important item to be studied, and other human behaviors, such as morality, do not merit attention. Therefore, scholars cannot even investigate the very interesting relationship between morality *and* power—which surely constitutes a loss to our general knowledge about power.

Second, the fact/value rule is usually seen to support the study of power as a value-free type of investigation. But as I have argued in some detail, this is an ideological position. The study of power, for example in the theory of realism, is soaked with values. A main consequence of my application of the sociobiological hypotheses to the prescriptive content of the negative arguments about international morality was the revelation that those arguments speak the language of group morality. And what is more unabashedly value-laden than the language of group morality?

Third, the fact/value rule implies that "shoulds" should not be discussed in universities because they should be discussed *elsewhere*, such as in the community or in the churches. This is one proposition with which I have a fair amount of sympathy. Earlier I quoted the international relations theorist John Garnett who said that if academics are tempted to moralize they should hang up their gowns and don cassocks instead. I support the ideal plan, that universities are meant not to preach but to teach, and are not meant to encourage political partisanship. But this *ideal* is not what we see in practice. We see universities accepting funding from governments to set up Strategic Studies on the one hand, and Peace Studies on the other. We see students and alumni insisting that universities divest from corporations that operate in South Africa. We see courses in "business ethics" being taught in graduate schools. We see academic journals that are readily identifiable as politically conservative, liberal, or radical in their editorial policy. In short, we see little consensus on the issue of keeping ethics and politics out of the universities.

For this reason, I think the fact/value rule loses its authority. My suggestion would be that we simply recognize the inevitable polemicism that goes on and make students aware of it, rather than telling them that it is not there. I think the student needs to seek a wide band of courses so that he can recognize prejudices and become critical of them. At the very least, a student of international relations should be exposed to both realist theory and normative theory.

Finally, I offer the general observation, in relation to the fact/value rule, that it is misleading or hypocritical to equate political science with pure science. As James Dougherty and Robert Pfaltzgraff note, the vocabulary of science includes such neutral words as "liquid," "vapor," and "magnetic," but political science words include such normative words as "democratic," "aggressive," "revolutionary," "violent," and "illegal."[29] Moreover, when we observe and analyze in political science, we are usually doing so in some sort of context, for instance, comparing one form of political organization to another. It is quite natural that we will see one as *better* than another, in a way that we would be unlikely to see "phosphate" as better than "magnesium" in the study of chemistry.

Overall, much more attention needs to be paid to the inherent limitations on, and the actual breaches of, the policy of being value-free or value-neutral in political science and international relations. To honor the rule blindly is not sensible.

A Venture into the Sociobiology of Ethics

The last context into which I attempt to place my book has to do with that subdivision of sociobiological writings that could be roughly called the sociobiology of ethics. I have already introduced this topic in Chapter 5's section on "Genes and Culture," and provided some of the historical background in Chapter 7's section on "The 'Evolutionary Ethics' Debate."

There are at least four different categories of writing on the sociobiology of ethics. The first and most essential are those sociobiological researches which are concerned with finding out how we evolved into ethical-minded creatures in the first place. These include the writings of Robert Trivers, E.O. Wilson, Richard Alexander, and Robert Bigelow which were discussed in the text. In my opinion these are among the most exciting social-theory contributions of all time, since they explain our moral nature—at least hypothetically.

Second, there are efforts by philosophers to see what this new work does, rather specifically, to older theories of ethics. The writings of Michael Ruse,[29] Camilo Cela-Conde,[30] and Robert Richards,[31] stand out here. I did not have the opportunity to discuss these in this book. A third set of writings is that of David Barash,[32] Lionel Tiger,[33] E.O. Wilson,[34] and others, which attempts to interpret one or more modern behaviors directly in terms of its evolutionary background, and perhaps to prescribe a solution to modern problems.

I imagine that my present study could be associated with the first category, insofar as it talks about the evolution of morality, and with the third category, to the extent that I have alluded to modern international behavior as an example of evolved intergroup behavior. However, I picture my work as belonging to yet a fourth category of sociobiology—of—ethics writings, of which there are only a few specimens that I know of. One is Richard Alexander's book, *The Biology of Moral Systems*, another is my previous book, *Human Evolution: a Philosophical Anthropology*,[35] and another is an unpublished essay by C. Scott Findlay and Charles J. Lumsden entitled "Evolutionary Ethics and the Evolution of Moral Behavior."[36] The unifying theme of these writings is their emphasis on *moral creativity*. They state or imply that the most significant conclusion to be drawn from the new knowledge of how we evolved is that *responsibility for future ethical invention is ours*. Of course, knowledge of how we evolved gives us some hint as to what ethics we will invent, but the process is more or less open-ended.* Alexander, for example, recommends that we recognize that morality is *a solution to conflicts of interest* and "get on with it."

In describing my international-morality thesis as a venture into the sociobiology of ethics, what I have in mind particularly is my conclusion that the positive position on international morality supersedes the negative position—on sociobiological grounds. I claim that although humans have the evolved predispositions (and, for that matter, the cultural traditions) suitable for both the practice of group morality and the practice of standard morality, the latter has an edge over the former when the two clash. That edge consists of the fact that standard morality leads inexorably

---

*By "open-ended" I do not mean unlimited or unconstrained. There is obviously a finite number of ways that individuals can form a cooperative society. Themes of reciprocity, promise-keeping, fair play, in short, some form of social contract, will inevitably be part of the invented morality. (I note that some theologians prefer to say that basic values are unveiled or "revealed," rather than invented by humans. I agree at least that they are inherent in social living and can be discovered by reason.)

to the development of abstract and universal ethical principles. In the end, moral rules *must* apply to all human transactions whether the actors be individuals or states.

I have emphatically made no prediction about anyone's ability to *enforce* moral rules on the transactions between states. States may continue to succeed in bamboozling people about their moral immunity for an indefinite period of time. And it may remain quite difficult to find ways of punishing states that break the rules. Still, I claim, there will be efforts to overcome these problems since there is a *drive* in that direction. That drive, according to my interpretation of sociobiology, reflects a combination of our moralistic mentality and the momentum of our externalized ethical institutions.

A Note on the Built-in Obsolescence of this Thesis

A final comment should be made about the temporal context of this book—to wit, its subject matter is out of date. For reasons explained earlier I concentrated only on *academic* arguments about international morality, and these undoubtedly lag behind the times. Three observations about those arguments can be made. First, they emphasize high politics over low politics—they are too concerned with the identity of the state and all that this entails. Second, they virtually ignore the economic dimension, despite the fact that there is tremendous intertwining of international politics and economics today. Third, most of the twelve arguments, being philosophical—in the sense of pointing to the essence of things—do not make any allowance for the fact that society changes over time. With the exception of world-order theory (which is perhaps *too* doggedly contemporary) they do not take into account the facts of the world in the late twentieth century.

It seems obvious that changes in the moral behavior of nations will come about less under the influence of these academic arguments than under the pressure of *new circumstances*. Let me name some of the most familiar such circumstances. One is simply the very new increase in population. The number of people in the world reached one billion for the first time around 1800 A.D. but by 1987 had multiplied to five times that figure. This is perhaps the greatest change in circumstance *Homo sapiens* has undergone, as a species. It would be incorrect to say that the effects of this are felt only *within* national borders. As Jones points out, in many Third World countries "the population rates far outrun the rates of economic growth, with the result that the quality of living per capita is actually declining . . ."[37] and that this breeds conflict which often has international implications—such as through war or migration.

A second great change in our species' circumstance concerns its changed environment. Certain once-abundant resources are no longer there in sufficient quantity for all, leading to various international tensions. Numerous parts of the environment are damaged through misuse or pollution. In many cases these environmental damages do not respect national borders and may even involve "the commons" such as the ocean and the atmosphere. This factor, along with new scientific understanding of ecological balance, brings about a sense of interdependence. It becomes harder to identify "we" and "they." Thus, many of the premises associated with national sovereignty or national interest are rendered meaningless.

A third change in our species' circumstance is more cultural than biological. I refer to the great increase in communication that results from travel, from electronic transmission of information, and from the rapid increase in literacy. Suddenly one can know what's going on anywhere (one can also mis-know, if misinformation is spread) and ideas that were once germane to particular cultures—such as democracy or feminism—get exported to very foreign settings. This, too, has complex implications for the doctrines of nationalism, and the theory of cultural pluralism.

No doubt there are many more than just these three changes in our species' circumstance that could be listed here, but this suffices to demonstrate that my thesis has a limited temporal context. The negative position that "there is not and cannot be a moral relationship among states" may already be a museum piece insofar as states and other groups are no longer as able as they once were to operate independently.

I do wish to imply that this new global interdependence has caused cosmopolitan morality to come into practice. Rather, we are between two worlds. There is much retreating to the old group morality—often of a desperate kind. And there is much reaching out to design a new civilization. Quincy Wright puts the present alternatives as follows:

> The sovereignty of the state must be limited by appropriate laws and institutions in the military, political, and economic fields, in order that all peoples may advance in freedom and welfare through international cooperation for the common interest. The alternative appears to be a further isolation of national cultures and economies and a general diminution of human freedom and standards of living.[38]

Wright goes on to say that the chaos that results from extreme claims of sovereignty and ideological intolerance, and the wars that result from this, are incompatible with the progress of civilization in a rapidly shrinking world.[39]

Humans have had varying degrees of success in the past in finding ways of living together, by inventing moral rules of social restraint. I do not think there is any *a priori* reason to believe that we are foredoomed when it comes to the matter of inventing a civilization that requires international morality.

NOTES

Chapter One: Introduction

1. Jack Donnelly, "Human Rights: the Impact of International Activity," *International Journal*, Vol. XLIII, No. 2, Spring 1988, p. 252.

2. Hans J. Morgenthau, *Politics among Nations*, Knopf, New York, 1948, p. 3.

Chapter Two: The Negative Position

1. Raymond Gettell, *History of Political Thought*, Century, New York, 1925, p. 140.

2. Niccolo Machiavelli, *The Prince*, trans. by W.K. Marriott, introduced by Herbert Butterfield, Everyman Library, Dent, London, 1958, Ch. 15, p. 83.

3. *Ibid*, p. 85.

4. Hans Morgenthau, *Dilemmas of Politics*, University of Chicago Press, Chicago, 1958; *In Defense of the National Interest*, Knopf, New York, 1951.

5. Morgenthau, *Dilemmas of Politics*, p. 64.

6. Stanley Hoffman, "An American Social Science: International Relations," *Daedalus*, Vol. 106, No. 3, 1977, p. 44.

7. John C. Garnett, *Commonsense and the Theory of International Politics*, Macmillan, London, 1984, p. 72.

8. George Kennan, *American Diplomacy 1900-1950*, Secker and Warburg, London, 1952, p. 100, and George Kennan, "Morality and Foreign Policy," *Foreign Affairs*, Vol. 64, Winter, 1986, pp. 205-219.

9. Michael Banks, "The Inter-Paradigm Debate" in Margot Light and A.J.R. Groom, eds., *International Relations: A Handbook of Current Theory*, Frances Pinter, London, 1985, p. 13.

10. Stanley Hoffman, *Duties beyond Borders*, Syracuse University Press, Syracuse, New York, 1981, p. 25.

11. Marshall Cohen "Moral Skepticism and International Relations," *Philosophy and Public Affairs*, Vol. 13, No. 4, 1984, p. 300.

12. Charles Beard, *The Idea of National Interest*, Macmillan, New York, 1934.

13. Noam Chomsky and Edward S. Herman, *The Washington Connection and Third World Fascism*, South End Press, Boston, 1979.

14. Stanley Hoffman, *Duties Beyond Borders*, p. 229.

15. R.J. Vincent, "Western Conceptions of a Universal Moral Order," in Ralph Pettman, *Moral Claims in World Affairs*, Australian National University Press, Canberra, 1979, p. 74; Henry Kissinger, *A World Restored*, Baylis, London, 1957, pp. 322-332.

16. Thomas Hobbes, *Leviathan*, George Routledge, London, 1887, Chapter 13.

17. *Ibid*, Chapter 13, page 65.

18. *Ibid*.

19. Andrew Bard Schmookler, *The Parable of the Tribes*, University of California Press, Berkeley, California, 1984, pp. 21-30.

20. Hedley Bull, *The Anarchical Society: A Study of Modern World Politics*, Columbia University Press, New York, 1977, pp. 23-52.

21. Ian Brownlie, "International Law, Human Rights and Indigenous Peoples," Lecture at University of Adelaide, 28 March, 1985.

22. Banks, "Inter-Paradigm Debate," p. 12.

23. Robert O. Keohane and Joseph S. Nye, Jr., *Power and Interdependence: World Politics in Transition*, Little Brown and Co., Boston, 1977, pp. 3-6.

24. Sissela Bok, "Distrust, Secrecy, and the Arms Race," *Ethics*, Vol. 95, No. 3, April 1985, p. 713.

25. *Ibid*. p. 721.

26. David Luban, "The Legacy of Nuremberg," QQ: *Report from the Center for Philosophy and Public Policy*," University of Maryland, College Park, Maryland, Vol. 6, No. 1, Winter, 1986, p. 11.

27. F.H. Hinsley, *Sovereignty*, 2nd edition, Cambridge University Press, Cambridge, 1986, pp. 69-73.

28. *Ibid*, p. 159.

29. *Ibid*, pp. 161-180.

30. Andrew Linklater, "Men and Citizens in International Relations," *Review of International Studies*, Vol. 7, 1981, pp. 27-28.

31. Samuel von Pufendorf, *The Law of Nature and Nations*, Clarendon, Oxford, 1934, p. 1068, quoted in Andrew Linklater, "Rationality and Obligation in the States-system: the Lessons of Pufendorf's Law of Nations," *Millenium: Journal of International Studies*, Vol. 9, No. 3, Winter 1980-81, p. 223.

32. Linklater, "Men and Citizens," p. 27.

33. Leo Kuper, *Genocide: Its Political Rise in the Twentieth Century*, Penguin, London, 1981, p. 183.

34. Maurice Cranston, *What Are Human Rights?*, Bodley Head, London, 1973, p. 81.

35. Kuper, *Genocide*, pp. 164-165, 170-173.

36. Leo Kuper, *The Prevention of Genocide*, Yale University Press, New Haven, Connecticut, 1985, pp. 168-170.

37. Stanley Hoffman, "The Problem of Intervention," in Hedley Bull, ed., *Interventions in World Politics*, Clarendon, Oxford University Press, Oxford, 1984, p. 13.

38. Cohen, "Moral Skepticism," p. 372.

39. Charles Beitz, *Political Theory and International Relations*, Princeton University Press, Princeton, New Jersey, 1979, p. 8.

40. *Ibid*, p. 66.

41. Plato, *Republic*, Introduction by A.D. Lindsay, Dent, London, 1935, Book 2.

42. Jean Jacques Rousseau, *The Social Contract*, translated by Maurice Cranston, Penguin, Harmondsworth, 1968, p. 64.

43. J.W. Gough, *The Social Contract: A Critical Study of Its Development*, 2nd edition, Clarendon Press, Oxford, 1957, p. 169.

44. Rousseau, *Social Contract*, p. 37.

45. Gough, *Social Contract*, p. 170.

46. *Ibid*, p. 169.

47. Quoted in Stanley Hoffman, *Janus and Minerva*, Westview, Boulder, Colorado, 1986, p. 376.

48. Johann Gottfried von Herder, *Reflections on the Philosophy of the History of Mankind*, Introduction by Frank E. Manuel, University of Chicago Press, Chicago, 1968, pp. xxiii-xxiv.

49. Linklater, "Men and Citizens," p. 29.

50. *Ibid*.

51. Heinrich von Treitschke, *Politik Vol. 2*, Max Correlius, Leipzig, 1897, p. 534, quoted in Raymond Aron, *Peace and War: A Theory of International Relations*, translated by Richard Howard and Annette Baker Fox, Weidenfeld and Nicolson, London, 1966, p. 591.

52. Aron, *Peace and War*, p. 586.

53. Ernest Gellner, *Nationalism*, Blackwell, Oxford, 1983, p. 1.

54. *Ibid*, p. 2.

55. *Ibid.*

56. John Dunn, *Western Political Theory in the Face of the Future*, Cambridge University Press, Cambridge, 1979, p. 55.

57. Pierre L. van den Berghe, *The Ethnic Phenomenon*, Greenwood Press, Westport, Connecticut, 1981, p. 27.

58. Dunn, *Western Political Theory*, p. 74.

59. *Ibid.* p. 57.

60. James F. Chidress, "Niebuhr's Realistic Pragmatism," in Richard Harries, ed., *Reinhold Niebuhr and the Issues of Our Time*, Mowbray, London, 1986, p. 124.

61. J.E. Hare and Carey Joynt, *Ethics and International Affairs*, St. Martins, New York, 1982, p. 34; Kenneth Thompson, "Beyond National Interest: A Critical Evaluation of Reinhold Niebuhr's Theory of International Politics," *The Review of Politics*, Vol. 17, No. 2, April, 1955, quoted in Gordon Harland, *The Thought of Reinhold Niebuhr*, Oxford University Press, New York, 1960, p. 192.

62. Reinhold Niebuhr, *Man's Nature and His Communities*, Bles, London, 1966, p. 15.

63. Reinhold Niebuhr, *Moral Man and Immoral Society*, Scribners, New York, 1932, pp. 84-85.

64. *Ibid*, pp. 87-88.

65. *Ibid*, pp. 88.

66. *Ibid.*

67. *Ibid*, p. 91.

68. *Ibid*, p. 93.

69. *Ibid*, p. 107.

70. *Ibid*, p. 108.

71. *Ibid*, p. 104.

72. *Ibid*, p. 105.

73. R.M. Hare, *Freedom and Reason*, Oxford University Press, Oxford, 1963, p. 157.

74. *Ibid*, p. 158.

75. Childress, "Niebuhr's Realistic Pragmatism," p. 124.

76. Garnett, *Commonsense*, p. 141.

77. *Ibid.*

78. Michael Banks, "The Evolution of International Relations Theory," in Michael Banks, ed., *Conflict in World Society*, St. Martins, New York, p. 4.

79. *Ibid.*

80. Adda Bozeman, *The Future of Law in a Multicultural World*, Princeton University Press, Princeton, New Jersey, 1971, p. xv.

81. *Ibid.*

82. Ortego y Gasset, *History as a System and Other Essays Toward a Philosophy of History*, New York, 1941, p. 210, quoted in Bozeman, *Future of Law*, p. xiv.

83. Bozeman, *Future of Law*, p. 162.

84. *Ibid*, p. 6.

85. *Ibid*, p. 38.

86. *Ibid*, pp. 37-38.

87. *Ibid*, pp. 162-163.

88. *Ibid*, pp. 11-12.

89. *Ibid*, p. 25.

90. *Ibid*, p. 29.

91. R.J. Vincent, *Human Rights and International Relations*, Cambridge University Press, Cambridge, 1986, p. 42.

92. Lucian W. Pye, with Mary W. Pye, *Asian Power and Politics*, Harvard University Press, Cambridge, Massachusetts, 1985, p. xi.

93. Hedley Bull, "Human Rights and World Politics" in Pettman, *Moral Claims in World Affairs*, p. 90.

94. Max Stackhouse, *Creeds, Society and Human Rights*, Eerdmans, Grand Rapids, Michigan, 1984, p. 246.

95. James Piscatori "Human Rights in Islamic Political Culture," in Kenneth Thompson, ed., *The Moral Imperatives of Human Rights*, University Press of America, Lanham, Maryland, 1980, p. 143.

96. *Ibid.*

97. *Ibid*, p. 144.

98. The U.N. Universal Declaration of Human Rights, in Ian Brownlie, ed., *Basic Documents on Human Rights*, Clarendon, Oxford, 1971, pp. 106-112.

99. Stanley Hoffman, *Duties Beyond Borders*, p 122.

100. Asmarom Legesse "Human Rights in African Political Culture," in Thompson, *Moral Imperatives of Human Rights*, 124.

101. *Ibid.*

102. *Ibid.*

103. *Ibid*, p. 125.

104. *Ibid*, pp. 125-126.

105. *Ibid*, p. 126.

106. Julius Nyerere, *Uhuru na Ujamaa: Freedom and Socialism*, Oxford University Press, London, 1968, p. 325, quoted in Legese, "Human Rights in African Political Culture," p. 131.

107. Stackhouse, *Creeds, Society and Human Rights*, pp. 277-278.

108. Mark J. Hoffman, "Normative Approaches" in Light and Groom, *International Relations*, p. 31 referring to G. Goodwin in Trevor Taylor, ed., *Approaches and Theory in International Relations*, Longmans, London, 1978.

109. Machiavelli, Niccolo, *The Prince and the Discourses*, Random House, New York, 1950, pp. 64-66, quoted in Ralph Pettman "Moral Claims in World Politics," in Pettman, *Moral Claims in World Affairs*, p. 23.

Chapter Three: The Positive Position

1. Cicero, *De Re Publica, De Legibus*, trans. by Clinton Walker Keyes, Heinemann, London, 1928, The Laws.

2. Aristotle, *Ethics*, trans. by J.A.K. Thomson, Penguin, N.Y., revised ed. 1976, p. 63.

3. Richard Regan, S.J., *The Moral Dimension in Politics*, Oxford University Press, New York, 1986, p. 16.

4. Anthony A. Long, "Ethics of Stoicism," in Philip Wiener, ed., *Dictionary of the History of Ideas: Studies of Selected Pivotal Ideas*, Vol. IV, Charles Scribner's Sons, New York, 1973, p. 319; David E. Hahm, *The Origins of Stoic Cosmology*, Ohio State University Press, Columbus, Ohio, 1977.

5. E. Vernon Arnold, *Roman Stoicism*, Cambridge University Press, Cambridge, 1911, pp. 282-284.

6. Luban, "The Legacy of Nuremberg," p. 10.

7. Roger Scruton, *A Dictionary of Political Thought*, Pan, London, 1982, p. 317.

8. Geoffrey Stern, "Morality and International Order," in Alan James, ed., *The Bases of International Order, Essays in Honour of C.A.W. Manning*, Oxford University Press, London, 1973, p. 140.

9. Richard Falk, "The Grotian Quest," in *The End of World Order: Essays on Normative International Relations*, Holmes and Meier, New York, 1983, pp. 26-27.

10. *Ibid*, p. 38.

11. Martin Wight, "Why Is There No International Theory?" in Herbert Butterfield and Martin Wight, eds., *Diplomatic Investigations*, Allen and Unwin, London, 1966, p. 30.

12. Emmerich de Vattel, *The Law of Nations*, a new edition by Joseph Chitty, Sweet, London, 1834, p. x.

13. Linklater, "Rationality and Obligation," p. 223.

14. Wight, "Why Is There No International Theory?" p. 29.

15. Peter Medawar, *The Future of Man*, Methuen, London, 1960, p. 100.

16. Pettman, "Moral Claims in World Politics," p. 25.

17. Luban, "The Legacy of Nuremberg," p. 10.

18. Richard Falk, *Human Rights and State Sovereignty*, Holmes and Meier, New York, 1981, p. 140.

19. R.J. Vincent, "Western Conceptions of a Universal Moral Order," in Pettman, *Moral Claims in World Affairs*, p. 74.

20. Judith Lichtenberg, "National Boundaries and Moral Boundaries: A Cosmopolitan View," in Peter G. Brown and Henry Shue, eds., *Boundaries: National Autonomy and Its Limits*, Rowman and Littlefield, Totowa, New Jersey, 1981, p. 94.

21. Michael Donelan, "The Community of Mankind," in James Mayall, ed., *The Community of States*, Allen and Unwin, London, 1983, p. 151.

22. T.H. Green, *Prolegomena to Ethics*, Oxford, 1916, p. 237, quoted in Linklater, "Men and Citizens," p. 33.

23. H.B. Acton, *Kant's Moral Philosophy*, St. Martin's, New York, 1970, p. 21.

24. Linklater, "Men and Citizens," p. 31.

25. *Ibid*, p. 33.

26. Donelan, "Community of Mankind," p. 154.

27. Beitz, *Political Theory and International Relations*, pp. 134-135.

28. *Ibid*, p. 128.

29. *Ibid*, pp. 3-4.

30. Henry Shue, *Basic Rights: Subsistence Affluence and U.S. Foreign Policy*, Princeton University Press, Princeton, New Jersey, 1980, p. 17.

31. *Ibid*, p. 112.

32. *Ibid*, pp. 41-46, 61-64.

33. Richard Barnet, "Human Rights Implications of Corporate Food Policies," in Paula Newberg, *The Politics of Human Rights*, New York University Press, New York, 1980, pp. 145, 155.

34. Karl Popper, *The Open Society and Its Enemies, Vol 2: Hegel to Marx.* Routledge and Kegan Paul, London, 1945, pp. 235-237.

35. Michael Sandel, *Liberalism and the Limits of Justice*, Cambridge University Press, Cambridge, 1982, p. 181.

36. Bull, *Anarchical Society*, p. 87.

37. Terry Nardin, *Law, Morality, and the Relations of States*, Princeton University Press, Princeton, New Jersey, 1983, p. 233.

38. Frederick Copleston, S.J., *A History of Philosophy, Vol. VI, Wolff to Kant*, Burns and Oates, London, 1964, pp. 106-109.

39. F.H. Hinsley, *Power and the Pursuit of Peace*, Cambridge University Press, Cambridge, 1963, pp. 46, 72, 86.

40. *Ibid*, pp. 144-146.

41. Bull, *Anarchical Society*, p. 109.

42. Henry Kissinger, *Years of Upheaval*, Little Brown, Boston, 1982, p. 50.

43. *Ibid*.

44. *Ibid*.

45. Bull, *Anarchical Society*, p. 109.

46. *Ibid*, pp. 39-40.

47. *Ibid*, p. 108.

48. *Ibid*, pp. 106-108.

49. W.H. Smith, "Justice: National, International or Global?" in Pettman, *Moral Claims in World Affairs*, p. 111.

50. Evan Luard, *History of the United Nations, Vol. I*, Macmillan, London, 1982, pp. 4-6.

51. Hoffman, *Janus and Minerva*, p. 373.

52. Brian Porter, "Patterns of Thought and Practice: Martin Wight's 'International Theory,'" in Michael Donelan, ed., *The Reason of States*, Allen and Unwin, London, 1978, pp. 64-68.

53. *Ibid*, p. 72.

54. Falk, "Grotian Quest," p. 30.

55. Beitz, *Political Theory and International Relations*, pp. 143-153.

56. Aron, *Peace and War*, p. 734.

57. Hedley Bull, in "The Grotian Conception of International Society," in Butterfield and Wight, *Diplomatic Investigations*, p. 73.

58. James Turner Johnson, *Just War Tradition and the Restraint of War*, Princeton University Press, Princeton, New Jersey, 1981, p. xxix.

59. *Ibid.*

60. *Ibid*, pp. 75-78, 94-103.

61. Hugo Grotius, *The Freedom of the Seas*, translated by Ralph Van Deman Magoffin, edited by James Brown Scott, Oxford University Press, New York, 1916, p. 74.

62. Vattel, *Law of Nations*, pp. 378-379.

63. Hoffman, *Duties Beyond Borders*, p. 46.

64. Charles R. Beitz, Marshall Cohen, Thomas Scanlon and A. John Simmons, eds., *International Ethics: a Philosophy and Public Affairs Reader*, Princeton University Press, Princeton, New Jersey, 1985, Part IV The Moral Status of the Nation-State.

65. For example, Geoffrey Goodwin, ed., *Ethics and Nuclear Deterrence*, Croom Helm, London, 1982; Nigel Blake and Kay Pole, *Dangers of Deterrence: Philosophers on Nuclear Strategy*, Routledge and Kegan Paul, London, 1983; Joseph S. Nye, Jr., *Nuclear Ethics*, Norton, New York, 1986.

66. For example, National Conference of Catholic Bishops, *The Challenge of Peace: God's Promise and Our Response*, United States Catholic Conference, Washington, D.C., 1983; James G. Blight, "Limited Nuclear War? The Unmet Psychological Challenge of the American Catholic Bishops," *Science, Technology, and Human Values*, Vol. 10, Issue 4, 1985, pp. 3-16.

67. Geoffrey Best, "International Humanitarian Law: Principles and Practices," in Goodwin, *Ethics and Nuclear Deterrence*, p. 162.

68. *Ibid.*

69. Richard J. Miller, *The Law of War*, D.C. Heath, Lexington, Massachusetts, 1975, quoted in Best, "International Humanitarian War," 158-159.

70. *Ibid.*

71. John Burton, *International Relations—A General Theory*, Cambridge University Press, Cambridge, 1965, p. 268-269.

72. Hoffman, *Duties beyond Border*, p. 56.

73. Field Marshal Lord Carver, *A Policy for Peace*, Faber and Faber, London, 1982, pp. 101-102, quoted in Nigel Blake and Kay Pole, "Introduction: A Skeptical Look at the Nuclear Debate," in Blake and Pole, *Dangers of Deterrence*, p. 1.

74. Alan James, "Law and Order in International Society," in *Bases of International Order*, p. 80.

75. David P. Forsythe, *Human Rights and World Politics*, University of Nebraska Press, Lincoln, Nebraska, 1983, p. 9.

76. Tom Farer, ed., *Toward a Humanitarian Diplomacy: A Primer for Policy*, New York University Press, New York, 1980.

77. J.E.S. Fawcett, "Human Rights: the Applicability of International Instruments," in F.E. Dowrick, *Human Rights: Problems, Perspectives and Texts*, Saxon House, Westmead, England, 1979, pp. 78-88.

78. Hedley Bull, "Human Rights and World Politics."

79. *Ibid*, p. 87.

80. Kuper, *Prevention of Genocide*, p. 30.

81. "Universal Declaration of the Rights of Peoples," in Richard Falk, Samuel S. Kim, and Saul H. Mendlowitz, *Toward a Just World Order*, Vol I., Westview, Boulder, Colorado, 1982. pp. 432-434.

82. Eugene Kamenka, "Human Rights: People's Rights," *Bulletin of the Australian Society of Legal Philosophy*, Vol. 9, No. 33, June 1985, pp. 148-159.

83. *Ibid*, p. 153.

84. A.J.M. Milne, "The Idea of Human Rights: A Critical Inquiry," in Dowrick, *Human Rights*, p. 30.

85. Shue, *Basic Rights*, pp. 35-64.

86. Jeremy Bentham, quoted in Eugene Kamenka, "The Anatomy of an Idea," in Eugene Kamenka and Alice Ehr-Soon Tay, eds., *Human Rights*, Edward Arnold, Melbourne, 1978, p. 10.

87. Alasdair MacIntyre, *After Virtue*, Duckworth, London, 1981.

88. Vincent, *Human Rights and International Relations*, p. 125.

89. Walter S. Jones, *The Logic of International Relations*, 6th edition, Scott Foresman, Glenview, Illinois, 1988, p. 688.

90. Grenville Clark and Louis Sohn, *World Peace through World Law*, 2nd edition, Harvard University Press, Cambridge, Massachusetts, 1960.

91. Richard Falk, "Contending Approaches to World Order," in Falk, Kim, Mendlowitz, *Just World Order*, p. 161.

92. Ali Mazrui, *A World Federation of Cultures: An African Perspective*, Free Press, New York, 1977.

93. Johan Galtung, *The True Worlds: A Transnational Perspective*, Free Press, New York, 1980.

94. Falk, "Contending Approaches to World Order," p. 147.

95. Robert Johansen, *The National Interest and the Human Interest*, Princeton University Press, Princeton, New Jersey, 1980, p. 24.

96. *Ibid.*

97. Falk, "Contending Approaches," 162.

98. Falk, Kim, Mendlowitz, *Just World Order*, p. 56.

99. Falk, "Contending Approaches," p. 152.

100. *Ibid*, p. 157.

101. *Ibid*, p. 152.

102. *Ibid*, p. 160.

103. *Ibid*, p. 162.

104. Robert Johansen, "The Elusiveness of a Humane World Community," in Falk, Kim, Mendlowitz, *Just World Order*, p. 211.

105. Hoffman, *Duties beyond Borders*, p. 193.

106. Falk, "Contending Approaches," p. 152.

107. *Ibid*, p. 147.

108. *Ibid*, p. 150.

109. Rajni Kothari , "Towards a Just World," *Alternatives, A Journal of World Policy*, Vol. 5, No 1, 1979, reprinted in Falk, Kim and Mendlowitz, *Just World Order*, p. 583.

110. Ajami, "Human Rights and World Order Politics," p. 31.

111. *Ibid.*

112. Cornelia Navari, "Diplomatic Structure and Idiom" in Mayall, *Community of States*, pp. 28-33.

113. Richard Falk, "Why Has the Peace Movement Failed?", Foundation Lecture, University of Adelaide, June 17, 1985.

114. Ernst B. Haas, *The Uniting of Europe: Political, Social, and Economic Forces 1950-1957*, Stanford University Press, Stanford, California, 1958.

115. Chris Brown, "Development and Dependency," *International Relations: A Handbook of Current Theory*, Frances Pinter, London, 1985, pp. 60-73.

116. George Brenkert, *Marx's Ethics of Freedom*, Routledge and Kegan Paul, London, 1983.

Chapter Four: Assessment of the Negative and Positive Positions

1. Donelan, "Community of Mankind," p. 153.

2. G. Bingham Powell, *Contemporary Democracies: Participation, Stability, and Violence*, Harvard University Press, Cambridge, Massachusetts, 1982, pp. 2-7.

3. Gough, *Social Contract*, p. 15.

4. D. Erskine Muir, *Machiavelli and his Times*, Heinemann, London, 1936, p. 105.

5. Charles Edwards, *Hugo Grotius, the Miracle of Holland*, Nelson Hall, Chicago, 1981, p.

6. Charles Hinnant, *Thomas Hobbes*, Twayne, Boston, 1977, p. 22.

7. Stephen P. Turner and Regis A. Factor, *Max Weber and the Dispute Over Reason and Value: a Study in Philosophy, Ethics, and Politics*, Routledge and Kegan Paul, London, 1984, pp. 168-179.

8. Bull, *Anarchical Society*, p. ix.

9. Richard Falk, *The World Order Approach: Issues of Perspective, Academic Discipline and Political Commitment*, Wheatsheaf (in press).

10. Frank Manuel in the Introduction to Herder, *Reflections on Philosophy of History*, p. x.

11. *Ibid*, p. xv.

12. Grotius, *Freedom of the Seas.*

13. Hobbes, *Leviathan*, ch. 13, p. 64.

14. Jean-Jacques Rousseau, "A Discourse on Inequality," in *The Social Contract and Discourses*, translated and introduced by G.D.H. Cole, revised and augmented by J.H. Brumfitt and John C. Hall, Dent, London, 1973, p. 67.

15. Jean-Jacques Rousseau, *A Discourse on Inequality*, translated and with introduction by Maurice Cranston, Penguin, 1984, p. 116.

16. *Ibid*, p. 40.

17. Hoffman, *Duties beyond Borders*, p. 207.

18. K. Holsti, *The Dividing Discipline*, Allen and Unwin, London, 1985, p. 8.

19. Vincent, *Human Rights and International Relations*, p. 124.

20. Garnett, *Commonsense*, p. 86.

21. David Easton, *The Political System: An Inquiry into the State of Political Science*, Knopf, New York, 1953, p. 221, quoted in Garnett, *Commonsense*, p. 135.

Chapter Five: The Biology of Morality

1. E.O. Wilson, *Sociobiology—the Abridged Edition*, Harvard University Press, Cambridge, Massachusetts, 1980, p. 4.

2. See Hiram Caton and Frank K. Salter, *A Bibliography of Biosocial Science*, St. Alban's Press, Brisbane, Australia.

3. David Pilbeam, *The Evolution of Man*, Thames and Hudson, London, 1970, pp. 19-24.

4. Conway Zirkle, "Mendel and his Era," in Roland M. Nardone, ed., *Mendel Centenary: Genetics, Development and Evolution*, Catholic University of America Press, Washington, D.C., 1968, pp. 120-133.

5. David Patterson, "The Causes of Down Syndrome," *Scientific American*, Vol. 257, No. 2, August, 1987, p. 43.

6. James Watson, *The Double Helix*, Weidenfeld & Nicolson, London, 1968.

7. Ernst Mayr and William Provine, *The Evolutionary Synthesis*, Harvard University Press, Cambridge, 1981.

8. Theodosius Dobzhansky, *Genetics and the Origin of Species*, Columbia University Press, New York, 1937.

9. Mary-Claire King and Allan C. Wilson "Evolution at Two Levels in Humans and Chimpanzees," *Science*, Vol. 188, 1975, pp. 107-116.

10. Jane Goodall, *The Chimpanzees of Gombe*, Harvard University Press, Cambridge, Massachusetts, 1986.

11. Hamilton, "Genetical Theory of Social Behaviour," I, II, *Journal of Theoretical Biology*, Vol. 7, 1964, pp. 1-6 and 17-52.

12. Wilson, *Sociobiology—the Abridged Edition*, pp. 220-301.

13. *Ibid*, p. 152.

14. J.B.S. Haldane, "Population Genetics," *New Biology*, Vol. 18, 1955, pp. 33-34.

15. Hamilton, "Genetical Theory of Social Behaviour," p. 8.

16. Wilson, *Sociobiology—the Abridged Edition*, p. 179.

17. *Ibid*, p. 246.

18. John Maynard Smith, "Group Selection and Kin Selection," *Nature*, Vol. 201, 1964, pp. 1145-1147.

19. Richard Dawkins, *The Selfish Gene*, Oxford University Press, Oxford, 1976.

20. Richard Alexander, *The Biology of Moral Systems*, Aldine de Gruyter, Hawthorne, New York, 1987, pp.33-63; George G. Williams, "Pleiotropy, Natural Selection, and the Evolution of Senescence," *Evolution*, Vol. 11, 1957, pp. 398-411.

21. Wilson, *Sociobiology—the Abridged Edition*, pp. 247-250.

22. John Hurrell Crook, "The Sociobiology of Primates" in S.L. Washburn and Phyllis Dolhinow, *Perspectives on Human Evolution*, Holt, Rinehart and Winston, New York, 1972, pp.281-347.

23. George C. Williams, *Adaptation and Natural Selection*, Princeton University Press, Princeton, 1966, p. 94; Robert Trivers, "The Evolution of Reciprocal Altruism," *Quarterly Review of Biology*, Vol. 46, No. 4, 1971, pp. 35-57.

24. Frans De Waal, *Chimpanzee Politics*, Harper and Row, New York, 1982.

25. Richard C. Connor and Kenneth S. Norris, "Are Dolphins and Whales Reciprocal Altruists?" *American Naturalist*, Vol. 119, 1982, pp. 358-374.

26. Gerald Wilkinson, "Reciprocal Food Sharing in the Vampire Bat," *Nature*, Vol. 308, 1984, pp. 181-184, cited in Robert Trivers, *Social Evolution*, Benjamin/Cummings, Menlo Park, California, 1985, pp. 363-366.

27. Trivers, *Social Evolution*, "Chapter 4—the Group Selection Fallacy," pp. 67-85.

28. Wilkinson, "Vampire Bat," cited in Trivers, *Social Evolution*, pp. 365-366.

29. David Pilbeam, *The Ascent of Man*, Macmillan, New York, 1972, pp. 15-48; David Pilbeam, "Patterns of Hominoid Evolution," in Eric Delson, ed., *Ancestors: The Hard Evidence*, Alan Liss, New York, 1985, pp. 51-59.

30. John Gribbin and Jeremy Cherfas, *The Monkey Puzzle: Reshaping the Evolutionary Tree*, Pantheon, New York, 1982, pp. 29 and 247-258; see also Maitland A. Edy and editors of Time-Life Books, *The Missing Link*, Time Inc., New York, 1972, Chapter 7.

31. Donald Johanson and Maitland A. Edey, *Lucy: The Beginnings of Humankind*, Simon and Schuster, New York, 1981.

32. Mary Leakey, "Footprints in the Ashes of Time," *National Geographic*, Vol. 155, April, 1979.

33. Graham Richards, *Human Evolutions*, Routledge and Kegan Paul, London, 1987.

34. Delson, *Ancestors*, Section V, pp. 202-264.

35. Glynn Isaac, "The Food Sharing Behavior of Protohuman Hominids," in Glynn Isaac and Richard Leakey, eds., *Human Ancestors: Readings from Scientific American*, W.H. Freeman, San Francisco, 1979.

36. John Reader, *Missing Links*, Collins, London, 1981, p. 145.

37. Erik Trinkhaus and William W. Howells, "The Neanderthals," *Scientific American*, Vol. 241, No 6, 1979, pp. 94-105.

38. George Constable and the editors of Time-Life Books, *The Neanderthals*, Time, Inc., New York, 1972, p. 101.

39. Trivers, *Social Evolution*, pp. 386-389.

40. Carroll Izard "Emotions as Motivations: An Evolutionary-Developmental Perspective," in *Nebraska Symposium on Motivation*, Vol. 26, 1978, pp. 163-200.

41. Trivers, *Social Evolution*, p. 388.

42. De Waal, *Chimpanzee Politics*, p. 207.

43. Alexander, *Biology of Moral Systems*, p. 153.

44. Richard Alexander, "Biology and the Moral Paradoxes," *Journal of Social and Biological Structures*, Vol. 5, 1982, p. 390.

45. *Ibid.*

46. *Ibid*, p. 394.

47. Alexander, *Biology of Moral Systems*, p. 107.

48. *Ibid*, p. 102.

49. *Ibid*, p. 186.

50. *Ibid*, p. 102.

51. Jane Goodall, "Order Without Law," *Journal of Social and Biological Structures*, Vol. 5, 1982, pp. 353-360.

52. Charles Lumsden and E.O. Wilson, *Genes, Mind and Culture: the Coevolutionary Process*, Harvard University Press, Cambridge, Massachusetts, 1981, p. 202.

53. Charles Darwin, *The Descent of Man and Selection in Relation to Sex*, John Murray, London, new edition, 1901, p. 157.

54. Jane Goodall, *In the Shadow of Man*, Collins, London, 1971, p. 199-204; of Vernon Reynolds, *The Apes*, Cassell, London, 1967, p. 192.

55. William Ernest Hocking, *Human Nature and its Remaking*, Yale University Press, New Haven, 1918, p. 97.

56. *Ibid.*

57. *Ibid.*

58. George Edgin Pugh, *The Biological Origin of Human Values*, Routledge and Kegan Paul, London, 1978, p. 29-35.

59. E.O. Wilson, *On Human Nature*, Harvard University Press, Cambridge, Massachusetts, 1978, pp. 64-67.

60. Lumsden and Wilson, *Genes, Mind and Culture*, pp. 16-21, 251-253.

61. Peter Singer, "Ethics and Sociobiology," *Zygon: Journal of Religion and Science*, Vol. 19, 1984, p. 145.

62. Wilson, *On Human Nature*.

63. Richard Alexander and Donald W. Tinkle, "A Comparative Review," *Bioscience*, Vol. 18, 1968, p. 246.

64. Michael Ruse and E.O. Wilson, "Moral Philosophy as Applied Science," *Philosophy*, Vol. 61, 1986, p. 174.

65. *Ibid.*

Chapter Six: The Evolution of Intergroup Behavior

1. John Hurrell Crook, "The Sociobiology of Primates," pp. 281-347.

2. Irvin De Vore and K.R.L. Hall, "Baboon Ecology," in Irvin De Vore, ed., *Primate Behavior: Field Studies of Monkeys and Apes*, Holt, Rinehart and Winston, New York, 1965, p. 49.

3. Van Den Berghe, *Ethnic Phenomenon*, p. xi.

4. *Ibid*, p. 33.

5. *Ibid*, p. 140.

6. *Ibid.*

7. Gary R. Johnson, Susan H. Ratwik, and Timothy J. Sawyer, "The Evocative Significance of Kin Terms in Patriotic Speech," in Vernon Reynolds, Vincent Falger, and Ian Vine, eds., *The Sociobiology of Ethnocentrism: Evolutionary Dimensions of Xenophobia, Discrimination, Racism and Nationalism*, Croom Helm, London, 1987, p. 157.

8. *Ibid*, p. 158.

9. *Ibid*, p. 159.

10. Darwin, *Descent of Man*, p. 199.

11. Arthur Keith, *A New Theory of Human Evolution*, Watts, London, 1948.

12. Alexander and Tinkle, "A Comparative Review," pp. 245-248.

13. Robert S. Bigelow, *The Dawn Warriors: Man's Evolution towards Peace*, Little Brown, Boston, 1969.

14. Phillip V. Tobias, "The Evolution of the Human Brain, Intellect and Spirit," 1st Abbie Memorial Lecture, University of Adelaide, 12 October, 1979, p. 25.

15. Williams, *Adaptation and Natural Selection*, p. 14.

16. Robert Bigelow, "The Evolution of Cooperation, Aggression and Self-Control," *Nebraska Symposium on Motivation*, Vol. 20, 1972, pp. 3-5.

17. Alexander and Tinkle, p. 247.

18. *Ibid.*

19. *Ibid.*

20. Richard Alexander, *Darwinism and Human Affairs*, University of Washington Press, Seattle, Washington, 1979, p. 223.

21. Robert Carneiro, "A Theory of the Origin of the State," *Science*, Vol 169, pp. 733-738.

22. Bigelow, "Evolution of Cooperation," pp. 1-12.

23. *Ibid*, p. 8.

24. Robert Bigelow, "The Role of Competition and Cooperation in Human Evolution," in M.A. Nettleship, R.D. Givens, and A. Nettleship, eds., *War, Its Causes and Correlates*, Mouton, The Hague, 1975, p. 239.

25. *Ibid.*

26. Alexander, *Darwinism and Human Affairs*, p. 228.

27. Bigelow, "Role of Competition," p. 237.

28. Marilyn Keyes Roper, "A survey of the evidence for intrahuman killing in the Pleistocene," *Current Anthropology*, Vol. 10, 1969, pp. 427-459.

29. *Ibid*, pp. 450-459.

30. Johan M.G. van der Dennen, "The Ethnological Inventory Project: an antidote against some fallacious notions in the study of primitive war," paper delivered at the European Sociobiology Society Conference on the Sociobiology of Conflict, Tel Aviv, January 10-11, 1987.

31. *Ibid.*, p. 10.

32. *Ibid.*

33. Bigelow, "Evolution of Cooperation," pp. 7-8.

34. Alexander, *Darwinism and Human Affairs*, p. 227.

35. *Ibid.*

36. *Ibid*, p. 228.

37. *Ibid.*

38. *Ibid*, pp. 229-230.

39. Bigelow, "Evolution of Cooperation," p. 10.

40. David Sloan Wilson, "The Group Selection Controversy," *Annual Review of Ecology and Systematics*, Vol. 14, 1983, p. 159.

41. Elliott Sober, *The Nature of Selection: Evolutionary Theory in Philosophical Focus*, M.I.T. Press, Cambridge, Massachusetts, 1984, p. 226.

42. Vincent C. Wynne-Edwards, *Animal Dispersion in Relation to Social Behavior*, Oliver and Boyd, Edinburgh, 1962, pp. 18-19.

43. Williams, *Adaptation and Natural Selection*, p. 16.

44. Wilson, *Sociobiology—The Abridged Edition*, p. 54.

45. Wilson, "Group Selection Controversy," pp. 180-187.

46. Wilson, *Sociobiology—The Abridged Edition*, p 51.

47. John Maynard Smith, "Group Selection," *Quarterly Review of Biology*, Vol. 51, 1976, p. 279.

48. *Ibid*, p. 278, 279.

49. *Ibid*, p. 279.

50. Wilson, *Sociobiology—The Abridged Edition*, pp. 298-299.

51. *Ibid*, p. 299.

52. Richard D. Alexander and Gerald Borgia, "Group Selection, Altruism, and the Levels of Organization of Life," *Annual Review of Ecology and Systematics*, Vol. 9, 1978, p. 470.

53. *Ibid.*

54. *Ibid.*

55. Wilson, *Sociobiology—The Abridged Edition*, p. 298.

56. Reynolds, Falger, and Vine, *Sociobiology of Ethnocentrism*.

57. Herbert Spencer, *The Principles of Ethics, Vol 1*, Williams and Norgate, London, 1892, p. 322, quoted in Umberto Melotti, "In-group/Out-group relations and the Issue of Group Selection," in Reynolds, Falger and Vine, *Sociobiology of Ethnocentrism*, p. 97.

58. Johan van der Dennen, "Ethnocentrism and In-group/Out-group Differentiation: A Review and Interpretation of the Literature," in Reynolds, Falger and Vine, *Sociobiology of Ethnocentrism*, pp. 1-47.

59. Irenàus Eibl-Eibesfeldt, *The Biology of Peace and War: Men, Animals and Aggression*, Thames and Hudson, 1979, p. 106.

60. Van der Dennen, "Ethnocentrism," p. 20.

61. *Ibid*, p. 18.

62. Goodall, *In the Shadow of Man*, pp. 199-204.

63. Muzafer Sherif, "Experiments in Group Conflict," *Scientific American*, Vol. 196, 1956, pp. 54-58.

64. P.G. Zimbardo, ed., *The Cognitive Control of Aggression*, Scott and Foresman, Glencoe, Illinois, 1969, cited in Van der Dennen, "Ethnocentrism," p. 29.

65. *Ibid*.

66. R.I. Watson, "Investigation into Deindividuation Using a Cross-cultural Survey Technique," *Journal of Personality and Social Psychology*, Vol 25, No. 3, 1973, pp. 343-345, cited in Van der Dennen, "Ethnocentrism," pp. 29-30.

67. Erik Erikson, *Childhood and Society*, Norton, New York, revised edition, 1964, cited in Van der Dennen, "Ethnocentrism," p. 41.

68. Van der Dennen, "Ethnocentrism," p. 39.

69. Heiner Flohr, "Biological Bases of Social Prejudices" in Reynolds, Falger and Vine, *Sociobiology of Ethnocentrism*, p. 194.

70. *Ibid*.

71. Ian Vine, "Inclusive Fitness and the Self System. The Roles of Human Nature and Sociocultural Processes in Intergroup Discrimination," in Reynolds, Falger, and Vine, *Sociobiology of Ethnocentrism*, p. 62.

72. *Ibid*.

73. W.A. Elliott, *Us and Them*, University of Aberdeen Press, Aberdeen, 1986, pp.81-83.

74. *Ibid*, p. 79.

75. Keith, *New Theory of Human Evolution*, p. 115; pp. 122-123.

76. *Ibid*, p. 63.

Chapter Seven: Cautions Regarding the Use of Sociobiology

1. Arthur Caplan, *The Sociobiology Debate*, Harper and Row, New York, 1978.

2. Niko Tinbergen, "On War and Peace in Animals and Man," *Science*, Vol. 160, June 28, 1968, pp. 1411-1418, reprinted in Caplan, *Sociobiology Debate*, p. 87.

3. Quoted in Marshall Sahlins, *The Use and Abuse of Biology*, University of Michigan Press, Ann Arbor, Michigan, 1976, p. 103.

4. Abraham Edel, "Attempts to Derive Definitive Moral Patterns From Biology," in *Ethical Judgment: the Use of Science in Ethics*, Macmillan, New York, 1955, pp. 115-121, reprinted in Caplan, *Sociobiology Debate*, p. 111-112.

5. Thomas H. Huxley, *Evolution and Ethics*, Appleton, New York, 1894, pp. 23-45, reprinted in Caplan, *Sociobiology Debate*, pp. 27-34.

6. Peter Kropotkin, *Mutual Aid: A Factor in Evolution*, McClure Phillips, New York, 1903.

7. Eduard Bernstein, "Ein Schüler Darwin's als Vertheidiger des Socialismus," *Die Nue Zeit*, 1890-1891, Vol. 9, pp. 171-177, cited in Robert J. Richards, "A Defense of Evolutionary Ethics," *Biology and Philosophy*, Vol. 1, 1986, p. 267.

8. Science for the People, "Sociobiology—Another Determinism," in Caplan, *Sociobiology Debate*, pp. 280-290.

9. Wilson, *Sociobiology—The Abridged Edition*, p. 3.

10. *Ibid.*, p. 4.

Chapter Eight: Critique of the Traditional Arguments

1. Hans J. Morgenthau and Kenneth Thompson, *Politics among Nations*, 6th edition, Knopf, New York, 1985, p. 12.

2. Martin Wight, "Why Is There No International Theory?" p. 26.

3. *Ibid*, p. 17.

4. *Ibid*, p. 20-21.

5. *Ibid*, p. 26.

6. *Ibid*, p. 33.

7. *Ibid.*

8. *Ibid.*

Chapter Nine: International Morality and Its Obstacles

1. Cohen, "Moral Skepticism and International Relations," p. 309.

2. Aron, *Peace and War*, p. 609.

3. Kennan, "Morality and Foreign Policy," p. 216.

4. *Ibid.*

5. *Ibid*, p. 217.

6. *Ibid.*

7. Kuper, *Prevention of Genocide*, p. 160.

8. "Kissinger's Personal Instructions," *New Statesman*, November 21, 1980, pp. 6-7.

9. Edward Herman, *The Real Terror Network*, South End Press, Boston, 1982, pp. 141-145.

10. E.F. Carritt, *Ethical and Political Thinking*, Clarendon, Oxford, 1947, p. 143.

11. J.D.B. Miller, "Morality, Interests and Rationalisation," in Pettman, *Moral Claims in World Affairs*, p. 45.

12. *Ibid.*

13. Darwin, *Descent of Man*, p. 194.

14. Peter Singer, *The Expanding Circle: Ethics and Sociobiology*, Farrar, Straus and Giroux, New York, 1981, p. 93.

15. Popper, *Open Society*, Vol. II, p. 235.

16. *Ibid*, p. 240.

17. James S. Fishkin, *The Limits of Obligation*, Yale University Press, New Haven, Connecticut, 1982, p. 7.

18. *Ibid*, p. 171.

19. Peter Singer, "Famine, Affluence and Morality," *Philosophy and Public Affairs*, Vol. 1, 1972, reprinted in Beitz et al., *International Ethics*, p. 259.

20. Shue, *Basic Rights*.

21. Tom Barry, Beth Wood and Deb Preusch, *Dollars and Dictators: A Guide to Central America*, the Resource Center, Albuquerque, New Mexico, 1983; Susan George, *How the Other Half Dies*, Penguin, New York, 1976; Chomsky and Herman, *The Washington Connection*.

22. Donelan, "The Community of Mankind," p. 141.

23. Amnesty International, *Political Killings by Governments*, 10 Southampton Street, London, 1983, p. 33.

24. *Ibid*, p. 27.

25. Hoffman, *Janus and Minerva*, p. 376.

26. Hannah Arendt, *Eichmann in Jerusalem: A Report on the Banality of Evil*, Viking, New York, 1964.

27. Bhikhu Parekh and R.N. Berki, eds., *The Morality of Politics*, Allen and Unwin, London, 1972, p. 7.

28. *Ibid*, p. 8.

29. Thomas Nagel, "Ruthlessness in Public Life," in Stuart Hampshire, ed., *Public and Private Morality*, Cambridge University Press, Cambridge, 1978, p. 75.

30. Morton Mintz, *At Any Cost: Corporate Greed, Women, and the Dalkon Shield*, Pantheon, New York, 1985, quoted in Robin Henig, "Corporate Conscience and the Bottom Line," *Guardian Weekly*, December 29, 1985, p. 13.

31. Lionel Tiger, *The Manufacture of Evil*, Harper and Row, New York, 1987, p. 5.

32. *Ibid*.

33. Parekh and Berki, *Morality of Politics*, p. 7.

34. Hare and Joynt, *Ethics and International Affairs*, p. 47.

35. E.H. Carr, *The Twenty Years' Crisis: 1919-1939*, Macmillan, London, 1966, p. 236.

36. Barry, Wood, and Preusch, *Dollars and Dictators*, p. 122.

37. J.N. Figgis, *From Gerson to Grotius*, Cambridge, 1923, pp. 74-77, quoted in Miller, "Morality, Interests and Rationalisation," p. 40.

38. *Ibid*.

39. Hans Morgenthau, *In Defense of the National Interest*, Knopf, New York, 1952, p. 242.

40. Michael Joseph Smith, *Realist Thought from Weber to Kissinger*, Louisiana State University Press, Baton Rouge, Louisiana, 1986, p. 235.

41. Joseph S. Nye, Jr., "Ethics and Foreign Policy," An Occasional Paper/Aspen Institute for Humanistic Studies, Wye Plantation, Queenstown, Maryland, p. 2.

42. *Ibid*.

43. *Ibid*.

44. *Ibid*, p. 6.

45. *Ibid*.

46. Michael Walzer, *Just and Unjust Wars*, Basic Books, New York, 1977, p. 12.

Chapter 10: An Afterword concerning Context

1. Walter S. Jones, *The Logic of International Relations*, 6th edition, Scott Foresman, Glenview, Illinois, 1988, pp. 263-264.

2. Garnett, *Commonsense and the Theory of International Relations*, p. 110.

3. Smith, *Realism from Weber to Kissinger*, p. 221, referring to Robert O. Keohane, "Theory of World Politics: Structural Realism and Beyond," in Ada K. Finifter, ed., *Political Science: the State of the Discipline*, American Political Science Association, Washington D.C., 1984.

4. James E. Dougherty and Robert L. Pfaltzgraff, Jr., *Contending Theories of International Relations*, Harper and Row, New York, 1981, pp. 6-7.

5. Garnett, *Commonsense and the Theory of International Relations*, p. 37.

6. John Spanier, *Games Nations Play*, 3rd. edition, Holt, Rinehart and Winston/Praeger, New York, 1978, p. viii.

7. Smith, *Realism from Weber to Kissinger*, p. 224.

8. *Ibid.*

9. Dougherty and Pfaltzgraff, *Contending Theories in International Relations*, p. 14.

10. Keohane and Nye, *Power and Interdependence*.

11. Raymond Vernon, *Sovereignty at Bay*, Basic Books, New York, 1971.

12. Richard Barnet and Ronald Muller, *Global Reach*, Simon and Schuster, New York, 1974.

13. Spanier, *Games Nations Play*, p. 356.

14. Morgenthau, *Politics among Nations*, p. 15.

15. John Vasquez, *The Power of Power Politics*, Pinter, London, 1983, p. 50.

16. *Ibid.*

17. Arnold Wolfers, "National Security as an Ambiguous Symbol," *Political Science Quarterly*, No. 67, 1952, pp. 481-502, quoted in Vasquez, *Power of Power Politics*, p. 51.

18. Werner J. Feld, *International Relations: A Transnational Approach*, Alfred, Sherman Oaks, California, 1979, p. 13.

19. Chadwick F. Alger, "International Relations: the Field," in David L. Sills, ed., *International Encyclopaedia of the Social Sciences*, Vols. 7 and 8, Macmillan Co. and the Free Press, New York, 1968, p. 62.

20. *Ibid.*

21. Smith, *Realism from Weber to Kissinger*, p. 222.

22. Spanier, *Games Nations Play*, p. 66.

23. Henry Kissinger, quoted in Smith, *Realism from Weber to Kissinger*, p. 225.

24. Spanier, *Games Nations Play*, p. 289.

25. William D. Coplin, *Introduction to International Politics*, 3rd. edition, Prentice Hall, Englewood Cliffs, New Jersey, 1980, p. 3.

26. Hans Morgenthau, *The Decline of Democratic Politics*, University of Chicago Press, Chicago, 1962, p. 121, quoted in Smith, *Realism from Weber to Kissinger*, p. 219.

27. Garnett, *Commonsense and the Theory of International Relations*, p. 90.

28. Dougherty and Pfaltzgraff, *Contending Theories in International Relations*, p. 35.

29. Michael Ruse, *Taking Darwin Seriously*, Blackwell, London, 1986.

30. Camilo Cela-Conde, *On Gods, Genes, and Tyrants: the Biological Causation of Morality*, Kluwer, Hingham, Massachussetts, 1987.

31. Robert Richards, "A Defense of Evolutionary Ethics," *Biology and Philosophy*, 1986, Vol. 1, pp. 265-293.

32. David Barash, *The Hare and the Tortoise: Culture, Biology, and Human Nature*, Penguin, London, 1986.

33. Lionel Tiger, *The Manufacture of Evil*, Harper and Row, New York, 1987.

34. E.O. Wilson, *On Human Nature*, Harvard University Press, Cambridge, Massachusetts, 1978.

35. Mary Maxwell, *Human Evolution: A Philosophical Anthropology*, Columbia University Press, New York and Croom Helm, London, 1984.

36. C. Scott Findlay and Charles J. Lumsden, "Evolutionary Ethics and the Evolution of Moral Behavior," (unpublished).

37. Jones, *The Logic of International Relations*, p. 670.

38. Quincy Wright, "International Law," *Encyclopedia Americana, International Edition*, Vol. 15, Grolier, Danbury, Connecticut, 1981, p. 310.

39. *Ibid.*

SELECTED BIBLIOGRAPHY

Ajami, Fouad, "Human Rights and World Order Politics," *Working Paper Number 4. World Order Models Project.* Institute for World Order, New York, 1978.

Alexander, Richard, *Darwinism and Human Affairs*, University of Washington Press, Seattle, Washington, 1979.

Alexander, Richard, *The Biology of Moral Systems*, Aldine de Gruyter, Hawthorne, New York, 1987.

Alexander, Richard, and Donald W. Tinkle, "A Comparative Review," *Bioscience*, Vol. 18, 1968, pp. 245-247.

Alger, Chadwick, "International Relations: the Field," in David L. Sills, ed., *International Encyclopedia of the Social Sciences*, Vols. 7 and 8, Macmillan and Co. and the Free Press, New York, 1968, pp. 60-69.

Aron, Raymond, *Peace and War: A Theory of International Relations*, translated by Richard Howard and Annette Baker Fox, Weidenfeld and Nicolson, London, 1966.

Ashley, Richard K. "The Poverty of Neo-Realism," *International Organization*, Vol. 38, 1984, pp. 225-286.

Banks, Michael, "The Inter-Paradigm Debate," in Margot Light and A.J.R. Groom, eds., *International Relations: A Handbook of Current Theory*, Frances Pinter, London, 1985.

Banks, Michael, "The Evolution of International Relations Theory," in Michael Banks, ed., *Conflict in World Society*, St. Martin's, New York, 1985.

Barash, David, *The Hare and the Tortoise: Culture, Biology, and Human Nature*, Penguin, London, 1986.

Barnet, Richard, "Human Rights Implications of Corporate Food Policies," in Paula Newberg, ed., *The Politics of Human Rights*, New York University Press, New York, 1980.

Barry, Tom, Beth Wood, and Deb Preusch, *Dollars and Dictators: A Guide to Central America*, the Resource Center, Albuquerque, New Mexico, 1983.

Beitz, Charles, *Political Theory and International Relations*, Princeton University Press, Princeton, New Jersey, 1979.

Beitz, Charles, Marshall Cohen, Thomas Scanlon, and A. John Simmons, eds., *International Ethics; a Philosophy and Public Affairs Reader*, Princeton University Press, Princeton, New Jersey, 1985.

Best, Geoffrey, "International Humanitarian Law: Principles and Practices," in Geoffrey Goodwin, ed., *Ethics and Nuclear Deterrence*, Croom Helm, London, 1982.

Bigelow, Robert, "The Evolution of Cooperation, Aggression and Self-Control," *Nebraska Symposium on Motivation*, Vol. 20, 1972, pp. 1-57.

Blight, James G. "Limited Nuclear War? The Unmet Psychological Challenge of the American Catholic Bishops," *Science, Technology, and Human Values*, Vol. 10, Issue 4, 1985, pp. 3-16.

Bok, Sissela, *A Strategy for Peace: Human Values and The Threat of War*, Pantheon, New York, 1989.

Bok, Sissela, "Distrust, Secrecy, and the Arms Race," *Ethics*, Vol. 95, April 1985, pp. 712-727.

Bozeman, Adda, *The Future of Law in a Multicultural World*, Princeton University Press, Princeton, New Jersey, 1971.

Brenkert, George, *Marx's Ethics of Freedom*, Routledge and Kegan Paul, London, 1983.

Brown, Chris, "Development and Dependency," in Margot Light and A.J.R. Groom, eds., *International Relations: a Handbook of Current Theory*, Frances Pinter, London, 1985.

Brown, Lester, *World without Borders*, Random House, New York, 1972.

Brown, Peter G. and Henry Shue, eds., *Boundaries: National Autonomy and its Limits*, Rowman and Littlefield, Totowa, New Jersey, 1981.

Brownlie, Ian, "International Law, Human Rights and Indigenous Peoples," Lecture at University of Adelaide, 28 March, 1985.

Brownlie, Ian, ed., *Basic Documents on Human Rights*, Clarendon, Oxford, 1971.

Bull, Hedley, *The Anarchical Society; A Study of Modern World Politics*, Columbia University Press, New York, 1977.

Bull, Hedley "The State's Positive Role in World Affairs," *Daedalus*, Vol. 108, 1979, pp. 111-123.

Bull, Hedley, ed., *Interventions in World Politics*, Clarendon Press, Oxford, 1984.

Bull, Hedley, and Adam Watson, eds., *The Expansion of International Society*, Clarendon, Oxford, 1984.

Butterfield, Herbert, and Martin Wight, eds., *Diplomatic Investigations*, Allen and Unwin, London, 1966.

Caplan, Arthur, ed., *The Sociobiology Debate*, Harper and Row, New York, 1978.

Carneiro, Robert, "A theory of the origin of the state," *Science*, Vol. 169, 1970, pp. 733-738.

Carr, E.H., *The Twenty Years' Crisis: 1919-1939*, Macmillan, London, 1966.

Caton, Hiram, and Frank K. Salter, *A Bibliography of Biosocial Science*, 2nd edition, St. Albans Press, Brisbane, Australia, 1988.

Cela-Conde, Camilo, *On Genes, Gods and Tyrants: The Biological Causation of Morality*, Kluwer, Hingham, Massachusetts, 1987.

Childress, James F., "Niebuhr's Realistic Pragmatism," in Richard Harries, ed., *Reinhold Niebuhr and the Issues of Our Time*, Mowbray, London, 1986.

Chomsky, Noam, and Edward S. Herman, *The Washington Connection and Third World Fascism*, South End Press, Boston, 1979.

Cohen, Marshall, "Moral Skepticism and International Relations," *Philosophy aand Public Affairs*, Vol. 13, 1984, pp. 299-346.

Connor, Richard C., and Kenneth S. Norris, "Are Dolphins and Whales Reciprocal Altruists?", *American Naturalist*, Vol. 119, 1982, pp. 358-374.

Constable, George, and the editors of Time-Life Books, *The Neanderthals*, Time, Inc., New York, 1972.

Copleston, Frederick S.J., *A History of Philosophy, Vol. VI: Wolff to Kant*, Burns and Oates, London, 1964.

Crawford, J.R., guest editor, "Special Issue: The Rights of Peoples," *Bulletin of the Australian Society of Legal Philosophy*, Vol. 9, June, 1985.

Darwin, Charles, *The Descent of Man and Selection in Relation to Sex*, John Murray, London, new edition, 1901.

Dawkins, Richard, *The Selfish Gene*, Oxford University Press, Oxford, 1976.

Delson, Eric, ed., *Ancestors; The Hard Evidence*, Alan Liss, New York, 1985.

Deutsch, Karl, *Nationalism and Social Communication*, M.I.T. Press, Cambridge, Massachusetts, 1953.

De Waal, Frans, *Chimpanzee Politics*, Harper and Row, New York, 1982.

Donelan, Michael, "The Community of Mankind," in James Mayall, ed., *The Community of States*, Allen and Unwin, London, 1983.

Donelan, Michael, ed., *The Reason of States*, Allen and Unwin, London, 1978.

Donnelly, Jack, *The Concept of Human Rights*, Croom Helm, London, 1985.

Donnelly, Jack, "Human Rights: the Impact of International Activity," *International Journal*, Vol. XLIII, No. 2, Spring, 1988.

Dougherty, James E. and Robert L. Pfaltzgraff, Jr., *Contending Theories of International Relations*, Harper and Row, New York, 1981.

Dowrick, F.E., ed., *Human Rights: Problems, Perspectives and Texts*, Saxon House, Westmead, England, 1979.

Dunn, John, *Western Political Theory in the Face of the Future*, Cambridge University Press, Cambridge, 1979.

Edwards, Charles, *Hugo Grotius, the Miracle of Holland*, Nelson Hall, Chicago, 1981.

Ellis, Anthony, ed., *Ethics and International Relations*, Manchester University Press, Manchester, 1986.

Falger, V.S.E., "Sociobiology and Political Ideology: Comments on the Radical Point of View," *Journal of Human Evolution*, Vol. 13, 1984, pp. 129-135.

Falk, Richard, *Human Rights and State Sovereignty*, Holmes and Meier, New York, 1981.

Falk, Richard, "The Grotian Quest," in *The End of World Order: Essays on Normative International Relations*, Holmes and Meier, New York, 1983.

Falk, Richard, "Lifting the Curse of Bipartisanship," *World Policy Journal*, Vol. 1, 1983, pp. 127-157.

Falk, Richard, Samuel S. Kim, and Saul H. Mendlowitz, *Toward a Just World Order*, Vol. I, Westview, Boulder, Colorado, 1982.

Farer, Tom, ed., *Toward a Humanitarian Diplomacy: A Primer for Policy*, New York University Press, New York, 1980.

Fetzer, James, ed., *Sociobiology and Epistemology*, Reidel, Dordrecht, Netherlands, 1985.

Forsythe, David P., *Human Rights and World Politics*, University of Nebraska Press, Lincoln, Nebraska, 1983.

Garnett, John C., *Commonsense and the Theory of International Politics*, Macmillan, London, 1984.

Gellner, Ernest, *Nationalism*, Blackwell, Oxford, 1983.

Gilpin, Robert, "The Richness of the Tradition of Political Realism," *International Organization*, Vol. 38, 1984, pp. 287-305.

Goodwin, Geoffrey, ed., *Ethics and Nuclear Deterrence*, Croom Helm, London, 1982.

Hamilton, William D. "Genetical Theory of Social Behaviour," I, II, *Journal of Theoretical Biology*, Vol. 7, 1964, pp. 1-16 and 17-52.

Hare, J.E., and Carey Joynt, *Ethics and International Affairs*, St. Martin's, New York, 1982.

Herman, Edward, *The Real Terror Network*, South End Press, Boston, 1982.

Hinsley, F.H., *Power and the Pursuit of Peace*, Cambridge University Press, Cambridge, 1963.

Hinsley, F.H., *Sovereignty*, 2nd edition, Cambridge University Press, Cambridge, 1986.

Hobbes, Thomas, *Leviathan*, George Routledge, London, 1887.

Hocking, William Ernest, *Human Nature and its Remaking*, Yale University Press, New Haven, 1918.

Hoffman, Mark J., "Normative Approaches," in Margot Light and A.J.R. Groom, eds., *International Relations: A Handbook of Current Theory*, Frances Pinter, London, 1985.

Hoffman, Stanley, "An American Social Science: International Relations," *Daedalus*, Vol. 106, 1977, pp. 41-60.

Hoffman, Stanley, *Duties beyond Borders*, Syracuse University Press, Syracuse, New York, 1981.

Hoffman, Stanley, *Janus and Minerva*, Westview, Boulder, Colorado, 1986.

Holsti, K., *The Dividing Discipline*, Allen and Unwin, London, 1985.

Howard, Michael, *The Causes of War and Other Essays*, Temple Smith, London, 1983.

Huxley, Thomas H., *Evolution and Ethics*, Appleton, New York, 1984, reprinted in Arthur Caplan, ed., *The Sociobiology Debate*, Harper and Row, New York, 1978.

James, Allan, ed., *The Bases of International Order*, Essays in Honour of C.A.W. Manning, Oxford University Press, London, 1973.

Johansen, Robert, *The National Interest and the Human Interest*, Princeton University Press, Princeton, New Jersey, 1980.

Johnson, Gary R., Susan H. Ratwik, and Timothy J. Sawyer, "The Evocative Significance of Kin Terms in Patriotic Speech," in Vernon Reynolds, Vincent Falger, and Ian Vine, eds., *The Sociobiology of Ethnocentrism: Evolutionary Dimensions of Xenophobia, Discrimination, Racism and Nationalism*, Croom Helm, London, 1987.

Johnson, James Turner, *Just War Tradition and the Restraint of War*, Princeton University Press, Princeton, New Jersey, 1981.

Jones, Walter S., *The Logic of International Relations*, 6th edition, Scott, Foresman, Glenview, Illinois, 1988.

Kamenka, Eugene, and Alice Ehr-Soon Tay, eds., *Human Rights*, Edward Arnold, Melbourne, 1978.

Kant, Immanuel, *Perpetual Peace*, translated by M. Campbell Smith, Allen and Unwin, London, 1903.

Kennan, George, "Morality and Foreign Policy," *Foreign Affairs*, Vol. 64, Winter, 1986, pp. 205-219.

Keohane, Robert O., ed., *Neorealism and Its Critics*, Columbia University Press, New York, 1986.

Keohane, Robert O., and Joseph S. Nye, Jr., *Power and Interdependence: World Politics in Transition*, Little Brown, Boston, 1977.

Kissinger, Henry, *The Years of Upheaval*, Little Brown, Boston, 1982.

Kitcher, Philip, *Vaulting Ambition*, M.I.T. Press, Cambridge, Massachusetts, 1985.

Kothari, Rajni, "Towards a Just World," *Alternatives, A Journal of World Policy*, Vol. 5, No. 1, 1979, reprinted in Richard Falk, Samuel S. Kim, and Saul H. Mendlowitz, *Toward a Just World Order*, Vol. I, Westview, Boulder, Colorado, 1982.

Kuper, Leo, *Genocide: Its Political Rise in the Twentieth Century*, Penguin, London, 1981.

Kuper, Leo, *The Prevention of Genocide*, Yale University Press, New Haven, Connecticut, 1985.

Lichtenberg, Judith, "National Boundaries and Moral Boundaries: A Cosmopolitan View," in Peter G. Brown and Henry Shue, eds., *Boundaries: National Autonomy and Its Limits*, Rowman and Littlefield, Totowa, New Jersey, 1981.

Light, Margot, and A.J.R. Groom, eds., *International Relations: A Handbook of Current Theory*, Frances Pinter, London, 1985.

Linklater, Andrew, "Rationality and Obligation in the States-system; the Lessons of Pufendorf's Law of Nations," *Millenium: Journal of International Studies*, Vol. 9, Winter, 1980-81, pp. 215-228.

Linklater, Andrew, *Men and Citizens in the Theory of International Relations*, St. Martin's, New York, 1982.

Luban, David, "The Legacy of the Nuremberg," *QQ: Report from the Center for Philosophy and Public Policy*, University of Maryland, College Park, Maryland, Vol. 6, Winter, 1986.

Lumsden, Charles, and E.O. Wilson, *Genes, Mind and Culture: the Coevolutionary Process*, Harvard University Press, Cambridge, Massachusetts, 1981.

Machiavelli, Niccolo, *The Prince*, translated by U.K. Marriott, introduced by Herbert Butterfield, Everyman Library, Dent, London, 1958.

Maxwell, Mary, *Human Evolution: A Philosophical Anthropology*, Columbia University Press, New York, and Croom Helm, London, 1984.

Mayall, James, ed., *The Community of States*, Allen and Unwin, London, 1983.

Maynard Smith, John, "Group Selection and Kin Selection," *Nature*, Vol. 201, 1984, pp. 1145-1147.

Mayr, Ernst, and William Provine, *The Evolutionary Synthesis*, Harvard University Press, Cambridge, 1981.

Miller, J.D.B., "Morality, Interests and Rationalisation," in Ralph Pettman, ed., *Moral Claims In World Affairs*, Australian National University Press, Canberra, 1979.

Milne, A.J.M., *Freedom and Rights*, Allen and Unwin, London, 1968.

Morgenthau, Hans, *In Defense of the National Interest*, Knopf, New York, 1952.

Morgenthau, Hans, *Dilemmas of Politics*, University of Chicago Press, Chicago, 1958.

Morgenthau, Hans, *Scientific Man versus Power Politics*, Chicago University Press, Chicago, 1946.

Morgenthau, Hans J., and Kenneth Thompson, *Politics among Nations*, 6th edition, Knopf, New York, 1985.

Nagel, Thomas, "Ruthlessness in Public Life," in Stuart Hampshire, ed., *Public and Private Morality*, Cambridge University Press, Cambridge, 1978.

Nardin, Terry, *Law, Morality, and the Relations of States*, Princeton University Press, Princeton, New Jersey, 1983.

Niebuhr, Reinhold, *Moral Man and Immoral Society*, Scribners, New York, 1932.

Nye, Joseph S., Jr., "Ethics and Foreign Policy," An Occasional Paper/Aspen Institute for Humanistic Studies, Wye Plantation, Queenstown, Maryland.

Parekh, Bhikhu, and R.N. Berki, eds., *The Morality of Politics*, Allen and Unwin, London, 1972.

Passmore, John, *The Perfectibility of Man*, Scribners, New York, 1970.

Pettman, Ralph, ed., *Moral Claims in World Affairs*, Australian National University Press, Canberra, 1979.

Popper, Karl, *The Open Society and Its Enemies, Vol. 2: Hegel to Marx*, Routledge and Kegan Paul, London, 1945.

Porter, Brian, "Patterns of Thought and Practice: Martin Wight's 'International Theory'," in Michael Donelan, ed., *The Reason of States*, Allen and Unwin, London, 1978.

Powell, G. Bingham, *Contemporary Democracies: Participation, Stability, and Violence*, Harvard University Press, Cambridge, Massachusetts, 1982.

Pugh, George Edgin, *The Biological Origin of Human Values*, Routledge and Kegan Paul, London, 1978.

Pye, Lucian W., with Mary W. Pye, *Asian Power and Politics*, Harvard University Press, Cambridge, Massachusetts, 1985.

Reader, John, *Missing Links*, Collins, London, 1981.

Regan, Richard, S.J., *The Moral Dimension in Politics*, Oxford University Press, New York, 1986.

Reynolds, Vernon, *The Apes*, Cassell, London, 1967.

Reynolds, Vernon, Vincent Falger, and Ian Vine, eds., *The Sociobiology of Ethnocentrism: Evolutionary Dimensions of Xenophobia, Discrimination, Racism and Nationalism*, Croom Helm, London, 1987.

Richards, Graham, *Human Evolution*, Routledge and Kegan Paul, London, 1987.

Richards, Robert, "A Defense of Evolutionary Ethics," and responses by C. Cela-Conde, A. Gewirth, W. Hughes, L. Thomas, and R. Trigg, *Biology and Philosophy*, Vol. 1, 1986, pp. 265-337.

Rose, Steven, Leon J. Kamin, and R.C. Lewontin, *Not in Our Genes*, Penguin, New York, 1984.

Ruse, Michael, *Taking Darwin Seriously*, Blackwell, London, 1986.

Ruse, Michael, and E.O. Wilson, "Moral Philosophy as Applied Science," *Philosophy*, Vol. 61, 1986, pp. 173-192.

Sandel, Michael, *Liberalism and the Limits of Justice*, Cambridge University Press, Cambridge, 1982.

Scruton, Roger, *A Dictionary of Political Thought*, Pan, London, 1982.

Shaw, R. Paul and Yuwa Wong, *Genetic Seeds of Warfare*, Unwin Hyman, London, 1989.

Shue, Henry, *Basic Rights: Subsistence, Affluence, and U.S. Foreign Policy*, Princeton University Press, Princeton, New Jersey, 1980.

Singer, Peter, "Famine, Affluence and Morality," *Philosophy and Public Affairs*, Vol. 1, 1972, reprinted in Charles Beitz, Marshall Cohen, Thomas Scanlon, and A. John Simmons, eds. *International Ethics: a Philosophy and Public Affairs Reader*, Princeton University Press, Princeton, New Jersey, 1985.

Singer, Peter, "Ethics and Sociobiology," *Zygon: Journal of Religion and Science*, Vol. 19, 1984, pp. 141-158.

Smith, Michael Joseph, *Realist Thought from Weber to Kissinger*, Louisiana State University Press, Baton Rouge, Louisiana, 1986.

Smith, W.H., "Justice: National, International or Global?" in Ralph Pettman, ed., *Moral Claims in World Affairs*, Australian National Press, Canberra, 1979.

Sober, Elliott, *The Nature of Selection: Evolutionary Theory in Philosophical Focus*, M.I.T. Press, Cambridge, Massachusetts, 1984.

Spanier, John, *Games Nations Play*, 3rd edition, Holt, Rinehart and Winston/ Praeger New York, 1978.

Stackhouse, Max, *Creeds, Societies and Human Rights*, Eerdmans, Grand Rapids, Michigan, 1984.

Sterling, Richard W., *Ethics in a World of Power: the Political Ideas of Friedrick Meinecke*, Princeton University Press, Princeton, New Jersey, 1958.

Thompson, Kenneth, *Masters of International Thought*, Louisiana State University Press, Baton Rouge, Louisiana, 1980.

Thompson, Kenneth W., ed., *The Moral Imperatives of Human Rights: A World Survey*, University Press of America, Lanham, Maryland, 1980.

Tiger, Lionel, *The Manufacture of Evil*, Harper and Row, New York, 1987.

Trivers, Robert, "The Evolution of Reciprocal Altruism," *Quarterly Review of Biology*, Vol. 46, 1971, pp. 35-57.

Trivers, Robert, *Social Evolution*, Benjamin/Cummings, Menlo Park, California, 1985.

van den Berghe, Pierre L., *The Ethnic Phenomenon*, Greenwood Press, Westport, Connecticut, 1981.

van den Berghe, Pierre L., *Stranger in Their Midst*, University of Colorado Press, Boulder, Colorado, 1989.

van der Dennen, Johan, "Ethnocentrism and In-group/Out-group Differentiation: A Review and Interpretation of the Literature," in Vernon Reynolds, Vincent Falger, and Ian Vine, eds., *The Sociobiology of Ethnocentrism: Evolutionary Dimensions of Xenophobia, Discrimination, Racism and Nationalism*, Croom Helm, London, 1987.

Vasquez, John, *The Power of Power Politics: a Critique*, Frances Pinter, London, 1983.

Vincent, R.J., "*Realpolitik*," in James Mayall, ed., *The Community of States*, Allen and Unwin, London, 1983.

Vincent, R.J., *Human Rights and International Relations*, Cambridge University Press, Cambridge, 1986.

Waltz, Kenneth, *Theory of International Relations*, Addison-Wesley, Reading, Massachusetts, 1979.

Walzer, Michael, *Just and Unjust Wars*, Basic Books, New York, 1977.

Walzer, Michael, "The Moral Standing of States: A Response to Four Critics," *Philosophy and Public Affairs*, Vol. 19, 1980, pp. 210-229.

Wight, Martin, *Power Politics*, edited by Hedley Bull and Carsten Holbraad, Penguin, Hammondsworth, 1977.

Williams, George C., *Adaptation and Natural Selection*, Princeton University Press, Princeton, New Jersey, 1966.

Wilson, E.O., "On the queerness of social evolution," *Bulletin of the Entomological Society of America*, Vol. 19, 1972, pp. 20-22.

Wilson, E.O., *On Human Nature*, Harvard University Press, Cambridge, Massachusetts, 1978.

Wilson E.O., *Sociobiology: the Abridged Edition*, Harvard University Press, Cambridge, Massachusetts, 1980.

Index